Quest For Excellence

Hanover Shoe Farms:
The First 75 Years

Dean A. Hoffman

To Jackie From Mark W. Edam [signature]

THE RUSSELL MEERDINK COMPANY, LTD.
Neenah, Wisconsin

ISBN 0-929346-74-2

Library of Congress Cataloging-in-Publication Data

Hoffman, Dean A., 1949-
    Quest for excellence : Hanover shoe farms' first 75 years / Dean A. Hoffman.
      p. cm.
    ISBN 0-929346-74-2
      1. Hanover Shoe Farms (Hanover, Pa.)--History. I. Title.

SF339.5.U6 H64 2002

                           2002032678

Published by

The Russell Meerdink Company, Ltd.
1555 South Park Ave.
Neenah, WI 54956
(920) 725-0955 Worldwide • (800) 635-6499 U.S. & Canada
www.horseinfo.com

Printed in the United States of America

Dedication

This book is dedicated to Lawrence B. Sheppard, John F. Simpson, and the men, women and horses that have contributed to the greatness of Hanover Shoe Farms over the past 75 years. I particularly applaud the current leadership of Hanover Shoe Farms for its continuing quest for excellence.

Table of Contents

Introduction

The first horse I purchased was a Hanover-bred. She was a daughter of Adios from The Old Maid, rather uptown breeding a few decades ago, but she was definitely the ugly sister in the family. To Charlotte Sheppard she was a cull. But to me she represented one of the breed's greatest families, and I was delighted to bask in the reflected glory of Hanover Shoe Farms.

In 1984, I was asked to come to the winner's circle during the Grand Circuit meet at The Red Mile for some unknown reason. I saw John Simpson, Jr. and artist Bill Orr there, but I didn't have a clue why I was there. Then Simpson produced one of Orr's huge conformation paintings from its hiding place behind a hedge. It depicted Best Of All, a teenage idol of mine who had gone to stud at Hanover. Best Of All had died seven weeks earlier and I had written a heartfelt tribute to him in the September issue of *Hoof Beats*.

John F. Simpson, Sr. was blind by then and couldn't read, but when he listened to the words I wrote, he sensed immediately the abiding affection I had for the horse. He could identify with that bond for he, too, felt a deep bond for certain horses. In a gesture of generosity that stunned me, Simpson decided to give me the painting of Best Of All that had been hanging in the main office at Hanover. He enlisted his oldest son to do the honors.

That painting occupies a place of honor in my home now, and I value it dearly. As I was to learn, John F. Simpson was a complex man who could be both unreasonably critical and unbelievably kind.

While I never knew Lawrence Sheppard, I came to know Simpson well in the last decade of his life and I knew I was in for a treat when I heard his voice and the words, "Hello, Buckeye" on the phone.

John Simpson didn't like finishing second. He was enough of a realist to know that it was part of life, but too much of a perfectionist to ever accept it. I had lunch with him a few months before he died and it was obvious how much his health had declined. But the mind was still like a rapier, slashing people and ideas he didn't like, giving full vent to his strong opinions.

The intensity and passion that John F. Simpson displayed was the only way he knew how to live, and in that respect he'd had a good mentor in Lawrence Sheppard. It was their passion that guided Hanover Shoe Farms through most of its first 75 years.

Dean A. Hoffman
Columbus, Ohio
Summer 2001

*Also featured on the cover, this photo shows the main entrance
of Hanover Shoe Farms*

Chapter 1

Dynasty

It covers the fertile fields southwest of the Borough of Hanover, Pennsylvania, like a huge patchwork quilt, its sheer size and complexity impossible to ignore. As you drive the narrow, two-lane county roads, everywhere you look there are signs of Hanover Shoe Farms.

Likewise, everywhere you look in harness racing there are signs of Hanover Shoe Farms. You can see the Hanover influence at every racetrack in North America. In fact, if you checked the winner's circle at one of the dozens of pari-mutuel tracks or hundreds of county and state fair tracks in North America, you'd unquestionably find horses whose pedigrees have been influenced by Hanover Shoe Farms.

You don't need to confine that claim to one continent because the same is true wherever harness horses are raced — in Scandinavia, New Zealand, Italy, Germany, Australia, Russia, and elsewhere. The Hanover influence is felt worldwide.

After its inception in 1926, Hanover Shoe Farms quickly grew to be the dominant power in harness racing, outstripping the magnificent nurseries in Kentucky's Bluegrass, many of which were established fountains of speed long before Hanover began.

Any businessman, coach, or athlete will tell you that while it's certainly a great accomplishment to rise to the top in your chosen field, it's an even greater accomplishment to remain on top. By that definition, Hanover Shoe Farms leaves you searching for a word more powerful than "dynasty."

Every year since the United States Trotting Association in Columbus, Ohio, began maintaining records on the leading breeders in harness racing, only one name has stood at the top of the list: Hanover Shoe Farms.

In the year 2000, horses bred by Hanover won more than $19 million at tracks across North America. They were simply carrying on the Hanover tradition. From the time the USTA began keeping records through 2001, the aggregate earnings of Hanover-bred stock are almost $400 million. The offspring of the Hanover stallions over the years total nearly $1 billion.

That's a total that no other horse farm — of any breed — can equal.

Breeding horses is a business fraught with pitfalls, suitable only for those willing to endure heartbreaks at every step of the process and willing to adopt a long-term perspective. Hanover Shoe Farms and the people who operate it have met those tests. From its start in the Roaring Twenties, through the Great Depression, World War II, 14 different Presidents, and radical changes in harness racing, Hanover Shoe Farms remains steadfast in its quest for excellence.

Hanover Shoe Farms began breeding horses before Lindbergh flew the Atlantic, before Babe Ruth swatted 60 homers in a season, and before Al Jolson starred in the first talking motion picture.

Hanover began breeding horses before the first Hambletonian was contested, when harness racing was a relic of American's agrarian roots and almost four decades before pari-mutuel racing came to Pennsylvania.

Hanover Shoe Farms is a single entity, despite the "s" at the end of the name. While the real estate consists of many separate parcels of land, it is unified under the Hanover banner.

The historic main farm lies a few miles south of Hanover and consists of two stallion barns, a few foaling barns, residences, and the main office.

The stallion barns are safe and sturdy, but not the showplaces that some breeders have built for their sultans at stud. At Hanover, all the horses — stallions, mares, sucklings, and yearlings — are treated like horses. That may not seem like a novel concept, but many farms that breed racehorses pamper their products needlessly. Ask anyone at Hanover and they'll tell you that they're breeding racehorses, not show horses or fragile porcelain figurines.

In addition to the main farm, there are 27 separate farms spread out hither and yon across the adjoining southern Pennsylvania countryside. To drive from the farm furthest south, near the Maryland State line, to the northernmost farm requires you to cover about 10 miles. Each farm consists of a residence, one or two barns, and a couple of fields. It takes almost 90 full-time employees to keep Hanover operating each day.

This real estate inventory doesn't cover Hanover's yearling farm, which is located to the west, much closer to the historic town of Gettysburg than it is to Hanover. Nor does it include the fairgrounds in the Borough of Hanover itself.

In total, Hanover Shoe Farms consists of 3,200 acres. The patchwork quilt is indeed very large.

Chapter 2

Building The House Of Hanover

They were both blunt, intense, autocratic, and didn't give a damn about winning any popularity contests. They were seldom diplomatic; they were often dictatorial.

They were also passionately committed to harness racing, and together they built the greatest breeding farm that horse racing has ever known.

Lawrence Baker Sheppard and John Frazer Simpson were cast from the same mold, the mold that produces men more known for their accomplishments than their charm.

To understand the growth and success of Hanover Shoe Farms, you must first understand these two extraordinary men because they were the twin pillars upon which Hanover's longevity has been built.

If Sheppard and Simpson were alive, they would undoubtedly balk at having too much attention paid to their accomplishments. "Write about the horses," they'd probably both insist. "The horses built Hanover Shoe Farms."

That's only half true. Certainly the horses have carried the name Hanover around the world, but without the relentless quest for excellence by these two men there would be no Hanover Shoe Farms.

In creating today's House of Hanover, Lawrence Sheppard was the builder. He provided the blueprint, laid the foundation, and built a solid basic structure. John Simpson was the remodeler, preserving what was best, but adding and updating as needed. That process continues today under a new generation of leadership.

Lawrence Sheppard was a short, blunt businessman with bulldog determination. Decades after his death in 1968, the principles of Lawrence Sheppard still silently guide the men and women who operate Hanover Shoe Farms. In his essay *Self Reliance*, Ralph Waldo Emerson captured that influence when he wrote, "An institution is the lengthened shadow of one man."

Lawrence B. Sheppard and John F. Simpson at the track in DuQuoin, Ill.
(Photo courtesy of the U.S. Trotting Association)

Since Lawrence Sheppard's death in 1968, there have been adjustments made at Hanover to accommodate time and tide and changes in the sport, but the shadow cast by this extraordinary man is indeed quite long.

Lawrence Sheppard was born in 1897 into a world about to turn its back on the horse-and-buggy days of the 19th century and march bravely into an industrialized new century, driving automobiles and flying in airplanes. But Lawrence Sheppard fell in love with horses early in life and that passion became the focal point of his life.

He was the son of Harper D. Sheppard, who had achieved extraordinary success in the shoe business through ambition, energy, and ingenuity. Born in 1868 and orphaned at age 13, Harper was sent to live and work on plantations in North Carolina with an uncle.

At age 17, Harper Sheppard shed his family ties and moved to Baltimore, working briefly there as a clerk before spending a year in Texas in the late 1880s. The days of the great cattle drives were coming to a close, but a Texan's life was still inextricably bound to his horse. Harper Sheppard grew to love horseflesh during his days in the West, much the same as his son would a generation later.

He then returned to Baltimore where he went to work for a prosperous shoe merchant named Charles Heiser. He immediately made a favorable impression on the boss with his enterprise and intellect.

That was in 1889, and Sheppard stayed with Heiser's Baltimore plant for five years, learning the shoe business from the inside. At age 28 he apparently decided it was time to learn the shoe business from the outside, so Sheppard joined a Boston firm as a traveling shoe salesman.

He beat the bushes up and down the Atlantic coast, calling on retailers from the state of Delaware to Key West, Florida. Along the way he took Henrietta Dawson Ayres as his wife and started a family.

When his son Lawrence was just an infant, Harper Sheppard heard from his old boss Charles Heiser, who was now making and selling shoes in the hamlet of Hanover, Pennsylvania. His once-thriving business was in trouble, and Heiser was at a loss for a solution. There were rumblings of discontent among the shareholders, and Heiser thought that Harper Sheppard might be his salvation.

Young Sheppard traveled to Hanover to assess the situation. The business outlook was indeed grave, but the shoes the firm produced were high quality and marketable. What the company needed was better management, and the shareholders turned to Sheppard and made him an offer.

If he would sign on as an assistant manager, he would be paid a salary of $100 a month. To ensure that Sheppard had a stake in making the firm profitable, the shareholders insisted that he invest $500 of his own money.

Harper Sheppard had seen and met too many challenges in his young life to be daunted by such a proposal, so he put up the money, rolled up his sleeves, and went to work.

It was soon apparent that Harper Sheppard, not Charles Heiser, was the right man. As the company's fortunes began to turn around, shareholders deferred to Sheppard's wishes, giving Heiser the cold shoulder at times. Inevitably, animosity built between Heiser on one side and Sheppard and the shareholders on the other. On Dec. 20, 1899, Heiser cleaned out his office, packed his bags, and left, severing all ties to the shoe company.

13

On Christmas Day, 1899, as children across America were unwrapping presents, Harper Sheppard couldn't wait to unwrap the Charles Heiser Shoe Co. from the constraints that had led it to the brink of bankruptcy.

Sheppard was joined in his new venture by Clinton N. Myers, whose father had been a shareholder in Heiser's failing business. Sheppard and Myers were both young men anxious to become successful businessmen in the coming century.

Young Lawrence Sheppard rides through the streets of Hanover in 1909

They knew that merely adopting Heiser's methods was a formula for failure, so they decided that they would be both manufacturer and retailer, passing the costs of the middleman on to the consumer in savings.

Heiser's name was no more suitable than his methods, so the shareholders simply switched the firm's name to recognize the new partners. It was now The Sheppard & Myers Co.

The first retail store selling Sheppard & Myers shoes opened on June 30, 1900, in York, Pennsylvania, 20 miles east of Hanover. Harper Sheppard took the train from Hanover to York for the big event while Clinton Myers hitched an old gelding named "Doc" to the family buggy and drove over.

Soon a second Sheppard & Myers store was opened in Reading, Pa. Then the partners opened a retail outlet in the big city of Philadelphia.

They were off and running. While Harper Sheppard stayed in Hanover and paid attention to the manufacturing end, Clinton Myers was often out searching for locations for new stores to sell their shoes. In time, the production and retailing would be split into two firms: The stores would continue to be known as Sheppard & Myers, Inc. and the factory then became The Hanover Shoe Co.

The shoes they sold were all leather and retailed for $2.50. Customers quickly recognized that Hanover-made shoes were a good investment. It seemed that you couldn't wear them out. You simply replaced the soles and heels and continued to wear them.

This attention to quality paid dividends with the public and the business grew rapidly. That meant an ever-greater demand for shoes, and soon the limited production facilities in Hanover were woefully inadequate.

In 1901, construction began on a three-story factory in Hanover and it was still going up when the partners realized that another floor was necessary. Make that a four-story factory, they told the builders.

Business was flourishing, and soon even the new factory was bulging at the seams. Another plant was needed and Sheppard and Myers spotted a site on Carlisle Street in Hanover, adjacent to the Pennsylvania Railroad and thus ideal for shipping. Because of delays in acquiring all the needed real estate, work didn't begin on the new factory until early in 1910. Once that factory was up and running, there was an ongoing need for other plants, other stores.

Harper Sheppard was doing more than just building factories. In 1913, he built a magnificent 27-room mansion in Hanover, which served as his home for almost four decades. In 1998, the mansion was restored and is now used as a bed and breakfast.

Sheppard and Myers were successful beyond their wildest dreams by the time World War I rolled around. Now they could devote some of their time and energies to other enterprises.

Harper Sheppard's expertise in footwear and proximity to Washington, D.C., made him a valuable member of the Shoes, Leather, and Rubber Goods Branch of the Quartermaster Corps. He offered his advice on how to fit the doughboys with proper boots, a service that his son Lawrence would also perform in the next world war.

Sheppard and Myers bought a local print shop that had published a daily paper in Hanover and modernized its presses and equipment. Soon a new paper, the *Hanover Evening Sun*, replaced the old one. Harper Shepherd was its president until his death; the paper continues to serve the community of Hanover and surrounding areas.

These years of prosperity weren't all work and no play for the astute businessmen. Both Sheppard and Myers admired and valued trees greatly, and they encouraged the planting of more than two million trees over 1,300 acres of the Hanover watershed. (Clinton Myers loved trees so much that he developed his own arboretum with more than 800 species.)

What really bound Sheppard and Myers besides their business acumen in shoes, however, was their love of a good horse. They kept a few horses for pleasure driving and racing, as many prosperous men did in that era. It was almost de rigeur for businessmen of that era to have some driving or racehorses. Those who enjoyed sitting behind a fast-stepping trotter organized themselves into Gentleman's Driving Clubs around the country.

Their horses gave Sheppard and Myers great pleasure, and served practical purposes, too. Horses were still often used for transportation well into the 20th century. Harper Sheppard drove a horse-drawn buggy to his office each day long after automobiles had become commonplace.

Young Lawrence Sheppard was smitten with horses when he spent two summers at Yellowstone National Park in Wyoming as a teenager. Tourists saw the nation's first national park in its pristine splendor then, riding horses to venture where cars couldn't go. It was young Sheppard's job to care for those horses. And he loved every minute of it.

Many driving horses in that era carried the blood of a racing trotter somewhere in their ancestry, but trotting races were limited to the fairs in the summer. A horse that pulled the family to church on Sunday might be entered in some races at the local fairs during the summer.

Lawrence Sheppard

Harper Sheppard and Clinton Myers jumped into the sport of harness racing with enthusiasm, driving a horse now and then in competition, and buying a few each year. They campaigned under the name of the Hanover Shoe Stable.

While his father was making his fortune in the shoe business, young Lawrence Sheppard was busy making grades in school. He graduated from Haverford College in 1917, then later went on to the University of Virginia, heeding his father's admonition to become a lawyer. There was, however, a war raging in the fields of France. When President Wilson and Congress gave the word, America's fighting forces entered the fray. Lawrence Sheppard was among them. He became a naval aviator, serving 18 months before being mustered out after the war had ended.

With that duty behind him, young Lawrence was ready to make up for lost time.

He married the former Charlotte Cassin Newton of San Antonio, Texas, finished law school, passed the bar, and was qualified to practice.

Except that Lawrence Sheppard never intended to practice law. It was nice to have that training and that sheepskin, but the wheels of justice moved a bit too slowly for the energetic young man. He followed his father's footsteps, first in the shoe business and then in the horse business. After all, Harper had given his son a filly named June Patchen when he was 11 years old and the youngster was driving in races as a teenager. He loved horses, and he loved the racing world.

Once Lawrence became a partner in the racing stable, he could see that there was a problem. The horses his father and Mr. Myers owned had been decent enough. They were pleasant to drive and be around, and occasionally they'd even win a race. Sure, they didn't pay for their keep, but the partners considered their horses just a hobby.

Lawrence Sheppard didn't see it that way. He felt that they were wasting both their time and money keeping horses that were second-rate at best. Lawrence Sheppard didn't see the purpose of being second-rate in anything, and certainly not in racing. They didn't give trophies to the horse that finished second.

In 1922, Harper Sheppard went to the Caribbean on vacation while partner Clinton Myers went off on his own vacation. They had earned it through their hard work. Lawrence was left in charge of the stable.

"I guess I was a nut," Lawrence recalled many years later, "but anyhow, I immediately did what I had longed to do. I sold the whole works, every lousy horse. When Dad came home, he saw red, but didn't say much. I told him that he and Mr. Myers couldn't part with any horse, no matter how bad, and as a result he had a stable full of critters not worth a damn."

Once the initial shock had worn off, Harper Sheppard and Clinton Myers gave the boy a free hand in rebuilding the stable. Lawrence chose carefully. The outstanding doubled-gaited performer Baron Worthy joined the stable, and was soon followed by Peter Manning, the reigning champion trotter. He was a gelding and past his prime, but owning the fastest trotter ever gave Hanover instant prestige.

Peter Manning had looped the Lexington mile track in 1:56-3/4 in 1922, setting a speed standard for trotters that would last until 1937. For Hanover his appearances were limited mostly to exhibitions at fairs in Pennsylvania. He was a headliner, a known star that brought out the crowds, and he gave Hanover Shoe Stable its first brush with championship horses. Lawrence Sheppard liked that feeling.

The Sheppards, father and son, and Myers decided to breed as well as race trotters. Breeding horses is a long-term proposition. You can buy a ready-made horse and race it tomorrow, but to build a breeding operation takes years, even decades. The normal route is to acquire mares slowly, perhaps add a stallion or two, and practice being patient.

Lawrence Sheppard was not particularly the patient type, however. He had other ideas.

The world was relatively calm in the spring of 1926. Prohibition was the law of the land, but some young people must have been finding the hooch because a report issued by the American Association of University Professors condemned football as promoting "drinking, dishonesty, and neglect of academic work."

"Silent Cal" Coolidge ran the country from the White House with a laissez-faire philosophy. *The Great Gatsby*, F. Scott Fitzgerald's novel celebrating the flapper age, was a hot item in bookstores, and Bobby Jones ruled the links in golf.

On the morning of Friday, May 28, of that year, Paul Carr, a correspondent for *The Trotter & Pacer* magazine, was in Hanover and he noticed considerable commotion in the vicinity of the train station.

"It didn't take long to find out that it had something to do with horses," wrote Carr, "and a moment later I saw a half-dozen colts being led down the road . . ."

Carr and other onlookers watched as 23 youngsters, mostly yearlings but also a few two- and three-year-olds, were unloaded.

What they were watching was far more than just a routine arrival of horses shipped by rail. They were, in fact, watching the start of a dynasty.

The scene at the railroad station was the culmination of some fast footwork by the junior member of the Hanover Shoe Stable partnership. The horses being unloaded had previously belonged to noted breeder Alexander B. Coxe of Paoli, Pa., who had died a month earlier. The grieving widow was left to disperse of her husband's beloved horses — 69 of them in total — in the thick of the breeding season. The timing couldn't have been worse for Mrs. Coxe.

Lawrence Sheppard's timing couldn't have been better. While other breeders tried to cherry pick the stallions Dillon Axworthy or Dillon Volo and the best broodmares from the Coxe holdings, Lawrence Sheppard demonstrated a trait that would mark his career. He knew this was an opportunity to take a giant leap forward. While other breeders pondered, Sheppard acted.

He had a bold and forthright proposal for Mrs. Coxe. He would buy all of them, he told her. The whole outfit — lock, stock, and barrel.

The simplicity of the deal appealed to Mrs. Coxe. So did Sheppard's offer of $150,000. It was a clean transaction, one that assured the continuation of the breeding program her husband had fostered so long and so lovingly. Besides, the horses would be going only 100 miles from Paoli to Hanover.

An agreement was reached.

The trade press called the coup the "largest transaction ever in trotting flesh" and one turf journal remarked that "Almost overnight Hanover, a small city in southern Pennsylvania, has become a star-marked spot on the harness horse map."

Dillon Axworthy, one of 69 horses purchased from the Coxe farm by Lawrence Sheppard

Dillon Axworthy and driver Joe Serrill

There probably hadn't been that much excitement in town since that hot summer day in 1863 when Union and Confederate troops clashed in Hanover as a precursor to the monumental struggle about to take place in nearby Gettysburg.

Hanover had been a sleepy farming community since it was first settled in the early 1700s by German immigrants. Scotch, English, and Irish pioneers later moved into the area, but to pay homage to the original farmers in the area, the town was named after a city in Germany (although an "n" was dropped in the process). The borough was officially incorporated in 1815.

When Harper Sheppard appraised the parcel of horses that his son bought from Mrs. Coxe, he realized what a bargain had been struck. He was justifiably proud of his son's determination in snaring the Coxe horses. He told Lawrence, "Young man, you'll never do a better bit of business than you have done today."

After arriving in Hanover by rail, the horses were led through the streets until they reached the fairgrounds, where the Hanover racing string was already stabled. A flurry of last-minute activity made sure that enough stalls were ready for the first contingent of new tenants.

Lawrence Sheppard was in such a hurry to buy the Coxe mares that he had no place to house all of them. The fairgrounds were only a holding facility until more permanent quarters could be found. The stallions Dillon Axworthy and Dillon Volo stayed at Coxe's Nawbeek Farm in Paoli because they had obligations to finish the breeding season.

The Coxe broodmares were split between Nawbeek and breeding farms in Kentucky, and they would remain in those locations until the facilities in Hanover were ready for occupancy.

Harness racing lore has Lawrence Sheppard establishing Hanover Shoe Farms, but we must remember that he was the junior partner in Hanover Shoe Farms at this point. The real founders were Harper Sheppard and Clinton Myers. The senior Sheppard would remain an owner until his death in 1951, while Myers was involved with the farm until his death three years later.

The senior partners, however, deferred to the young dynamo on matters relating to horses. From the time he snared the Coxe horses, Lawrence Sheppard was running the show at Hanover Shoe Farms, and he was anxious to get the show started.

Miss Bertha Dillon and Joe Serrill

Chapter 3

The Founding Mother

Great breeding farms are always closely identified with the stallions that have resided there, sending forth hundreds or even thousands of offspring to carry their name far and wide. The influence of a great stallion is inestimable as it lasts for generations and can pervade pedigrees for decades.

Ironically, the horse that lifted the banner of Hanover Shoe Farms above its rivals in the early years was not a stallion, but instead a broodmare. Her name was Miss Bertha Dillon.

So extraordinary was her success that she established a powerful female family that quickly became known as the "Hanover Sisters" or simply the "Hanover" family.

Some of Lawrence Sheppard's initial stallions at Hanover were not successful. They came and went, leaving only a shallow imprint on the breed, but the mark left by Miss Bertha Dillon and her descendants was indelible.

All you need to know are the names Bret Hanover, Mack Lobell, and Peace Corps to understand the type of horses that came from the family that Miss Bertha Dillon established.

The lessons learned from Miss Bertha Dillon are still valuable today because no one at Hanover has ever forgotten that while the glamour boys in the stud barn may get most of the attention, the real nucleus of any breeding farm is its broodmare band.

Ask Jim Simpson, the president of Hanover Shoe Farms, to summarize the farm's philosophy and he will say simply, "Broodmares." It's one lesson he knows the farm cannot afford to forget.

When Lawrence Sheppard bought Miss Bertha Dillon, she was 12 years old, middle aged for a broodmare, and past the period when some people think a mare's procreative prowess peaks. But Miss Bertha Dillon's best years were ahead of her.

Miss Bertha Dillon came to A.B. Coxe from a family of trotters developed at Riverside Stock Farm in Berlin, Wisconsin. If the females in this family shared one trait, it was their willful disposition.

Harness historian John L. Hervey could trace this trait back at least to Medio, the great-grandam of Miss Bertha Dillon and now revered as a foundation mare.

Medio was an aloof mare "without any of the gentle traits that broodmares so often exhibit," wrote Hervey. Even during her later years, after she had gone blind, Medio stood apart from her pasture mates, "asking for neither caresses nor kind words from anybody."

Medio's 1891 daughter named Marble inherited her mother's disposition. On the track she was so unpredictable, wrote Hervey, "The day she took her record, her driver was sweating blood with anxiety, regarding just what she might take a notion to do next."

In 1906, Marble produced a filly named Miss Bertha C after the daughter of J.B. Chandler, trainer of the Riverside Stock Farm trotters. The torch was passed to a new generation, you might say, and this torch was flaming hot.

Hervey recalls visiting Riverside Stock Farm once to see the horses in training. Chandler opened the door to Miss Bertha C's stall and Hervey began to step in.

"Hold on there!" he shouted to Hervey. "This is about the meanest filly that the Lord ever made."

Living up to those words, Miss Bertha C sprang at the two men "as if to eat us alive," recalled Hervey. Her ears were laid back, her mouth wide open, and there was fire in the filly's eyes.

Chandler grabbed a thick club kept handy for such occasions and he shook it at Miss Bertha C, threatening, "Get back there, you hussy, or I'll give you a taste of this!"

When she was retired from the track, Miss Bertha C was bred to the handsome Dillon Axworthy. The resulting filly named Miss Bertha Dillon arrived on April 7, 1914, just two months before an assassination in Sarajevo would ignite World War I.

Miss Bertha Dillon was a beauty in every respect on the track, winning her share of stakes races and winning the admiration of everyone who saw her. She was the type of mare that no breeder could let escape from his grasp and A.B. Coxe retired Miss Bertha Dillon after she got a 2:02-1/4 mark at age four.

On April 1, 1919, Miss Bertha Dillon was bred to Moko, an aging patriarch at Walnut Hall Farm. He was nearly at the end of his tether as a stock horse and the manager of Walnut Hall advised Coxe to breed her to another stallion if she failed to conceive.

She did indeed come back into season and was switched to the robust young stallion Peter Volo. She promptly got in foal.

That first foal was named Dillon Volo and Joe Serrill, who trained Coxe's horses, later told fellow horsemen that this colt was the best one his boss had ever bred. One of Dillon Volo's front feet became infected, however, and he was not trained until he was a four-year-old. He got a 2:11-1/2 record with scant preparation, and he was used mostly for breeding purposes.

Miss Bertha Dillon was barren the next two seasons to the cover of Peter The Great and in 1923 she had her second foal, a filly by Chestnut Peter. She went back to the court of Peter Volo that season.

The result of that mating was a 1924 colt named Sandy Flash, and he was entrusted to Thomas W. Murphy, the premier trainer of Standardbreds of that era. Murphy had developed innumerable champions, and he stated that he felt Sandy Flash was the equal if not the superior of any youngster he had ever trained. The colt's career, however, died aborning when he injured a ligament in front.

When Sandy Flash was sold with the other Coxe horses to Hanover Shoe Farms in 1926, the Hanover crew decided to leave him with Murphy in hopes that the wizard could find a way to keep him sound. Sandy Flash was given a 2:14-3/4 mark by Murphy in March of 1927 over a track in Macon, Georgia. Soon thereafter Sandy Flash was withdrawn from training, and later that year Murphy stunned the world of harness racing by announcing that he, too, was withdrawing from the sport.

Miss Bertha Dillon's 1925 foal was Miss Bertha Worthy by Lee Worthy.

At the end of 1927, Miss Bertha Dillon's four foals had records of 2:11-3/4, 2:14-3/4, 2:21, and 2:29h. It was hardly an auspicious start for a broodmare, even by the standards of the Roaring Twenties.

Things changed quickly, however, when Miss Bertha Dillon's three daughters by Peter Volo took to the track. While the stock market was crashing in the autumn of 1929, the stock of Miss Bertha Dillon was soaring into the stratosphere.

Hanover's Bertha was the most gifted of the trio. When she made her debut on the track as a two-year-old in 1929, horsemen weren't sure if they had ever seen a filly blessed with such speed.

Joseph I. Markey, a veteran reporter for *The Horse Review* in Chicago, knew that he had never seen anything to compare to Hanover's Bertha. It was Markey who was among the first to sing — and write — the praises of Lou Dillon when she appeared early in the century. Lou Dillon, Markey had told all within earshot, was the 2:00 trotter that horsemen had waited so long for.

Markey was proven right in 1903 when Lou Dillon sprinted to a 1:58-1/2 record. Some 26 years later, Markey thought he saw in Hanover's Bertha the first trotter capable of 2:00 speed as a two-year-old.

A two-year-old trotting in 2:00? That seemed implausible, but people said the same thing when Markey had touted Lou Dillon. Hanover's Bertha zoomed to a 2:02 mile in 1929, and it seemed possible she could chip two seconds off that mark. Lameness, however, prevented her from attaining that special place in the sport's history. It would be another 15 years before the breed would gain its first 2:00 juvenile trotter, and that champion was also a Hanover product.

Hanover's Bertha to halter

Joe Markey died in the spring of 1930, so he sadly never lived to see Hanover's Bertha win the Hambletonian. The purse in the Hambletonian was $56,859, an enormous sum in that era, and its purse wouldn't climb back to that level for another two decades.

More important than the purse was the fact that Hanover's Bertha was Lawrence Sheppard's ticket to becoming a major player in the trotting sport. His bold move in acquiring the Coxe mares had already paid off in spades, and the 32-year-old businessman had every reason to smile as he stood next to his wife Charlotte after the Hambo. His only son, Lawrence, Jr., was on hand that day, too.

Hanover's Bertha and Berry to jog cart
(Photo courtesy of Len Wetherall)

Shortly after winning the Hambletonian, Hanover's Bertha trotted the first 2:00 mile ever in an official race in winning the Kentucky Futurity.

Horsemen praised the extraordinary filly for her fluid gait, refinement, and speed. Hanover's Bertha gave legitimacy to the fledgling breeding operation in Pennsylvania.

Or did the credit really belong to Miss Bertha Dillon? After all, Hanover's Bertha wasn't the only daughter of Miss Bertha Dillon who was making headlines in 1930.

While Hanover's Bertha was winning the big three-year-old races, she had younger and older siblings that also trotted into the world record tables.

Her younger sister, the two-year-old Charlotte Hanover, became the fastest freshman trotting filly ever in a two-heat race when she trotted in 2:04 twice in the same afternoon. The four-year-old Miss Bertha Hanover took a time trial record of 2:00 that same season, the fastest mile ever by a trotting mare of her age.

The next year Charlotte Hanover further enhanced her mother's resume when she entered the 2:00 list with a time trial mark of 1:59-1/2 as a three-year-old.

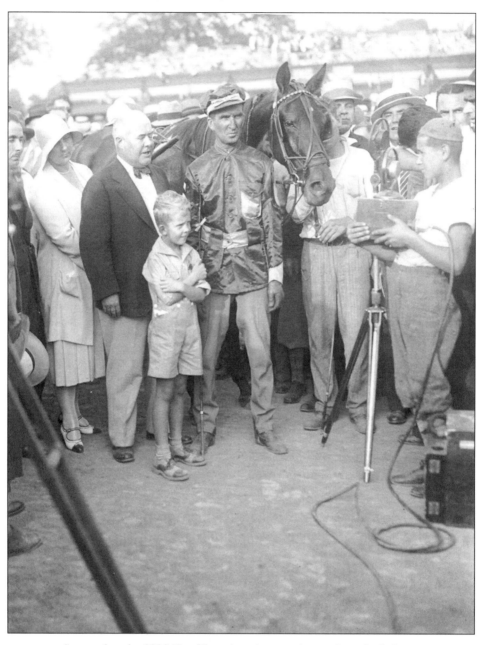

Scene after the 1930 Hambletonian victory; shown, from far left, are Lawrence Sheppard, Charlotte Sheppard, little Sonny (Lawrence Jr.), Tom Berry and the winner, Hanover's Bertha

Hanover's Bertha's win at the 1930 Kentucky Futurity -— the first 2:00 mile ever trotted in a race. Hanover's Bertha was undefeated in her three-year-old season. If there had been a Triple Crown in 1930, she would be the only filly Crown winner.

Miss Bertha Hanover and Tom Berry at Lexington
(Photo courtesy of P.W. Moser)

To put that in proper historical perspective, it should remembered that when the 1930 racing season started, only 10 trotting mares had entered the "charmed list," as the 2:00 list was then called. For one mare to produce three consecutive daughters with 2:00 marks was all but incomprehensible.

In the four seasons that Hanover Shoe Farms owned her, Miss Bertha Dillon had gone from a disappointing princess to a dazzling queen.

Miss Bertha Hanover, Hanover's Bertha, and Charlotte Hanover were heralded far and wide as the "2:00 Sisters" or, more commonly, the "Hanover Sisters." Lawrence Sheppard had truly hit the mother lode in Miss Bertha Dillon and if none of the other Coxe mares contributed a whit to Hanover's accomplishments, the farm's broodmare band was clearly on its way.

Hanover's first yearlings sold in 1926 and averaged $253. The farm was in business, but it still had a long way to go. And Lawrence Sheppard was anxious to get there.

He was young, but Sheppard knew that a stock farm needed stallions to generate a steady stream of stud fees.

The greatest Standardbred farm of that era, Walnut Hall Farm in old Kentucky, had gained fame when the unraced stallion named Moko proved to be a sire of exceptional speed.

Later Guy Axworthy, San Francisco, and Peter Volo took up residence in Walnut Hall's stone stallion barn, and their offspring proved enormously successful on the racetrack and enormously popular in the sale ring.

Tom Berry and Lawrence Sheppard
holding trophy

The formula seemed clear: Get the right stallions, breed them to fashionable mares, and the world — at least the harness horse world, that is — will beat a path to your farm's front gate.

The reason that the right stallions were important, of course, is that they could sire dozens of foals each year while a mare could produce but one. Through the sheer weight of his numbers, a stallion was usually far more influential than a mare.

Part of the package of Coxe horses was Dillon Axworthy, the sire of Miss Bertha Dillon and an established stallion. Sheppard knew that having Dillon Axworthy would put Hanover Shoe Farms on the map for breeders, but he also knew that you didn't build for the future with a 16-year-old stallion.

Dillon Axworthy would suffice temporarily, he knew, but he had to lasso some younger stallions with broad appeal.

Just a few months after the Coxe mares were acquired, a great new stake for three-year-old trotters, the Hambletonian, was first raced, and the first winner of that rich event was Guy McKinney.

This was the type of

Guy McKinney at Lexington

stallion Lawrence Sheppard wanted at Hanover, and soon the young Hambletonian winner was starting his breeding career in Pennsylvania. After concluding his first season in the stud, Guy McKinney entered the 2:00 list with a 1:58-3/4 effort in Phoenix, Arizona.

Sandy Flash, the promising son of Peter Volo—Miss Bertha Dillon, was also offered for public service at Hanover, as were The Great Volo, a brother to Peter Volo, and Bunter.

Still, even as an economic depression settled over the land in the 1930s, casting millions out of work and causing many businesses and banks to fold, Lawrence Sheppard was bullish on trotting and eager to upgrade his stallions.

The axiom for success in the stock market has always been to "buy low, sell high." Shrewd investors know to buy on the bad news, and sell on the good news.

Certainly there was bad news aplenty in harness racing during the Depression and Lawrence Sheppard used that to Hanover's advantage.

Many wealthy men were abandoning the breeding of trotters, including some who owned the great farms of Kentucky. After William M. Wright of the Calumet Baking Powder fame died in 1931, his son Warren decided to switch to breeding Thoroughbreds, and dispersed Calumet Farm's harness horses.

The most coveted stallion in the Calumet consignment was the 15-year-old Peter The Brewer, and when he walked into the ring he was the object of a bidding duel between Sheppard, tobacco magnate W. N. Reynolds, and bloodstock agent W. J. Rosemire. In the end, it was Sheppard who had the final bid at $15,000.

One of the major buyers at the Calumet dispersal was Henry Knight of Almahurst Farm in Kentucky, but by 1936 Knight was ready to throw in the towel himself. He decided to disperse his Standardbreds at the Old Glory Sale in New York.

The centerpiece of the Almahurst dispersal was Mr. McElwyn, a robust, owl-headed champion on the track and in the stud barn. European buyers had been plucking off some of America's choicest trotters during the Depression and it was feared that the 15-year-old Mr. McElwyn would be sold "across the pond."

Once again, however, Lawrence Sheppard was at the sale with his checkbook. Sheppard had been breeding some of his best mares, including Hanover's Bertha, to Mr. McElwyn at a stud fee of $200, so he decided it would be nice to have the great stallion as a resident at Hanover. When the bidding reached $15,000, Lawrence Sheppard was out, but he raised his hand one final time and bought the horse known as "Mr. Mac" for $15,500.

Mr. McElwyn to halter at Lexington track

Sheppard's timing was impeccable. The next two Hambletonian winners were both by Mr. McElwyn, and both were products of Hanover broodmares. Yes, he'd certainly bought the right horse in Mr. McElwyn, and that stallion's blood was to be found in Hanover pedigrees for decades to come.

After taking so much joy from seeing Hanover's Bertha win the Hambletonian, Lawrence Sheppard decided he rather liked winning the Hambletonian. To win that race became the goal of both his racing operation and the standard by which he judged stallions. What he really wanted, of course, was to win the Hambletonian with a colt that could retire at Hanover.

Sheppard thought his best chances of getting another Hambletonian winner would come through Miss Bertha Dillon. He knew he had mined a rich vein in the petite chestnut mare. The young businessman was ultimately proven right, but not exactly in the way he had hoped.

After producing four straight fillies, Miss Bertha Dillon delivered a colt in 1929. He was simply named Hanover and great hopes were vested in him, but he died in March 1931 as a two-year-old.

In 1930, Miss Bertha Dillon had a foal that didn't fit the mold of her older sisters for a very good reason. She was sired by Guy McKinney, not Peter Volo, and her name was Bertha Hanover. She was a chestnut like her mother, and although she trotted herself, her legacy would ultimately be limited to pacers. (They were, however, extremely fast pacers.)

In 1931, another Peter Volo filly arrived, this one christened Bertha C. Hanover. She was a stakes filly of the first order, but the dearth of distaff events during the Depression forced her to compete against colts and she was seldom up to that task.

In 1932, Lawrence Sheppard's dream colt arrived. He was by Peter Volo from Miss Bertha Dillon. He certainly had the right pedigree. He also had the right framework; his textbook conformation would make any trainer's mouth water.

Sheppard also saw that this colt had the right name; he named the youngster after himself. Lawrence Hanover's career path, Sheppard hoped, would lead him to many winner's circles during his racing days and then lead him straight home to a stall in the stud barn at Hanover.

The colt, however, proved to be just as bull-headed as his namesake in the early stages of training. He was entrusted to the master horseman Dr. Hugh M. Parshall, a veterinarian-turned-horse trainer. The colt got his early lessons at Pinehurst, North Carolina, in the winter of 1933-34.

Lawrence Hanover's work ethic was highly suspect. When hooked to a breaking cart, he would simply lie down. He pulled that trick day after day until Parshall decided to educate the colt.

A local farmer came to the training center regularly with a double cart pulled by a mule and a draft horse.

"Take that mule out of there," Parshall told the farmer. His stablehands then hitched Lawrence Hanover in double harness with the draft horse. When the farmer asked the pair to step out on a cinder path that ringed the track, once again Lawrence Hanover took a dive.

Parshall yelled, "Go on!" to the farmer, and the stout draft horse simply dragged Lawrence Hanover about 50 yards before the colt scrambled to his feet. He decided he didn't like those cinders biting him in the rear end, and tried that stunt only a few more times before he learned his lesson.

If his work ethic was initially lacking, there was never much question about Lawrence Hanover's ability. In 1934, Parshall won with the colt in 2:02, tying the world record for two-year-old trotters set by his older sister Hanover's Bertha.

A world champion daughter, and now a world champion son! Miss Bertha Dillon had done it again! Lawrence Sheppard walked a little taller whenever he thought about his namesake.

But there was trouble in paradise. Lawrence Hanover was a good one, but there was a better two-year-old trotter that season. He was a gangly, gunmetal gray gelding with a fitting name: Greyhound.

Lawrence Hanover had trouble beating Greyhound as a two-year-old, but Sheppard hoped that things would be different the following year.

They weren't. Greyhound still dominated his class. Sheppard was desperate for his namesake to win the Hambletonian and he took the colt away from Parshall and gave him to Henry Thomas.

Lawrence Hanover was no match for Greyhound in the Hambletonian, but the crusty old Thomas did win Sheppard's favor when Lawrence Hanover beat Greyhound one heat at the New York State Fair in Syracuse.

That fall at Lexington, Greyhound stayed in the barn while the Kentucky Futurity was raced. Officially, the word was that he had kicked while jogging one day and got a leg over the shaft of his jog cart. The ensuing soreness prevented him from racing. Some people felt, however, that Greyhound's owner, Colonel E.J. Baker, simply didn't want to risk having Lawrence Hanover beat him.

With Greyhound gone, Lawrence Hanover easily won the Kentucky Futurity.

There was never any doubt that Lawrence Hanover was going to stud at Hanover. He was assured of that opportunity by his pedigree, but he had also earned that opportunity by his ability.

Miss Bertha Dillon's final three foals failed to meet the high standards set by their older siblings, but her most celebrated daughter helped fill the void.

Gravestone of Miss Bertha Dillon

Shirley Hanover and Henry Thomas

Chapter 4

And A Child Shall Lead Them

In the spring of 1933, Hanover welcomed the first foal of its Hambletonian winner Hanover's Bertha. He was a colt by Truax, sire of the 1931 Hambo winner Calumet Butler. Sheppard was thrilled with the youngster and named him Brownie Hanover in honor of his close friend Bowman A. Brown, Sr., later founder of *The Harness Horse* magazine and one of the founders of The Standardbred Horse Sale Co.

In the 1936 Hambletonian, Brownie Hanover was no threat to Rosalind, but none of the others in the race were either and it was no disgrace to place 2-2 in the sport's greatest classic.

Lawrence Sheppard didn't fancy finishing second, and he felt the same way about it that John Nance Garner of Texas felt about being vice president under Franklin D. Roosevelt. Garner was so overshadowed by FDR that the Texan complained that the vice presidency wasn't "worth a bucket of warm [spit]."

Finishing second might have been acceptable for his father or Clinton Myers, but Lawrence Sheppard wasn't involved in racing to be the bridesmaid.

Hanover's Bertha made amends with her second foal, the nervous, flighty filly Shirley Hanover. Patiently brought to her peak by trainer Henry Thomas, Shirley was at her best on Hambletonian Day in 1937 and scampered to a straight-heat victory. Lawrence Sheppard's face lit up afterwards with a wide, sincere smile.

"Shirley had terrific speed," recalls Dick Thomas, Henry's son. "In the first heat of the Hambletonian, she had post seven and had the lead before they got to that first hairpin turn."

The Mr. McElwyn filly won by open lengths in each heat, making Hanover's Bertha the first Hambletonian winner to produce a Hambletonian winner. She retains that distinction at the start of the 21st century. Miss Bertha Dillon and her daughters were on their way to establishing a dynasty, a Hanover dynasty.

Playing a major role in the making of this dynasty was Henry Thomas, the tough-talking horseman hardened in the racing wars on the Plains State early in the century.

Son Dick Thomas recalls that his father and Lawrence Sheppard were alike in many ways and that led to a tempestuous relationship between them.

"Shep was a tough man to get along with," recalls Thomas. "I don't know how my father ever did it. Dad and Shep would yell back and forth all the time. I guess Shep liked that. He ruled Hanover with an iron hand; he was a tough man."

Lawrence Sheppard took enormous satisfaction from Shirley Hanover's victory in the Hambletonian. After all, what would be more rewarding than to breed and own a Hambletonian winner, especially if you had also stood next to her mother in the Hambletonian winner's circle?

Sheppard was proud of Shirley and the silverware she got for winning, but something was troubling him. Shirley Hanover may have won the Hambletonian that year, but Sheppard knew darn well that she wasn't the best three-year-old trotter of that season. That honor belonged to a colt campaigning under the name of Mr. Watt.

Let's retreat two years to the fall of 1935, when the final crop of Dillon Axworthy was auctioned at Harrisburg. In an era where the hot young sires were Volomite and Scotland, the offspring of the aging Axworthy stallion had little appeal. Still, Lawrence Sheppard took a liking to a Dillon Axworthy colt named Tony Hanover from the great mare Volga E. Sheppard showed little interest in another Dillon Axworthy colt named Dean Hanover.

"My father preferred Dean Hanover," recalls Dick Thomas. "Dad always rode the lead pony at Hanover, so he got to know those yearlings quite well."

Sheppard retained Tony Hanover, but the best he could do was get a mark of 2:04-1/2 on the pace. That wasn't the kind of horse that interested Lawrence Sheppard. Meanwhile, Dean Hanover was turning out to be exactly the kind of horse that interested Lawrence Sheppard.

Dean Hanover had sold for a mere $410 as a yearling and had been rechristened Mr. Watt by his purchaser. He showed remarkable ability as a two-year-old and returned to the races even better as a three-year-old in 1937.

Mr. Watt was not eligible to the Hambletonian, so that limited his earning capacity significantly, but Lawrence Sheppard wanted this horse at all costs.

"All costs" proved to be a check for $25,000 handed over to H. Stacey Smith, Mr. Watt's owner. The first thing that the publicity-minded Sheppard did was to restore the colt's original name of Dean Hanover. (In that era, which was prior to the formation of the U.S. Trotting Association, a horse's name could be changed even after he had raced.)

Lawrence Sheppard foresaw a great future for the son of Dillon Axworthy. He wanted the colt to carry his original Hanover name while he was making headlines. It didn't take long for Dean Hanover to make them.

He won the Ohio Governor's Cup, negotiating the half-mile track at the state fairgrounds in 2:06 with Henry Thomas in the bike.

He then shipped to his home state of Pennsylvania. Owner Sheppard, who had ridden many miles behind his horses over the years, slipped into the sulky and set a world record for three heats in winning the Reading Futurity. The miles were in 2:04-3/4, 2:06-3/4, and 2:06.

Henry Thomas watched from the sidelines that day and marveled at Dean Hanover's manners.

"My, he goes nice," the trainer mused. "Why, anybody could drive him — even a little girl."

Thus a daring idea was spawned. For it just so happened that Lawrence Sheppard had three little girls. One of them was an 11-year-old named Alma, who was crazy about her father's horses, and quite capable of handling them on the track. Henry Thomas approached Lawrence and Charlotte Sheppard to ask if they would agree to allow their daughter Alma to drive Dean Hanover in a time trial at Lexington.

Dean Hanover and Alma Sheppard

Certainly, the proud parents replied, as long as Thomas was sure she could handle the colt, and as long as Alma wanted to try.

Alma Sheppard was only 11 years old, but no stranger to a sulky. She was born the same year that her father started Hanover Shoe Farms and she had grown up around the trotters and pacers. If any little girl was qualified to drive Dean Hanover, it was Alma Sheppard.

It was one thing, however, for her to jog and train her father's horses, but it was quite another to drive the best three-year-old trotter in the country. Alma had given her own mare Nimble Hanover a 2:09-1/4 record, but she might have to go 10 seconds faster driving Dean Hanover.

Alma leapt at the chance. She took the lines for her first workout behind Dean Hanover three days before their scheduled time trial. She wore her father's orange and blue driving colors with the sleeves rolled up. Her driving hat was a little too big, but no one seemed to care.

Dean Hanover was pulling a sulky made especially for Alma. It measured just 27 inches high and 48 inches wide.

Years later Dick Thomas marvels at a horse using such a small sulky. "Just think of a big trotting colt going to a sulky that confined," he mused. "That's how pure gaited Dean Hanover was. I've never had a trotter go with a sulky less than 50 inches wide."

On the appointed day, Dean Hanover was officially programmed to beat a time of 2:00-3/4, his winning time taken at Good Time Park during Hambletonian Week. Everyone knew that the real goal, however, was the 1:59-1/4 speed standard for sophomore trotters held jointly by the brother-sister team of Protector and The Marchioness.

Before the time trial, Henry Thomas, who would drive the prompter, an old horse named Grover, told Alma that he wouldn't trail too closely during the opening half. He feared that Dean Hanover would take too much hold for the 90-pound girl if the prompter got close.

As they waited for their rendezvous with history, the gruff veteran Thomas asked Alma if she were nervous. The little girl smiled and replied, "Deanie is a good horse, and we'll get along fine."

Alma's smile turned into a poker face when she turned Dean Hanover for the word. Suddenly the pair was off flying into the first turn. They reached the first quarter in 29-1/2 seconds.

"That's the way, Alma!" yelled Thomas, who was trailing with the prompter. But Alma probably didn't hear him because the driving cap had fallen down over her ears.

Henry Thomas, Dean Hanover and 11-year-old Alma Sheppard after the trial

Dean Hanover could certainly hear the prompter and he was racing to stay ahead, Dick Thomas recalls.

"Dean got over to the half in 58-1/2 seconds, which was unheard of at that time," he says. "Of course, Alma was just sitting there. She couldn't really rate Dean."

If Alma wasn't nervous before or during the time trial, Henry Thomas surely was. "Believe me, I was trembling," he admitted afterwards. "No Hambletonian had ever been like this."

When Dean Hanover crossed the wire and the 1:58-1/2 time was hung out on the judge's stand, a thunderous roar erupted from the crowd. A new world record! By an 11-year-old girl!

To put this in the proper context at the start of the 21st century, it would be the same as an 11-year-old girl driving a three-year-old trotter a mile in 1:51. Can anyone truly imagine such a feat?

Henry Thomas walked the prompter Grover back slowly in front of the grandstand, allowing the attention to fall on those who deserved it: Dean Hanover and Alma Sheppard. Thomas posed for photos holding Dean Hanover's head, but he avoided the microphone.

"There was something in my throat that stuck there and kept me from saying anything," he later explained. "I've been around a long time and I'm a hard guy, but if anybody had asked me to speak, I'd have cried."

In the twilight of his life, Henry Thomas looked back on a career with harness horses and said, "You can have my three Hambletonian wins for thrills. I'll take the little girl at Lexington and that mile in a million."

A week after Alma drove Dean in a time trial, father Lawrence took the lines and drove Dean Hanover to a three-heat victory at Lexington, trotting consecutive miles in 2:00-1/4, 2:00-3/4, and 2:00-3/4.

That world record lasted for decades, and was still in the books when Lawrence Sheppard died more than three decades later.

The wizened veterans of the harness turf found it all but impossible to comprehend what this girl and this horse had done. Driving a trotter at that rate of speed was something that demanded skill and years of experience. But Alma was a mere child.

John Hervey wrote, "Little Alma Sheppard has at a stroke become the most extraordinary child in the world to those who love horses or, for that matter, those who do not."

Hervey compared the young lass to child prodigies who had astonished the music world with their skills on the violin or piano. He then added, " . . . she has played upon an instrument far more complex and intricate, and drawn from it a song more wonderful than ever they could draw from theirs."

Is it any wonder that Dean Hanover was Lawrence Sheppard's favorite horse of all time?

Winning the Hambletonian was then the highest honor for a harness horse owner, but everyone knew you couldn't win it every year. Everyone, that is, except Lawrence Sheppard. He found his trips to the Hambletonian winner's circle in 1929 and 1937 to be intoxicating, and a man could come to like that, he reasoned. In the summer of '38, however, Sheppard found himself without a Hambo hopeful. So Henry Thomas found one for him in a mostly unlikely prospect.

The colt McLin was a son of Mr. McElwyn from the famous mare Ethelinda by Peter The Great. Anyone who watched him in his races knew that he had abundant ability. McLin would dazzle horsemen with his bursts of raw speed, then break stride and finish at the back of the pack. The woods are full of such horses that never live up to their potential.

But Henry Thomas spotted something in McLin that made him think he could find the key. He advised Sheppard to buy the horse, if possible, and the master of Hanover wrote out a check for $20,000. It seemed to be sheer foolishness. McLin had only won a single heat in his career.

For $20,000, Sheppard got the right to rename the horse and he simply tagged the "Hanover" to the colt's existing name.

Son Dick Thomas never knew exactly what his father changed to transform the flawed McLin into the flawless McLin Hanover that the trotting world saw on Hambletonian Day.

"Maybe Dad changed the colt's rigging before the Hambletonian," mused Dick Thomas many years later. "I just don't know."

Whatever Henry Thomas did worked because the newly minted McLin Hanover won the Hambletonian by open lengths, destroying colts he had previously chased.

Once again, there was the smiling visage of Lawrence Sheppard standing next to the Hambletonian winner. He was getting to be regular visitor there, and he liked it that way.

Whatever key Henry Thomas used with McLin Hanover opened the door to several astonishing performances. He went to Lexington that fall and won the Kentucky Futurity easily. Here was a horse with such incredible speed that he could easily become the fastest three-year-old trotter in history, and Thomas wanted to give the colt that chance in a time trial.

"I think McLin Hanover would have trotted in 1:57 or better," estimated Dick Thomas many years later. "His speed was unbelievable. He trotted eighths in 13-1/2 seconds. It was Hanover's practice to time trial everything in the stable when they got to Lexington."

Everything, that is, except McLin Hanover. Lawrence Sheppard decreed that there would be no time trial for McLin Hanover.

"He [McLin Hanover] would have beaten Dean Hanover's 1:58-1/2 world record so far it would have been funny," claims Thomas. "But Dean Hanover was Shep's all-time favorite."

No father would want to take his daughter's name out of the record books after only one year. Besides, Sheppard already had a stall in the Hanover stallion barn for Dean Hanover and he wanted him to keep his world record. No horse, certainly not even a Hambletonian winner like McLin Hanover, would ever usurp Dean Hanover's spot in Lawrence Sheppard's heart.

Sheppard saw to it that McLin Hanover, who was from the same Axworthy male line as Dean Hanover, wouldn't compete with Dean Hanover as a stallion either by selling the colt in the fall of 1938 to Count Orsi Mangelli of Italy.

Lawrence Sheppard didn't limit his aspirations for a Hambletonian winner to Hanover-sired stock. As the 1939 season began, it seemed certain that the two top candidates for the Hambletonian were Nibble Hanover, a son of Calumet Chuck, and Peter Astra, a Kentucky-bred son of Peter Volo.

Nibble Hanover, however, took ill that year and never made it to the races. That allowed Peter Astra to sweep through the stakes leading up to the Hambletonian.

On the eve of the Goshen classic, Sheppard approached Peter Astra's trainer, Doc Parshall, and asked if the colt was for sale. That decision, replied Parshall, was up to Peter Astra's owner. Sheppard said he would give $25,000 for the Hambo favorite, but owner Dr. L. M. Guilinger had dreamed of owning a Hambletonian winner and he refused the offer.

Peter Astra won the Hambletonian, and Sheppard's filly Cherry Hanover finished well back in the field.

(When Nibble Hanover returned to the races as an aged horse, he made up for lost time and he set a 1:58-3/4 mark in winning as a five-year-old. Lawrence Sheppard decided that he was the horse for Hanover, and when Nibble Hanover's days on the track were done, he was headed to Hanover. Peter Astra was a colossal failure as a stallion, while Nibble Hanover would contribute to the breed in a unique way.)

Sheppard's aggressive acquisition of stallions and mares resulted in a burgeoning broodmare band and ever-larger yearling consignments. Each fall horsemen tried to find their way to Hanover in October to look over the prospects headed for the auction.

One horse owner who didn't have far to travel was Mahlon Haines, who lived in nearby York. One day in the fall of 1939, as German troops were marching on Europe, Haines went to Hanover to visit the Sheppards and possibly see some horses. His impish personality belied the business sense behind the man. Haines billed himself as "The Shoe Wizard" and became a rich man in the same business that fueled Hanover Shoe Farms.

On this day, however, he spotted 17-year-old Lawrence Sheppard, Jr. ("Sonny" to all who knew him) and began tossing a baseball with him. Haines was doing his best to mimic the style of Carl Hubbell and the great pitchers of that day.

Haines paid little attention to Henry Thomas, who was exercising the Hanover yearlings, but he finally acknowledged the famed horseman by saying,

"Let me know when you bring out a good colt, and I'll watch him. I just want to show Sonny what Buck Newsom should have served up to those Reds in the seventh inning of that final game of the World Series."

Henry Thomas had little patience for baseball antics when it was time to show off sales yearlings, so he yelled to Haines, "You'd better put that ball away and watch all these colts, for they can all show plenty."

Hanover's broodmare band was growing with each passing year and by 1940 Hanover was offering 62 yearlings for sale. They represented such sires as Guy McKinney, Mr. McElwyn, Calumet Chuck, Peter The Brewer, and the brothers Sandy Flash and Lawrence Hanover.

Sheppard wanted to draw attention to a yearling named Gordon Hanover that year. The colt was a son of Calumet Chuck from the noted matron Miss Pierette. Horsemen couldn't help but admire this robust bay. Miss Pierette was already the breed's leading producer of 2:10 trotters, but Hanover wanted another credit for her. The farm offered this inducement to buyers:

We believe this to be one of our outstanding yearlings and possibly the best of the foals of Miss Pierette. We are therefore offering $100 to the owner and $25 to the driver if Gordon Hanover is given a Breeders Record of 2:10 or faster as a two-year-old or $50 to the owners and $25 to the driver if Gordon Hanover is given a Breeders Record of 2:10 as a three-year-old.

Gordon Hanover sold for $1,700, but, alas, he never won a race or took any kind of record. The 1940 Hanover consignment averaged $750, and the top item was the flashy chestnut Guy McKinney colt Al Hanover, named after Al Thomas, father of Henry Thomas. He sold for $3,700.

In 1941, Hanover gained another Hambletonian credit when Bill Gallon won the classic at Good Time Park. Because he didn't compete with the Hanover surname, few people realized that Bill Gallon had gone through the sale ring as a yearling under the name Ashley Hanover.

Bill Gallon was a son of Sandy Flash, and now the family of Miss Bertha Dillon not only had Hambletonian credits from its females, but also boasted a stallion that had sired a Hambo winner.

It was too late, however, to help Sandy Flash's stud career as he had been exported to Sweden in 1938. When his kid brother Lawrence Hanover showed up in the stud barn, Sheppard reasoned that there was no need for two horses with the same pedigree. Sandy Flash was older and had none of the racing credentials, so he had to find a new home.

Hanover sent some of its best mares to Lawrence Hanover, a stallion that was frequently referred to in the trade journals of that era as a "stallion who simply can't miss." Lawrence Sheppard, and everyone else in the sport, would get a lesson in just how unpredictable genetics can be. The result was one of the greatest disappointments of Sheppard's career as a horse breeder, according to Dick Thomas.

"Lawrence Hanover was the most beautiful horse you would ever want to see, but he wasn't worth a damn as a sire," recalls Thomas. "Lawrence's failure as a sire just about killed Shep."

Lawrence Hanover

Conformation of Billy Direct

Billy Direct winning at Good Time Park

Chapter 5

Two Stallion Kings And A Trotting Titan

When Lawrence Sheppard wanted something, he wasn't easily deterred. And what he wanted in the Hanover stallion barn were champions. In 1941 as the United States was spiraling toward involvement in World War II and other breeding farms were adopting a watch and wait attitude, Sheppard plunged ahead.

He had his sights set on two horses, the pacer Billy Direct and trotter Spencer Scott.

They were the fastest stallions on each gait in history and Lawrence Sheppard felt they belonged at Hanover.

The pacing stallion was already retired after a career in which he astonished horsemen with his blazing speed.

Foaled in Tennessee but developed in Maine, Billy Direct came into the spotlight in the summer of 1936 as a juvenile. He raced free-legged, without the aid of hobbles, and so overwhelmed his foes that he performed like an aged campaigner with his speed and assurance.

It was much the same in 1937 when he was a three-year-old. He was definitely a cut above his rivals and he concluded his racing season by pacing the fastest race mile in the history of the sport when he won in 1:58 at Lexington.

The fastest race mile ever — by a three-year-old? In an era when most Standardbreds were anything but natural athletes, it simply didn't make sense. And he got that record in the final heat of a three-heat event. Yes, Billy Direct was truly something special.

Billy Direct proved just how special he was when he returned to Lexington the following autumn. He was entered in a free-for-all pace with four contestants. This was before mobile starting gates were used, so the horses were required to score down across the track, making certain not to beat the inside horse away.

False starts — "recalls" in harness racing terminology — were common under the scoring system and confusion often prevailed. Such was the case at the start of that 1938 free-for-all pace. The starter said "Go!" and rang the recall bell almost simultaneously.

Two drivers decided to make a race of it; the other two pulled their mounts up, thinking they would have another chance. Officials were in a quandary, but decided that the race was official. The two horses that had pulled up were declared "distanced" and were prohibited from coming back for the second heat.

One man who had stopped was Vic Fleming, driver of Billy Direct. He knew that his horse was sharp and ready to go a good mile, but now he was declared out of the race. The frustrated Fleming didn't know what to do. Suddenly he had an inspired idea. He walked to the judge's stand and asked to go a time trial with Billy Direct. Time trials normally had to be programmed in advance, but under the circumstances the judges granted him permission. Fleming undoubtedly would have preferred to race for the $1,000 purse because money wasn't plentiful for pacers during the Depression, but a time trial would have to suffice.

That walk to the judges stand was one of the most important decisions of Vic Fleming ever made. He brought Billy Direct back to the track and sent his pacing whirlwind around the mile oval in 1:55, shocking the crowd.

The shocked spectators had just witnessed the first official 1:55 mile in history. Dan Patch had recorded the same time years earlier, but his mile was paced behind a running Thoroughbred prompter. Billy Direct did it on his own — amazing!

In 1940, Billy Direct was shuffled off to stud at Peninsula Farm in Freemont, Ohio. It was a nice farm, but it hardly seemed suitable for the fastest Standardbred in history. There were, however, few large breeding farms in that era and many of them harbored a prejudice against pacers. Pacers were seen as second-class citizens; many pacers were, in fact, failed trotters.

Hanover Shoe Farms had never stood a pacer, but Lawrence Sheppard decided it was time to change that. He never stood on tradition if he saw no practical reason to do so. The fact of the matter was that Billy Direct was the fastest pacer in the world and Hanover had to have him. In late 1941, Sheppard announced that Billy Direct was coming to Hanover.

Once Sheppard had the fastest pacing stallion in history, he needed a trotting bookend and found that horse in Spencer Scott, winner of the 1940 Hambletonian.

Unlike Billy Direct, Spencer Scott was born to privilege. His sire was Scotland, then at the apex of his fame as a stallion, while his dam was May Spencer, a daughter of the 1928 Hambletonian winner Spencer.

*Spencer Scott
and Fred Egan
at Lexington*

*Spencer Scott
conformation*

*(Photo courtesy of
Howard DeFreitas, USTA)*

Astute breeder Charles W. Phellis admired May Spencer, who was owned by his friend David Look of Castleton Farm in Kentucky. Phellis felt that the robust, masculine Scotland would be the perfect mate for May Spencer, and he told Look that if he bred her to Scotland, he would buy the resulting foal.

Phellis selected a winning combination and the colt with the combination name — Spencer from his grandsire and Scott from his sire — proved to be a dandy. Phellis judged horsemen as well as he judged horses and he placed Spencer Scott with his trusted trainer Fred Egan.

Spencer Scott won the Hambletonian in 1940 and the following year Egan took him to Lexington and scheduled him for a time trial. He wanted to find out just how fast his guy could trot.

One minute fifty-seven and one-fourth seconds later, Egan — and the world of trotting — knew how fast Spencer Scott could trot. His mile was the fastest ever by a trotting stallion.

None of this was lost on Lawrence Sheppard, of course, and soon he announced that Spencer Scott would be starting a new career as a sire at Hanover.

Billy Direct and Spencer Scott were to follow parallel paths in their breeding careers at Hanover, starting there in 1942 and achieving immediate success.

As overjoyed as Sheppard was to have the two stallion kings at Hanover, he shared the shock and sorrow that all Americans felt when they awoke on Sunday, December 7, 1941. As they listened to their radios, they realized that America would soon be involved in the horrors of war. Japanese fighter pilots attacked a naval base at Pearl Harbor in Hawaii and there was little doubt that this meant war. President Roosevelt and Congress confirmed it with a formal declaration.

With our boys soon going off to fight in the Pacific and European theaters, horse racing was an exceedingly low priority. Many young horsemen learned how to carry a gun instead of a training whip and some fairgrounds were taken over for use as military bases. Wartime rationing of gasoline and tires made shipping horses impractical in many cases, and it also made it difficult for racing fans to travel far to follow their favorite horses. Horse racing was an afterthought to most of America.

Many breeders had barely limped through the Depression years. In Kentucky, Samuel Look of Castleton was so virulently anti-Roosevelt that he had earlier decreed that he and his father David, a revered elder statesman, would not invest money in their horse business as long as FDR occupied the White House. Little did they realize Roosevelt would serve for a dozen years. Like many breeders, the Looks curtailed their horse operations further during World War II.

Hanover continued its breeding operations during the war, as did Walnut Hall Farm, the belle dame of the Bluegrass. The stallions Volomite and Scotland were the rage in trotting circles at that time. They had sired three of the first four Hambletonian winners in the 1940s and they had other trotting — and pacing — winners busting out all over.

It was difficult for Hanover to compete with the virtual stranglehold that the sons and daughters of Volomite and Scotland held. Mr. McElwyn was getting old and Dean Hanover was just getting started. Hanover wouldn't sell its first offerings by Billy Direct and Spencer Scott until 1944, so shoppers for Hanover yearlings had to content themselves with prospects by Dean Hanover, Mr. McElwyn, Calumet Chuck, and Lawrence Hanover.

Billy Dickerson, a wily old horsemen employed as a trainer by E. Roland Harriman's Arden Homestead Stable, found a butterball bay colt by Calumet Chuck from Tisma Hanover that caught his eye in the 1943 Hanover consignment. Dickerson liked him enough to buy him for his patron, and the youngster named Titan Hanover was taken south by young Harry Pownall to be schooled.

For many months, it appeared that Dickerson had picked a lemon. Titan Hanover stabbed a hind leg, a trait that causes trainers to shake their heads in a combination of dismay and disgust. "Stabbing" is a gait defect in which a horse jabs a hind leg abruptly to the ground in an attempt to avoid interference with a front leg. It often spells doom for a trotter's career.

Pownall patiently let Titan Hanover find his gait, and he eventually overcame the habit of stabbing. There was no way, however, the colt could overcome the fact that he was simply so darn small.

Pownall's preference for allowing his trotters to go with a low head made Titan seem even smaller, and the little guy was the laughingstock of the winter training colony. They would ultimately find, however, in the words of a phrase popular a half-century later, "It's not the size of the dog in the fight, but the size of the fight in the dog."

Or in Titan's case, the size of the fight in the horse. And Titan was indeed a fighter. As more and more demands were placed on him in the late spring and early summer of 1944, he handled them with ease and asked for more. He made a few mistakes along the way, as baby trotters will do, but after Pownall started racing Titan, the Brooklyn-born horseman knew he had a rare horse on his hands.

That September, Titan Hanover won in heats in 2:05-1/2 and 2:03-1/2 over the new half-mile track at Delaware, Ohio, beating the existing world record for one heat by 1-1/2 seconds and the two-heat record by 5-1/2 seconds.

Titan then went to Lexington and ripped off a pair of heats in 2:02-3/4 as if he were breaking sticks. His pursuers were struggling far behind him and Pownall was just buggy riding.

Harry Pownall started thinking. Titan, the young horseman was sure, could trot even faster if afforded the opportunity in a time trial. How fast? No one knew for sure, but there was only one way to find out. That was to put Titan against the fence with the encouragement of some Thoroughbred prompters and see what happened.

Conformation shot of Titan Hanover, with Kenny Hamm

In the back of Pownall's mind, and in the back of everyone's mind, was the outside chance that Titan could be the one, the one precocious trotter that the breed had waited for. No juvenile had ever stepped a mile in 2:00. Joe Markey had thought Hanover's Bertha capable of that feat 15 years earlier, but she was denied that chance.

But asking 2:00 speed of a mere baby seemed like a fool's errand. There had been many great trotters come down the pike in the first four decades of the 20th century. None of them had gone faster than 2:02. In fact, four trotters were tied at 2:02 and that seemed like the de facto limit of two-year-old speed.

Of course, none of them had ever trotted a race mile in 2:03-1/2 around four turns either, so Pownall scheduled Titan Hanover for a time trial.

The appointed day was October 4, 1944, and the little colt took to the track under the watchful eyes of horsemen from across America. They murmured their dissent. Sure, a little colt like Titan could get around the turns of a half-mile track like a hoop around a barrel, but how would he hold up when he looked down that long stretch?

They soon found out. Titan and Pownall were away swiftly and trotted through fast but consistent fractions. The first quarter was covered in 29-1/4 seconds, then next one in 29-1/2 seconds. He was ahead of the pace for a 2:00 mile, but could he sustain that tempo?

Titan Hanover finishes his 2:00 mile at Lexington in 1944

Rounding the far turn, Titan looked down that long stretch, the "heartbreak lane" that had scuttled the hopes of so many would-be champions. But instead of fading, the little guy was flying. Pownall rallied him, shouting and shaking the lines. On the little titan trotted.

He reached the wire under a head of steam and when the time of 2:00 was displayed the spectators stared in disbelief. A 2:00 two-year-old, and a trotter to boot! It simply seemed impossible.

As Titan trotted his way into history, Allied troops were sweeping across Europe. Americans could finally see an end to the war against Germany and Italy. Things on the home front were picking up, too, and that fall Hanover's yearling sale passed the $100,000 mark for the first time as 73 head averaged $1,496.

So dominant was Titan Hanover in his class that he

Titan after the 1945 Hambletonian

was barred in the betting in the 1945 Hambletonian despite drawing a starting post in the second tier. That really made no difference as Pownall left carefully with his champion, let the dust settle a bit, and then began weaving his way through trotting traffic.

When Titan reached the front, the race was over. No one was going to catch him now. The second heat was even easier.

Titan Hanover continued to race as an older horse and then found a home at Hanover Shoe Farms when he was retired. His extraordinary performances on the track made him popular with breeders in the post-war period, but when his first offspring were placed in training, they showed a nasty tendency to stab a hind leg.

Titan Hanover had overcome this fault through the patient training of Harry Pownall, but not every horse was Titan Hanover and not every trainer was Harry Pownall. Titan Hanover was ultimately judged a modest success at best as a stallion, but he did sire one horse that got Lawrence Sheppard a trip back to the Hambletonian winner's circle.

Chapter 6

Master Of Hanover

Both Lawrence Sheppard and Sonny Sheppard served their nation during World War II. The son was of prime age for the military, and he served as a pilot in the Army Air Corps.

Lawrence Sheppard served on the War Production Board, visiting European battlefields to determine how to improve the footwear of American soldiers. For his unselfish service to his country's cause, Sheppard was later awarded the Medal of Freedom for "exceptionally meritorious achievement . . . "

With the boys back from the war in 1945, America's economy exploded. Housing was needed for the young men, their wives, and the baby boom they created. Jobs were plentiful and optimism was abundant, as America was anxious to forget more than 15 years of economic depression and war.

Working men needed shoes, of course, and Lawrence Sheppard saw to it that many of them were shod with Hanover shoes, still a practical dress and everyday choice. Sheppard was particularly delighted to have his son join him in the shoe business after he was discharged from the service.

The economic boom swept harness racing along. The development of the mobile starting gate and the advent of night pari-mutuel palaces such as Roosevelt Raceway, Batavia Downs, Saratoga Raceway, and others signaled a whole new era in the sport.

Purses were edging up, too. The 1944 Hambletonian carried a purse of $33,577 but the next two renewals were contested for more than $50,000.

Lawrence Sheppard's perseverance during the hard times positioned Hanover Shoe Farms perfectly to ride the wave of this euphoria.

In 1946, Billy Direct's son Ensign Hanover took the inaugural edition of a new race in Ohio called the Little Brown Jug. The flashy chestnut was just one of many Billy Direct pacers turning heads at racetracks across the continent.

Spencer Scott, too, had hit big immediately as his son Rodney (sold as a yearling under the name Edwin Hanover) was the fastest two-year-old trotter of

Lawrence Sheppard in a pensive moment
(Photo courtesy of Wide World Photos)

1946 and won a heat in the 1947 Hambletonian. That fall a brother to Rodney named White Hanover had fetched a price of $42,000, making him the highest priced Standardbred yearling in history.

White Hanover and all the other Hanover yearlings were sold at the Standardbred Horse Sale, a venture that Sheppard started with Bowman Brown, Sr., a Harrisburg businessman and publisher of *The Harness Horse* magazine after the Old Glory Sale in New York ceased operation. With the quantity of Hanover yearlings growing each year, Sheppard needed to have a regular venue to sell them and thus a sale company was born.

As 1947 drew to a close, however, Lawrence Sheppard had mixed emotions. His two stallion kings, Billy Direct and Spencer Scott, had been smashing successes in the stud, but Billy had died unexpectedly that year and Spencer Scott went sterile, stunning financial losses for Hanover and greater losses for the breed.

Sheppard swallowed hard and accepted those losses, and, as he neared age 50, he was secure enough in his accomplishments to poke fun at himself.

On December 3, 1947, Sheppard spoke to the Horse and Mule Association of America, Inc and began his remarks by saying, "You have invited me 20 years too late to discuss with confidence as to how to breed good horses.

"I thought I knew most of the answers then, but as the years of experience accumulated, I began to doubt that I knew as much as I thought I did. I have finally reached the conclusion that I, in particular, and probably no one else, have any hard and fast theories, rules, or secrets that are worth a tinker's damn.

"I perhaps can be described as a 'ginner' for I am more or less against all formulas, theories, fads, fixations of all kinds, and particularly prejudices, not only as to breeding horses, but also as to raising and caring for them."

In a nutshell, that was the Sheppard philosophy.

Sheppard went on in his speech to say that he spent many nights reading discourses on why good horses could not be raised in New Jersey or California; why inbreeding is incestuous but line breeding is acceptable; and why the old-time horses were superior to the ones bred at that time.

"I wind up by getting mad all by myself with no one to listen to me," said Sheppard.

Sheppard pointed out that judicious inbreeding in the Standardbred had resulted in remarkable improvements in the time standard for the mile distance.

"The man who categorically said that inbreeding is no good is a fool," concluded Sheppard. "We really have only two principal foundation sires and both of these died only a comparatively short time ago. I refer to Peter The Great and Axworthy."

He added that some lesser strains, McKinney, Direct, and Electioneer through Abbedale, were scattered around.

Sheppard's comments were telling because Peter The Great and Axworthy male lines were primarily trotting lines while the blood of Direct and Electioneer were already enormously popular among pacing breeders. They would become more so in the post-war boom.

The man from Hanover acknowledged the progress that inbreeding had produced, but added, "Any man who says that secret of breeding good horses is to inbreed them is, I think, just as big or perhaps a bigger fool than the man who condemns all inbreeding."

Sheppard's experience showed him that some families and individuals could be crossed closely with good results and others couldn't. There were no hard and fast rules.

In his remarks, Sheppard went on to point out that good horses could be raised in a variety of areas "providing the soil is of such a nature that nutritious grasses, legumes, and feeds can be produced on it."

While Kentucky's Bluegrass was known as the heart of America's horse country, Sheppard said that the tradition of raising horses had as much to do with establishing that reputation as the soil, grass, water, and climate of Kentucky.

"I have watched from time to time with some amusement an occasional Kentucky breeder who decided to rest his oars on Kentucky's reputation, neglect his lands and the care and feeding of his stock," continued Sheppard. "With the result that he produces some of the sorriest, wormiest, small-boned, pot-bellied colts that I have ever seen. And then unsuccessfully sells them on the statement that they were born and raised in Kentucky."

Some buyers apparently liked the yearlings raised in Hanover, Pennsylvania, because when Imperial Hanover walked into the ring in 1949 at Harrisburg, the action didn't stop until the bids reached $72,000.

The price shocked breeders and horsemen. It was $30,000 more than the record set when White Hanover sold just two years earlier. Neither White Hanover nor Imperial Hanover ever amounted to much on the track, and it wasn't until a special Hanover yearling waltzed through the ring in 1958 that Imperial Hanover's record price was broken.

Lawrence Sheppard had been relentless in pursuing Billy Direct and Spencer Scott before the war, and after the war he focused his energies on another stallion prospect he wanted badly. He had secured the services of the 1947 Hambletonian winner Hoot Mon and the 1948 Jug winner Knight Dream, but he was soon to realize that even he didn't always get his way.

Because of his miracle mile with Alma Sheppard in the sulky, Dean Hanover had earned a permanent place in Lawrence Sheppard's heart. There never was, and never would be, another horse quite like Dean Hanover for him.

He was delighted to have Dean Hanover in the stud barn at Hanover and he enjoyed any success his offspring enjoyed. Many of the sons and daughters of Dean Hanover, however, lacked their sire's natural gait and ability. All too frequently they demonstrated a preference for the pace unless a trainer hung plenty of weight on their front feet.

One colt, however, was an exception. This son of Dean Hanover was foaled at Hanover in 1945 and went through the yearling sale the next fall. His name was Demon Hanover and he was an intelligent, perfect mannered, and a flawless racing machine — many of the things horsemen had said about Dean Hanover.

It's a good thing that Demon Hanover was so perfectly behaved because he was purchased by Harrison R. Hoyt, a Connecticut hat manufacturer who gave the youngster his early lessons on a quarter-mile track in a field near his home.

No one is sure if the colt trained Hoyt or if Hoyt trained the colt. With the results that they produced it didn't make much difference. The lightly-staked Demon Hanover swept through his two-year-old engagements with ease, taking a 2:05-1/2 mark at Lexington in the fall of 1947.

The ivory hunters came waving fistfuls of dollars at the amateur horseman Hoyt, all for the chance to lay claim to what was clearly the best colt of this crop.

No one wanted Demon Hanover more than Lawrence Sheppard. He had sold Dean Hanover as a yearling and bought him back a decade earlier, and now he wanted more than anything for history to repeat itself.

Harrison Hoyt and Demon Hanover

The problem is that Harrison Hoyt didn't want to sell. Nonsense, thought Lawrence Sheppard. Every man has his price. We'll just find out what Harrison Hoyt's price is. That fall Sheppard tried to buy the colt from Hoyt.

Thanks, but no thanks, said Hoyt.

Sheppard didn't like the fact that Hoyt wouldn't relent, but what really concerned him was his conviction that Demon Hanover would never reach his full potential in the hands of an amateur trainer and driver. Sheppard knew what a Hambletonian winner could mean to Dean Hanover's stud career, and he thought that Hoyt would be a lamb led to slaughter when the big stakes for three-year-olds were contested.

Sheppard tried another tack with Hoyt. He enlisted the services of veteran horseman Fred Egan, a Grand Circuit regular, to do his bidding. Egan cornered Hoyt at the Harrisburg sale and told him he had a deal too good to refuse.

"We'll take the horse to Florida and give him a long, slow prep for the Hambletonian," Egan told Hoyt. "I'll train him. Mr. Sheppard will pay all the expenses and all the stakes payments. You can keep the horse. All he wants is 10 percent of what the horse wins in the Hambletonian."

Egan paused to let all the details sink in, then asked Hoyt, "Now you can't refuse a deal that good, can you?"

"Yep," said Hoyt, and blithely walked away.

Sheppard was active in the National Shoe Manufacturers Association, even serving as its president, and that winter he attended a footwear convention. One of Harrison Hoyt's cousins in the shoe business met Sheppard, who was well known in the trade for his success in breeding horses. The man casually mentioned to Sheppard that he had a cousin who owned a Hanover horse.

"That's nice," said Sheppard, knowing full well that perhaps hundreds of people owned Hanover-bred horses.

They crossed paths later and Sheppard asked, "By the way, what Hanover horse does your relative own?"

"The name's Demon Hanover," the man said.

Sheppard blood pressure soared through the ceiling at the mere thought of the mad hatter who had refused his overtures.

"I wish to hell you'd get that cousin of yours to sell me Demon Hanover," Sheppard blurted out. "He stands about as much chance of winning the Hambletonian with that colt as you do of pitching for the New York Yankees."

In the early summer of 1948 Sheppard and E. Roland Harriman had joined forces — and checkbooks — in an effort to buy Demon Hanover. Sheppard traveled to Saratoga to offer Hoyt $75,000 for Demon Hanover. Once again, Hoyt refused. This time, however, he left the door open. A hundred thousand dollars, he told Sheppard, just might make a man change his mind.

Sheppard and Harriman huddled. They decided to use the wily old New York horseman Harry Whitney to approach Hoyt.

After Demon Hanover won his final prep for the Hambletonian at Saratoga, Whitney burst into the tack room where Hoyt was changing into his street clothes and blurted out, "Take a hunnert grand for that horse?"

"Nope," said Hoyt, and continued changing clothes.

Lawrence Sheppard just knew that Hoyt would be outfoxed and outdriven by the professionals on Hambletonian Day, and Dean Hanover wouldn't get his Hambletonian winner.

Sheppard was wrong. Demon Hanover and Harrison Hoyt just cruised to an easy victory in the Hambletonian. In the following years, the colt matured into a splendid free-for-aller widely admired by horsemen.

When it came time for Demon Hanover to retire, it was obvious that he wasn't going to stand at Hanover Shoe Farms, but racing fans were surprised to learn that Robert Critchfield of Gay Acres Farm in Ohio had purchased him for $82,500.

The initial foals by Demon Hanover were so impressive that he became the first Standardbred stallion syndicated, as is detailed later. Many of the major breeders took shares in Demon Hanover. Lawrence Sheppard did not.

Shortly, however, he would own half-interest in a colt destined to become one of the greatest sires of the century.

Chapter 7

Hitch Your Sulky To A Star

After they were thwarted in their efforts to buy Demon Hanover in 1948, Sheppard told Harriman, "Let's take that money and buy some colts." Harriman agreed, and later that year Harriman offered Sheppard half-interest in a yearling colt by Worthy Boy.

This colt was named Star's Pride and he would make Sheppard and Harriman forget all about their failed attempt to acquire Demon Hanover. In fact, the legacy of Star's Pride is so monumental that he is indisputably one of the greatest sires of the last century.

At the time of his death at age 30 in 1977, Star's Pride was the leading sire of Hambletonian winners with eight, and also the leading sire of Kentucky Futurity winners with 10. Harness racing may be well into the 21st century before any stallion can equal those totals.

Sheppard's ties to Star's Pride came quite by coincidence, as is so often the case in the world of horse racing.

In the fall of 1948, Harry Pownall went to a sale of mixed stock at Indianapolis, hoping that he might find a few Worthy Boy fillies to train and ultimately for Harriman to breed to Titan Hanover.

He spotted his old friend Sam Berger, who was then working for breeder Henry Warwick.

"Harry, Mr. Warwick's got a nice Worthy Boy colt I'd like you to look at," said Berger.

"I'm really not interested in any colts, Sam," said Pownall politely. "I'd like to buy some Worthy Boy fillies if I can."

Berger pleaded, "I sure wish you'd look at him, Harry. He's an awful nice colt."

Pownall relented, more as a favor to an old friend than out of an interest in a trotting colt. In retrospect, it would turn out to be one of the wisest decisions Harry Pownall ever made.

The colt was from Worthy Boy's second crop and out of Stardrift, a Mr. McElwyn mare that Pownall knew well from her days on the track.

"There was something about him that I liked," recalls Pownall. "He had a nice head on him and wasn't too big. So I called Mr. Harriman and told him I'd found a colt I liked."

"Let's bid on him," agreed Harriman.

Pownall couldn't stay to see Star's Pride sold, so he left instructions with trainer Jimmy Wingfield, who had gained fame as the groom of Greyhound, to bid on the yearling for him.

"Mr. Harriman said to go to $2,500 to get that colt," instructed Pownall. "But don't let a couple hundred stop you."

E.R. Harriman and Lawrence Sheppard at the Historic Track

(Photo courtesy of the Harness Racing Museum and Hall of Fame)

Pownall wasn't the only one who liked Star's Pride. His breeder Henry Warwick liked him, too, and he protected the colt past $2,500, but Wingfield stayed in the action. The Georgia horseman recalled the moment years later.

"Sep Palin was running the sale and I had worked for Sep a long time," remembered Wingfield. "When the bidding slowed down a little and I had the bid, Sep said to Henry Warwick, 'Let that boy have the colt. He'll do all right with him.'"

Star's Pride was hammered down to Wingfield for $2,950. Warwick was mightily upset when he learned that Wingfield was a proxy for the well-heeled Harriman. Had he known that, Warwick would have kept running the price.

Wingfield had exceeded his authorized limit by more than a "couple hundred" and he was a bit anxious as he called Pownall to tell him the price.

"Jeez, Jimmy," Pownall barked, "I'm gonna have to check with Mr. Harriman."

Harriman knew all too well how bidders could get carried away at auctions, so he agreed to take Star's Pride at $2,950.

Pownall left Star's Pride in Indianapolis, and Palin and his assistant Jimmy Laughlin gave the youngster his first lessons. Soon the colt found himself standing in his stall, trying to overcome a persistent sickness that put him well behind the other youngsters in the stable.

In February, Star's Pride was shipped to Florida to join Pownall's other two-year-olds. Pownall knew that the colt was lagging behind the class, but he liked him from the first time he sat behind him.

"When I first drove him, he was barefooted," said Pownall, "but he started off like a horse already shod. 'Gee, this colt's a natural,' I said to myself at the time."

Pownall reflected many years later on his first impressions of Star's Pride.

"I never had a colt that could do it as easy as he did," he points out. "I thought right then that he was a top colt."

Every horse owner with a promising two-year-old like Star's Pride finds reason to dream, but Lawrence Sheppard's fondest dream was shattered on an idyllic summer day in June of 1949 when his only son was killed in an airplane crash.

Many people say that Lawrence Sheppard was never the same man again. Paul Spears, who knew his boss well, said, "That almost killed him."

Sonny Sheppard had been the apple of his father's eye since his birth in 1922. As the only boy in a family with three sisters, young Sheppard was the logical heir to his father's positions in both the horse world and the business world.

Lawrence Sheppard was a man's man. He felt most comfortable when associating with men, whether they were businessmen or horsemen. His language could be a bit too salty for feminine tastes, and he wasn't a man easily reined in when expressing an opinion.

The son grew up to share his father's fancy for fine horses, but he was far friendlier than his father, smiling readily and making friends easily. He and an entire generation of young American men pitched in to help win World War II, then returned home to build a career. Lawrence Sheppard expected his son to work hard and earn the respect of his peers in the shoe business. And Sonny did just that.

He also jumped into harness racing in a big way as the sport expanded after the war. He loved to train and drive his own horses and he became widely known and popular with trainers and owners in the sport.

On June 14, 1949, Sonny was at Roosevelt Raceway on Long Island to drive his filly Marietta Hanover in a $400 event for two-year-old trotters. Mysteria, driven by Delvin Miller, won the event. Sonny and his filly finished fifth while his close friend Gene Pownall, brother of Harry Pownall, finished farther back. The mile went in 2:15.2.

Sonny stayed overnight with Pownall in Mineola, then went to Mitchell Field to start the flight back to Hanover. The weather was clear, and the day seemed perfect for flying. He was just west of Villanova, Pa., when he encountered some problems that forced him to land.

He received assistance at an airfield in making the needed repairs, then took off to the northwest. Suddenly, his engine stopped. The plane plunged into high-tension wires and crashed, bursting into flames. Sonny, who was one week away from celebrating his 27th birthday, was killed instantly.

Part of Charlotte and Lawrence Sheppard died that day, too.

Tributes poured in from political and business leaders, but perhaps the most poignant one came from F. R. Brilhard, manager of a Hanover Shoe store in Washington, D.C.

"The tragic news has been most shocking and had gotten us all down," wrote Brilhart. "Young Lawrence Sheppard was very popular and very well liked, not only in the executive offices, but by the people in and around the factory. He was one of the country's outstanding young executives, definitely on the way up."

One horseman who remembered Sonny Sheppard well was Dick Thomas, the son of Henry Thomas who grew up to be an accomplished horseman in his own right.

"We grew up together," recalls Thomas of Sonny Sheppard. "We were great friends. That night when Sonny came to Roosevelt Raceway, he forgot his driving pants, and I gave him a set of mine."

Losing a child is the greatest tragedy that can befall a parent, and for a father to lose his only son, a son who carried his name and shared his passions, was devastating. Lawrence Sheppard bore his grief with stoic silence, grimly going about the details of the requiem mass for Sonny and agreeing to help organize the Lawrence B. Sheppard, Jr. Memorial Drivers Fund.

The sole purpose of the fund was "to aid drivers who are either injured or ill and unable to follow their usual line of endeavor. There have been many cases in the past where deserving drivers were sorely hampered in their recovery and recuperation due to financial worries."

Lawrence Sheppard also memorialized his son in Goshen, New York, the sleepy village known as the "cradle of the trotter." When an old stable on Main Street opened in 1951 as the Hall of Fame of the Trotter, the main facility was named the Lawrence B. Sheppard, Jr. Memorial Building.

The fund and the memorial building were nice tributes, but there was still an enormous empty feeling inside Lawrence Sheppard.

Russell Williams was born five years after his uncle perished in a plane crash, but he says that the ghost of Sonny Sheppard loomed large over the family for many years thereafter.

"We kids were aware that Sonny had existed, but we would never ask about him or mention him because it would produce so much grief in the older generation," he says.

Understandably, Charlotte and Lawrence Sheppard never fully recovered from the tragic loss of their son.

"That was the defining moment in the lives of my grandparents," Williams says. "My grandfather saw everything that he built in the shoe business and horses passing to Sonny. That dream came to such an abrupt end. Both of my grandparents were devastated by it. They were able to support each other. My grandmother was really in mourning for years, but she pushed my grandfather to keep going."

Lawrence Sheppard once told his daughter Pat, "The only panacea for life's ills is hard work."

Hard work, and horses, too. Fortunately, Lawrence Sheppard had horses that would help heal the wounds.

Harry Pownall told him that his two-year-old colt Star's Pride had such natural ability that he quickly caught up and passed all of his stablemates but one. That one was Florican, a homebred Arden Homestead colt from their stakes-winning mare Florimel. Florican was practically a member of the Arden Homestead Stable family and he showed such talent that he was the one Pownall usually drove in races.

That meant that he had to find catch drivers for Star's Pride, and Lawrence Sheppard drove the colt at the Historic Track meeting in early July, shortly after his son's death.

"I felt he needed a little boost after what happened to Sonny," said Harry Pownall.

At first Star's Pride couldn't beat Florican, and Florican couldn't beat Lusty Song, but that trio of colts emerged from the class as the dominant ones. Gradually, Star's Pride caught and surpassed Florican.

In the fall of 1949, Sheppard once again climbed into the sulky behind Star's Pride and won with the colt in 2:06.1 at Lexington. He was a nice colt, but he seemed to be stuck with the label of "second best."

The second-best colt was good enough to attract the attention of Frances Dodge Van Lennep of Castleton Farm. Worthy Boy had been her first good trotter and now she wanted to buy his son Star's Pride. Before the 1950 Hambletonian, Castleton offered Sheppard and Harriman $60,000 for Star's Pride, but when the asking price was set at $75,000, Castleton passed.

Star's Pride was driven in the Hambletonian by 30-year-old Johnny Simpson of South Carolina, then a young horseman making a big name in the sport. Star's Pride valiantly chased Lusty Song and almost reached him, but once

Patricia Sheppard holding Hambletonian candidate Star's Pride, who finished second

again had to be content being second best. Later in the season, as Lusty Song's aching feet undermined his ability, Star's Pride marched to the head of the class.

As a four-year-old in 1951, Star's Pride was sidelined by three separate quarter cracks early in the season and he simply refused to train. He would jog the wrong way of the track, but he balked when Pownall turned him to go a mile.

"He was an intelligent horse and suddenly the thought came to me that Star's Pride was trying to tell me that he simply wasn't ready to go training miles," said Pownall later.

After extensive jogging, Star's Pride was ready for his first work mile. Pownall was hoping to go a mile around 2:20, but Star's Pride wasn't buying into the plan. He tore away and reached the half-mile marker in 1:04 and finished his mile in 2:09 with Pownall taking a strong hold on him,

"It dawned on me that Star's Pride was saying, 'Awright, I'm okay now and ready to train,'" explained Pownall later.

Star's Pride had a wonderful four-year-old season, even if he couldn't beat the gelding Pronto Don. Pownall believed that Star's Pride realized he couldn't beat him and quit trying. Florican was still racing, too, and it became apparent that he couldn't beat Star's Pride, but Florican never relented.

The stablemates were held over another year and campaigned again. The shining moment of their 1952 season came one hot afternoon at DuQuoin, Illinois, when they were two of the three entrants in a race. Track officials wanted to cancel the contest, but Pownall had been plotting and asked to showcase his horses. What the race lacked in quantity, he told them, it made up in quality. He assured them that Star's Pride and Florican would put on a good show.

It was a tailor-made opportunity to get fast race records on the two horses that were soon bound for stallion duty.

"So I whacked out a good mile with Star's Pride the first trip," says Pownall, "and Florican came on to win for Del Miller in 1:57.2. That was the world record for trotting stallions." It lowered the record set 11 years earlier by Spencer Scott.

The two reversed roles in the second heat with Florican doing the dirty work. Star's Pride collared his stablemate in the stretch and won in 1:57.1, lowering the stallion record set an hour earlier.

Despite his accomplishments, Lawrence Sheppard had reservations about Star's Pride as a stallion candidate. The horse didn't have the best set of feet and he was also known to whack his shins. Star's Pride was actually sold for export to Italy that year, but the buyer failed to come across with the money and the deal fell through.

Harriman and Sheppard were left with no recourse other than to retire Star's Pride at the end of the 1952 season, and the reception that the young Worthy Boy stallion got from breeders was decidedly chilly.

Tar Heel

Chapter 8

Hanover's Got To Have Them

In 1950 Delvin Miller campaigned a troika of freshman pacing colts that dominated every stake in sight. Alphabetically, they were Direct Rhythm, Solicitor, and Tar Heel. W. N. "Will" Reynolds, co-founder of the R. J. Reynolds tobacco empire with his brother, owned the latter pair. His nephew W. G. Reynolds owned Direct Rhythm.

Will Reynolds was one of harness racing's most beloved figures. He had been an enthusiastic patron of the sport for decades, remaining deeply involved with harness horses through the ups and downs of the Depression and war years. He was born a few months before the Battle of Gettysburg, acquired a love of horses early in life, and never lost that love.

R. J. Reynolds had died many years before his brother, and he once counseled him, "Always keep your horses, Will. They'll keep you young."

The man known as "Uncle Will" had spotted the extraordinary talent and ambition of Delvin Miller before World War II, and when the young horseman from Pennsylvania returned from the service, Reynolds hired him. Miller began working his no-nonsense brand of magic with the colts and fillies bred by Reynolds at his farm in North Carolina.

When Direct Rhythm, Solicitor, and Tar Heel were entered in a race, their opponents were racing virtually for fourth money. Some weeks Solicitor won; other times Tar Heel got the best of his stablemates. Direct Rhythm was the stable's third string colt, but he could usually outstep everything else on the track.

In the 1950 Fox Stake, then the richest race for two-year-old pacers, Solicitor won the first heat and Direct Rhythm was second. In the next heat, Tar Heel won with Direct Rhythm second again. A third-heat raceoff was needed. Solicitor got the nod, and the Reynolds family got most of the purse money.

If their foes thought that the new year might bring them new hope, Miller and his pacing troika soon showed otherwise. They were every bit as dominant as three-year-olds. Sadly, however, Uncle Will wasn't able to fully enjoy their success in person because his health was failing rapidly. He passed away in early September at age 88.

Tar Heel and the filly Meda had been entered in the Reading Futurity, but trainer Miller scratched them out of respect for his patron.

"I didn't want to race them while Mr. Reynolds was laid out," he explained.

This gracious gesture was entirely in keeping with Miller's personality, but it posed a challenge for Miller the horseman. The Reading Futurity was to be Tar Heel's final prep race for the Little Brown Jug, the most important event for three-year-old pacers. Sure, Tar Heel was unquestionably one of the best colts of the class, but without a final tightener before the Jug, who could say how he might perform?

Miller gave the Jug driving assignment behind Tar Heel to his friend Del Cameron while he took Solicitor himself. Benny Schue would drive Direct Rhythm.

Miller had driven Dudley Hanover to victory in the Jug the previous year and many people thought that he was forfeiting a chance to repeat when he relinquished the reins on Tar Heel. Miller was simply doing what was best for the horses.

"Anyone can drive Tar Heel," he explained. "Solicitor can be a handful at times, particularly at the start."

That proved prophetic in the first heat as Tar Heel got away smoothly at the start while Solicitor encountered problems. Tar Heel won the first round easily, with Direct Rhythm third and Solicitor fourth.

In the second heat, however, Solicitor displayed his Sunday school manners, pacing around the first turn flawlessly. He was positioned perfectly behind the pacesetting Tar Heel. When Miller moved out with Solicitor, it initially appeared that he was going right past his stablemate. But that never happened. Solicitor stalled, and Tar Heel went on to victory in the first 2:00 race mile ever on a half-mile track by a three-year-old.

Knowing horsemen who watched Delvin Miller carefully felt that he hadn't really tried to win with Solicitor. Incredible as it seemed to many, Solicitor could probably have paced faster than 2:00 if Miller had driven him full out.

Years later Miller admitted that he hadn't tried to win with Solicitor and gave a very logical explanation. He pointed out that if Solicitor had won, the entire field would have come back for a third heat. Who knows what would have happened in that heat, Miller argued. Besides, he wasn't cheating the bettors because Tar Heel and Solicitor were coupled in the mutuel pools. And both were owned by the Estate of W. N. Reynolds.

Tar Heel, driven by Del Cameron (front) and Solicitor, driven by Delvin Miller, at the Little Brown Jug

Little Brown Jug winner Tar Heel, with driver Del Cameron and Delvin Miller (far right, holding the trophy)

It was soon announced that the Reynolds horses would be dispersed at auction in Harrisburg that November to settle his estate. There were numerous broodmares, yearlings and weanlings, but the stars of the show were Tar Heel and Solicitor. No one knew just how much money they might bring, but everyone conceded that it was not a game for a poor man to play.

Lawrence Sheppard wasn't a poor man and he was among the many breeders casting covetous eyes on the pair.

Less than a decade earlier, Billy Direct had been the first pacing stallion to stand at Hanover. Sheppard could see that the future of the breed would belong to pacers. The explosion of pari-mutuel wagering after the war created a demand for reliable racing stock, and pacers were deemed more reliable than trotters.

Hanover, Sheppard knew, needed to beef up its pacing studs. Nibble Hanover had raced on the trot, but he'd proven to be a double-gaited producer as a stallion. He'd sired the 1948 Little Brown Jug winner Knight Dream and the Hambletonian winner Miss Tilly the next year. Nibble Hanover's distinction of siring the winners of the greatest classics on both gaits has never been equaled, and likely never will be.

Also, in siring a Jug winner in Knight Dream, Nibble Hanover started a three-generation link of Jug winners. Knight Dream sired a Jug winner in Torpid and Torpid sired a Jug winner in Vicar Hanover. Torpid and Vicar Hanover are names known to few in harness racing in the 21st century, but there is only one other three-generation span of winners in the Jug. That was started in 1965 by Bret Hanover and continued in subsequent generations by Strike Out (1972) and Hot Hitter (1979).

Knight Dream in Indianapolis

Solicitor sold first and the bidding continued on the son of King's Counsel for several minutes as auctioneer George Swinebroad alternately tried to coax or intimidate bidders, including Lawrence Sheppard, into offering more bids.

As the colt stood in the ring and the bidding dragged on, Swinebroad bellowed, "I'll sell 'im in the lobby of the Penn-Harris if I have to!" referring to the local hotel favored by horsemen.

At $96,000 Castleton Farm called it quits. Sheppard's $100,000 bid closed the door, and Solicitor was moved from the brown and gold colors of the Reynolds Stable to the orange and blue of Hanover Shoe Farms.

Immediately thereafter, Tar Heel waltzed into the ring and the fireworks started all over again. A group comprised of Leo McNamara, Octave Blake, and Percy Gray opened the bidding at $50,000. They were prepared to go as high as $80,000, but never got a chance as the bids flew relentlessly. They didn't stop even when they reached $100,000. The bidding just kept going, and Lawrence Sheppard kept going with it.

Industrialist Walter Michael of Ohio, acting on behalf of a four-man Ohio syndicate, bid $120,000. Sheppard then countered with $125,000, and Michael surrendered.

Noted writer Jim Harrison, then 30 years old, asked Sheppard after the sale which one of his new stallions would be the best sire. "How the hell should I know?" growled Sheppard. "All I know is that they're the two best young sire prospects in the country and Hanover's got to have them."

Solicitor ultimately would leave little in the way of a legacy, but Tar Heel's influence was large enough to compensate for a dozen Solicitors.

After the sale, Sheppard posed for a photo with Tar Heel. Delvin Miller, Tar Heel's first trainer, and John Simpson, the man who would take over the pacer's training as a four-year-old, flanked them.

Sheppard greatly admired the two young horse- men, and he began to see Simpson as a man who could play an important role in the future of Hanover. He also saw Simpson as a surrogate son because he was from the same generation as Sonny Sheppard. Unquestionably, John Simpson was one of the hottest young hands in the sport.

While Sheppard was chasing Tar Heel and Solicitor with such determination, Simpson was finishing that 1951 season with an unbeaten Hanover-bred three-year-old trotter.

His name was Ford Hanover, and he concluded his season by winning the Kentucky Futurity in straight heats, making it a perfect 11-for-11 season. Few horsemen ever have a horse good enough to go undefeated for a season and win at the highest levels in the sport. When they successfully campaign such a colt, they cannot help thinking about what a terrific sire he could become.

John Simpson didn't see Ford Hanover through those rose-colored glasses, but instead through the objective eyes of an astute young horseman. Better than anyone, he knew Ford Hanover's strengths, and his weaknesses.

"I didn't like Ford Hanover for a sire myself because he wasn't a clean-going horse," said Simpson later. "He paddled in front. He was overly big, too. It's true that you want a big horse for a trotter, but Ford Hanover wasn't put together that well. He was a big, loose, sloppy horse in many ways."

Simpson also knew that Ford Hanover's female line had not produced superior stallions.

Simpson talked to Lawrence Sheppard about Ford Hanover and was brutally frank in his assessment. Sheppard also didn't like the horse behind the headlines. Ford Hanover was on a ship to Italy at the end of the 1951 season.

Sheppard didn't like the horse, but he liked Ford Hanover's trainer. The businessman was a good judge of talent and John Simpson had made a favorable impression on him. He was not only a superb horseman, but he was also honest and outspoken. He was Lawrence Sheppard's kind of man.

John Frazer Simpson was a native of South Carolina, a state that has never been known as a hotbed of harness racing. Born in Chester, South Carolina, on the day after Christmas in 1919, the boy matured into a masterful horseman.

John Simpson seemed to have a special insight when appraising a horse. When selecting a yearling, he could see beneath its veneer to the inner workings. When sitting behind a horse, it didn't take him long to separate the exceptional from the ordinary.

John F. Simpson

Simpson was a rare horseman who operated a racing stable and later a breeding operation with equal success. In that accomplishment, he was helped immeasurably by confidence in his judgement and by an astute business sense.

First and foremost, however, John Simpson was a horse trainer. After blindness later forced him out of the sulky and into a desk chair, he still burned with desire to sit behind a fast horse.

That love came from his father, an Illinois horseman who went south to race some horses, fell in love, got married, and settled down in South Carolina. Young John grew up during the Depression when the dust was far more plentiful than the dollars a the bush-league southern fairs. The boy got his first few drives as a teenager, and he was hooked. He thought about harness horses night and day, and his life's work became clear to him.

John F. Simpson driving Tar Heel at Lexington
(Photo courtesy of the U.S. Trotting Association)

His parents, however, saw the value of a college education and insisted that he attend classes at Clemson College. He started his university studies in the fall of 1938, declaring an interest in animal husbandry and looking down the road toward becoming a veterinarian. When classes ended the next summer, he was back with the horses, working for trainer Earl Walker at Myrtle Beach.

Mrs. Simpson felt that there were better ways for her son to spend the summer and she summoned him home. No more racing, she insisted. Racing was what he enjoyed most, said her son. There's no future in it, she countered. Besides, he could get hurt driving dangerous horses on unsafe tracks.

Finally, they compromised: he would drive no more hobbled pacers. The young Simpson took that vow and went back to the horses. He lasted another year at Clemson before the allure of the horses simply became more than he could withstand.

In the summer of 1940, bankrolled in large measure by his uncle Joe Frazer, the 20-year-old Simpson boy went north of the Mason-Dixon to discover what racing was all about up there. He learned his lessons, paid his bills, and impressed some of the old-timers. And in the summer of 1941, he went back north again.

By this time, however, he had acquired a bride in Helen Faulk from his hometown of Chester.

Simpson's emergence as a professional horseman coincided with the advent of pari-mutuel raceways in New York State. Harness racing had shed its overalls and come to the big city and found success.

In the summer of 1942, Simpson became the youngest driver ever to score a 2:00 mile when he piloted My Birthday to win the $6,000 Maine Pacing Derby at the famed kite track at Old Orchard Beach, Maine. At the dawn of the 21st century, a 2:00 mile doesn't make a horse competitive in most qualifying races, but when My Birthday clocked his fastest mile he entered into an extremely exclusive club, that reserved for horses with 2:00 race records.

Simpson was soon to trade his racing silks for Uncle Sam's fatigues as he entered the service in October, 1942, serving as an infantry officer in the European Theater.

He was back in harness in 1946, and drove in his first Hambletonian two years later. The upstart from South Carolina was demonstrating that he would be a force in coming years. In 1951, his stable earned $375,000, more than any other operation in the sport. And John Simpson was only 32 years old.

He won 118 races that season, courtesy of such consistent performers as Ford Hanover, Duke Of Lullwater (a baby trotter that won 14 of 15 starts and $59,270), and Kimberly Mine, Ferman Hanover, and Silent Waters.

John Simpson was the consummate professional at the track, in complete control of his stable, and intensely earnest in his approach to training horses. While many other trainers were spending their summer afternoons on the golf course, John Simpson was taking care of business.

In that era, racing was still seasonal and when Simpson went into winter quarters in Florida he found time to indulge his passion for hunting.

"He would rather quail hunt than drive horses," says his son Jim. "He loved doing both, and they were compatible because hunting season was different than racing season."

Simpson had hunted some when he was a youngster growing up in South Carolina, but he allowed his interest to blossom into a passion in the 1950s when success on the track came his way. That prompted him later to purchase 8,600 acres near Orlando that he turned into a hunting camp stocked with quail, turkey, deer, and lakes with plenty of fish.

His son Jim remembers how much his father liked to entertain at the camp.

"We had each mayor of Orlando up for a hunting and fishing weekend about every year," he recalls. "We had many horsemen at the camp over the years."

"Dad preferred quail hunting, but he didn't limit it to that," says Jim. "He also hunted deer, turkey, and hogs. I recall that he went chukkar hunting in New Mexico a few times. He also loved bass fishing."

Despite living in Florida, John Simpson never developed an interest in golf. His son Jim laughs when he recalls Delvin Miller's attempt to get his sidekick involved in the game.

"Delvin bought him a pair of golf shoes years ago," Jim says. "He tried to get Dad interested in golf because Delvin loved it so much. Dad told me later that he went out with Delvin only once, and the leather in the golf shoes eventually turned green with mildew."

Hunting was a nice diversion during the off-season, but when the stakes season heated up in the summer, John Simpson focused entirely on his stable.

*(Left to right) Lawrence Sheppard, William B. Murray
and Sanders Russell at a USTA meeting*

Chapter 9

Leading An Industry

Just as he wanted his horses to lead the way on the track, Lawrence Sheppard wanted to lead the way in the trotting world and in the business world.

In 1951, he was elected president of the United States Trotting Association, the organization that had been formed in the late 1930s to bring some semblance of order to the mishmash of rules that governed harness racing.

Three organizations — the American Trotting Association, the United Trotting Association, and the National Trotting Association — joined with the Trotting Horse Club of America in 1938 to form a central organization that would maintain records and promulgate rules for the sport.

Lawrence Sheppard was its third president. He ran the U.S. Trotting Association just as he ran his shoe business or the horse farm: with integrity and with an iron fist.

He worked closely with Don R. Millar, a young man from Wisconsin who was the executive vice-president of the USTA. Millar was more than a mere administrator, however, as he had an abiding interest in the sport, particularly in breeding. When Sheppard and Millar got together to talk USTA business, sooner or later the conversation would drift to breeding, a topic they both preferred over the regulations and bureaucracy of the sport.

Sheppard could be hard-boiled and demanding with those who worked for him, but Millar came to know and admire Sheppard, and he remembers a side of Sheppard that few people saw.

"He was unusually kind and considerate with waiters in restaurants," said Millar, knowing all too well how powerful people often lorded it over those at the bottom of the socio-economic ladder.

Sheppard did have an extremely short fuse and wasn't afraid if others knew it. William B. Murray, master of Bonnie Brae Farms in Ohio, worked with Sheppard on many struggles during their years as directors of the U.S. Trotting Association, and yet he and Sheppard were complete opposites in temperament.

Murray was a soft-spoken man who once told a visitor to his home, "We never serve anything stronger than pink lemonade."

Murray admired Sheppard's convictions even if he didn't always admire his approach.

"One time I was walking through the grandstand at The Red Mile with Mr. Sheppard and he spotted a man he'd been feuding with," recalled Murray. "He just exploded, saying 'There's that dirty rotten, no good SOB!'"

Murray said that Sheppard then paused for a moment of reflection and said mused, "Now why was I was mad at him?"

Sheppard had several public battles with George Monahan, chief of the New York State Racing and Wagering Board. As president of the U.S. Trotting Association, Sheppard felt that the sport could regulate itself with minimal interference from the state bureaucracy, but it was a battle that he and harness racing were ultimately to lose.

The greatest challenge that Sheppard faced during his eight years at the helm of the USTA was an anti-trust suit brought by the federal government. That case was won, and a working agreement on racing regulation was reached between the state racing commissions and the USTA.

Grandson Russell Williams acknowledged that Lawrence Sheppard may have viewed racing through the perspective of the past. That led to some conflicts with the regulators and operators of the metropolitan pari-mutuel plants.

"His concept of integrity will never be outdated, but in some of his ideas about racing, he was still thinking in the 1930s," conceded Williams. "The growth of pari-mutuel racing led to the increasing influence of the state racing commissions and L.B. felt some real animosity toward them."

In Sheppard's battle with the state regulators, it was a case of "if you can't beat them, join them." When pari-mutuel wagering was approved in Pennsylvania in the early 1960s, Sheppard served as the first chairman of the Pennsylvania Harness Racing Commission. Ironically, Sheppard was a staunch Republican, but Democratic governor David Lawrence made the appointment.

Paul Spears worked for Sheppard for almost 15 years and says that the words that come to mind when describing him are pugnacious and irascible.

"He was a very, very difficult man," says Spears. "If he had it in for someone, that person was dead meat."

Spears says that many employees simply couldn't take the heat that the head man put on them. Spears admitted that he once cleaned out his desk at Hanover and was ready to resign when Sheppard lured him back.

One person who remembers Lawrence Sheppard in a much different light is Dale Welk, the farm's maintenance chief. He was literally born into the Hanover family as his father worked for the farm for over 45 years starting back in the early 1940s.

"I got to know Mr. Sheppard as a young boy," Welk recalls. "When my father was cleaning the snow off the Sheppards' driveway in the winter, Mr. Sheppard would invite me into his study. There were pictures on the wall and I'd ask him question after question about the pictures. He never got mad at me for asking so many questions."

One day, Welk says he sensed that Sheppard's fuse was getting shorter because he turned to the boy and said, "You sure ask a lot of questions. You think you're going to work here one day?"

Welk admits that his father idolized Lawrence Sheppard and repeatedly told his son, "If you were fair with Mr. Sheppard, he was fair with you. If you gave him a fair day's work, he treated you right."

Lawrence Sheppard may have had a tough, crusty exterior, but the company he ran was very enlightened in the area of employee benefits and about the need for the Hanover Shoe Co. to be a good citizen of the community.

In one sense, he was simply carrying on the tradition established by his father and C.N. Myers. After all, they had built the Hanover Hospital in 1925.

"The Hanover Shoe Co. had a retirement plan and what amounted to a worker's compensation program about 40 years before the federal government ever thought of these things," says Russell Williams.

In 1932, the Hanover area was in dire need of an impounding dam to provide water to the community, so Sheppard and Myers together put up the money to build the dam. They also funded the planting of approximately a million trees in the area surrounding the dam, and arranged for Secretary of the Interior Gifford Pinchot to dedicate the project. By the mid-1960s, the population of Hanover had grown so much that another impounding dam was needed and this time it was Lawrence Sheppard who made sure that it was built.

Spears says that Sheppard was so intense that he had few interests other than horses and shoes, but he recalls that Sheppard occasionally liked to go hunting or fishing. Neither pastime, however, evoked much passion in Sheppard.

Lawrence Sheppard was so deeply committed to his work that his grandson said it was a "big deal" if he was around for family festivities. He remembers what a memorable day it was when his grandfather once showed up to go swimming with his children and grandchildren.

Williams, who was born in 1954, remembers the reverence that other family members held for him.

"That was partly true reverence and partly fear," he recalls with a soft laugh. "Nobody wanted him mad. He was formidable when irritated."

Lawrence Sheppard lived the adage that "Early to bed, early to rise, makes a man healthy, wealthy, and wise."

"He left home before dawn on any working day," says Russell Williams, "and any working day to him was any day. He got back about supper time and then went to bed."

Before bedtime, he might watch a little television, but he was more likely to drift off after reading a book.

"He was interested in everything," says Russell Williams. "He had stacks of books in his bedroom, mostly historical biography. He loved history of all kinds. He liked to talk about the Indian trails in the Hanover area."

One TV show that Williams recalls his grandfather enjoying was Groucho Marx's *You Bet Your Life* which tickled the crusty businessman's funny bone.

"He had a sense of humor, but he didn't joke with the grandchildren," says Williams. "My grandmother saw the humorous side of everything and they were foils for each other. He didn't intimidate her at all, and we got to see her sense of humor when they were quarreling."

Jim Simpson was just a teenager when Lawrence Sheppard died, and a teenager with limited interest in harness racing, so his contacts with the farms' founder were sporadic at best.

"I was intimidated by him," admits Simpson. "I always made it a point to be very quiet around him. It's not like I was listening, as I wish I had been. I was always afraid of him."

One time when the boy saw a softer side of Sheppard was on a long automobile trip through Pennsylvania.

"I believe it was the year [1963] that The Meadows opened," recalls Simpson. "I caught a ride back to Hanover with Mr. Sheppard. What I remember most is that he talked about the Civil War in great detail. He was quite a student of the Civil War. Here's a man who is running so many different businesses and yet he's got time to be interested in the Civil War."

Lawrence Sheppard was fascinated with Standardbred pedigrees, but never pretended to be a geneticist. He did know that more stallions ultimately fail than succeed, and that meant that he had to have a constant stream of new stallions coming to Hanover. Some would make it; most would fail.

Two stallions proven by the mid-1950s were Hoot Mon and Adios, and they came to Hanover is unusual ways. On Hambletonian Day in 1947, Lawrence Sheppard was cheering with all his heart and soul to see Hoot Mon beaten by the Hanover-bred Rodney (Edwin Hanover). Sheppard applauded when the Big Train, as Rodney was known, rolled home first in the opening round.

The second heat, however, turned Sheppard's head and everyone else's in the crowd because a black streak named Hoot Mon scalded the kite-shaped track with the first 2:00 mile in Hambletonian history. Hoot Mon won the third heat and the trophy.

Hoot Mon was the property of Mrs. James B. Johnson's Castleton Farm in Kentucky, and Sheppard knew one of Hanover's Kentucky rivals was getting a good stud candidate in the son of Scotland.

Hoot Mon failed to stand training as a four-year-old in 1948, and, in a bizarre turn of events, he was sold to Hanover as a stallion. The man from Hanover was all too happy to grab him, and he was even happier when Hoot Mon's first crop contained the Hambletonian-winning filly Helicopter.

In 1955, two years after Helicopter scored an upset in the Goshen classic, a sprawly-gaited son of Hoot Mon named Scott Frost won the Hambletonian and the embryonic Triple Crown of trotting.

Hoot Mon was clearly on a roll, and he continued to roll along for Hanover. He sired eye-catching individuals. Ebby Hanover, a son of Hoot Mon named for Elbridge T. Gerry of Arden Homestead Stable, was the top-priced yearling in the sport in 1957 when he sold for $60,000. Two years later Bill Hanover, another Hoot Mon, was the sport's top ticket item at $50,000. In 1960, Mon Mite at $81,000 was the most valuable prospect at the yearling sales.

Two more of Hoot Mon's sons found the winner's circle in the Hambletonian. Blaze Hanover fought his way to a game four-heat triumph in 1960 and A.C.'s Viking took the DuQuoin classic in 1962.

By the early 1960s, however, Hoot Mon's fame was waning while the fame of his Hanover stablemate Star's Pride was quickly waxing.

Another stallion whose reputation was burgeoning along with Hoot Mon's in the mid-1950s was Adios, a slick-gaited, blocky stallion who was standing at Delvin Miller's Meadow Lands Farm in western Pennsylvania. From mares whose pedigrees were often nondescript, Adios was siring speed in measures never seen before. In 1953, the breed welcomed its first two-year-old colt and filly pacers to enter the 2:00 list. Their names were Adios Boy and Adios Betty.

By 1955, Delvin Miller seized a chance to make some money with Adios and give him access to much better mares. The Midas of Meadow Lands sold Adios to Hanover and Pennsylvania breeder Max Hempt, then bought back one third of the horse. The price for the stallion was an astonishing $500,000.

Adios bred his first large contingent of Hanover Shoe Farms mares in 1956 and it wasn't long before he simply smothered all of his opposition among pacing stallions. His offspring dominated the pacing stakes of that era.

Hoot Mon and Adios were proven, but the man from Hanover was hoping that Star's Pride and Tar Heel would find success, too.

There were no trumpet flourishes when Star's Pride and Tar Heel began serving mares at Hanover in 1953, but in retrospect there should have been because these two stallions proved to be of enormous significance for the farm in the coming decades.

There were also no trumpet flourishes when the first get of Star's Pride began to race, and one trainer prematurely condemned them as "a bunch of damn shin hitters."

Star's Pride got scant patronage in his early years at Hanover. For a breeder who studied his lessons carefully, however, the signs of greatness were there. Of the 46 foals in Star's Prides first three crops, 45 made it to the races, a remarkable accomplishment.

He ranked fifth in the pecking order among the trotting stallions at Hanover, behind Hoot Mon, Dean Hanover, Titan Hanover, and Nibble Hanover.

*Star's Pride as
a young stallion*

Lawrence B. Sheppard received an award in 1964 at the inauguration of the annual Lawrence B. Sheppard Pace for Two-Year-Olds, held at Yonkers Raceway. During the fifth annual pace, after Sheppard passed away, a scholarship fund for veterinary students at the University of Pennsylvania was inaugurated in his memory.

(Photo courtesy of Michael Cipriani, Yonkers Raceway)

Sheppard also knew that Star's Pride didn't have the best feet and he whacked his shins repeatedly. He seemed to have several strikes against him.

His second crop contained the filly Emily's Pride, winner of the 1958 Hambletonian in a three-heat contest. The other heat winner that afternoon at DuQuoin was Little Rocky, a son of Star's Pride.

While Emily's Pride and Little Rocky were dominating the three-year-old trotters, a two-year-old colt named Diller Hanover was humbling the freshman trotters. He, too, was by Star's Pride.

The world of trotting was never the same again. Certainly the book of Star's Pride was never the same again as breeders recognized that a new king was in their midst and clamored for bookings to him.

Diller Hanover gave Star's Pride his second Hambletonian winner in 1959 and legions of fast trotters by Star's Pride followed.

The unpredictable Matastar became the world's fastest trotting stallion in a 1:55.4 time trial in 1962.

Lawrence Sheppard beamed when he thought of the great things that Star's Pride had done, and could do in the future. He personally owned half of the horse in partnership with Roland Harriman, but he saw an advantage in Hanover Shoe Farms owning 100 percent of Star's Pride.

For his part, Harriman still owned Florican, then off to a good start as a stallion at Castleton Farm in Kentucky. He was agreeable to having Hanover pick up his half of Star's Pride. Harriman didn't personally need the income, but he was president of the American Red Cross and its efforts were very near and dear to his heart. So he donated his half-interest in Star's Pride to the Red Cross, and when

Hanover bought the remaining half of Star's Pride, the $100,000 check was made payable to the American Red Cross. Roland Harriman got a nice tax deduction out of the deal, and he retained breeding rights valued at $50,000 to Star's Pride.

Sheppard and accountant Paul Spears were every bit as sharp as Roland Harriman when it came to playing the tax laws, and Sheppard's plan involved a Catholic convent and the University of Pennsylvania's School of Veterinary Medicine.

Sheppard's children and grandchildren had been educated at a school operated by the Sisters of St. Joseph, and he learned that improvements were needed to bring the school up to state fire codes. The renovations were estimated to cost $50,000 and the nuns weren't certain they could raise that kind of cash quickly.

Also, the University of Pennsylvania was in need of funding for new facilities at its veterinary facility, which was an important cause to Sheppard.

Paul Spears was intimately involved in the case and remembers it well.

"The school was condemned by the state because it didn't have adequate fire protection," he says.

The plan that Sheppard devised was simple, daring, and, after years of litigation, was deemed legal.

On June 16, 1959, Sheppard wrote a personal letter to the convent and the university offering each one-third of his 50 percent interest in Star's Pride. That would give the nuns and the University of Pennsylvania one-sixth ownership in the stallion, a share valued at $50,000. There were no stipulations attached to the gift at all.

On the very same day, on Hanover Shoe Farms letterhead, Sheppard wrote a letter to the convent and to the university offering to purchase its interests in the horse for $50,000 each.

You can imagine the surprise of both the nuns and the university administrators when they opened the mail a few days later. They got a personal letter from Lawrence Sheppard giving them one-sixth of a horse called Star's Pride, and then a letter from the same man in his role as president of Hanover Shoe Farms offering to buy that interest for $50,000.

The nuns didn't know what to think, but they were particularly reluctant to become involved with a horse "directly involved in a betting scheme."

The Sisters of St. Joseph and the University of Pennsylvania were free to keep their interest in Star's Pride or to sell it to the highest bidder, but Sheppard knew that they needed cash. They readily accepted his offer to purchase their share.

Sheppard took a $50,000 charitable donation deduction for each of the two gifts.

He sold his other one-sixth interest to Hanover Shoe Farms, and reported that as a capital gain.

"Mr. Sheppard got audited by the IRS about every year," recalls Spears. "The auditor was a guy who was a member of the Catholic church in McSherrystown. He saw the way that we had done the deductions and he disallowed it. I told him he'd probably get excommunicated from the church for disallowing that. He said that he couldn't help it; he had to do his job."

Sheppard's gifts were initially not deemed valid, but in the case of Sheppard vs. United States, adjudicated in 1966, the Court of Claims upheld and even applauded Sheppard's imaginative use of the tax laws.

As Sheppard was tangling with the IRS, harness racing was growing with incredible speed. It boasted of being "America's fastest growing sport" in the 1950s, and one of the horsemen with the fastest growing reputation was a young trainer-driver from New Jersey named Stanley Dancer.

Raised on a dairy farm, Dancer quit school early to pursue his passion for horses and veteran horsemen saw that he possessed a unique talent when he sat behind a horse. He had a gift that few were given.

Lawrence Sheppard could see that, too, and he was impressed with the young man who was so dedicated to his career and to the sport. In 1957 Sheppard asked if the farm had ever named a foal after him. When Dancer said no, Sheppard said, "Well, you pick one out and we'll do it."

"Hanover's already got one," Dancer replied. "He's a weanling now. He's the Adios colt out of The Old Maid."

"No," said Sheppard. "The dam's name has to begin with D. Think about it and let me know."

A week later Dancer recalls that he got a letter from Sheppard a week later to inform him that the Adios colt out of The Old Maid had been registered as Dancer Hanover.

The young horseman was pleased because he knew all about Bachelor Hanover, a previous colt from The Old Maid and a standout pacer. Dancer had often catch-driven the colt for trainer Billy Haughton when Bachelor and the filly Belle Acton were entered in the same event.

Dancer Hanover grew up in the fields of Hanover to be a handsome, athletic-looking prospect and he was the headliner in the farms' 1958 consignment to Harrisburg.

On Nov. 6, there was an expectant buzz in the Pennsylvania Farm Show Arena as the hip numbers passed 900. The crowd began getting larger. They anticipated that some of the sport's big guns were about to commence firing.

Their target was hip number 914, Dancer Hanover. He was the yearling that everyone wanted but couldn't afford. No Standardbred yearling had ever sold for more than $72,000, but there were a lot of people who thought Dancer Hanover might break the record.

One man who was prepared to break the record was the colt's namesake, Stanley Dancer. In partnership with several others, he was ready to pay $75,000 to collar the colt.

When the pedigree reader finished extolling the merits of Dancer Hanover's family, which was scarcely necessary. Delvin Miller opened the action by tossing in a $25,000 bid. To put that in perspective, Hanover's yearlings had averaged $5,564 the previous year. And things were just getting started.

Immediately the bids began coming from around the arena and the former record of $72,000 was quickly eclipsed. The bids quickly passed Dancer's $75,000 limit.

"The only one of my partners who was with me that day at Harrisburg was Mr. Shriner of Taney Rainbow Farm," recalls Dancer. "When they were asking for $80,000, he told me to go ahead and bid again."

This went on for several more bids and suddenly auctioneer George Swinebroad was asking for an unprecedented $100,000 bid. Dancer nodded, and the crowd cheered. But the horse still wasn't sold.

The only other bidder left at this level was Californian Jim Camp, and he tried one more time to discourage Dancer with a $102,000 bid. Now Swinebroad was asking for $105,000.

"Give it to them," Shriner told Dancer.

"No, Mr. Shriner, you're the only one here," protested Dancer. "The others don't want the colt at that kind of money."

"Don't worry about it," said Shriner. "I'll take all of him."

Dancer nodded to indicate his $105,000 bid. Camp capitulated. The hammer fell and the spectators again applauded wildly.

They had reason to applaud because no Standardbred — or Thoroughbred — yearling had ever sold for such a sum. It was announced that Dancer would own one-sixth of the colt and handle the training chores.

It helps to put Dancer Hanover's record price into perspective when you learn the next two highest yearlings sold at Harrisburg that year were Bullet Hanover at $30,000 and Blaze Hanover at $27,000. (Those bids represented money well spent because Bullet Hanover won the 1960 Little Brown Jug just a few weeks after Blaze Hanover had won the Hambletonian.)

Another way to grasp the impact of Dancer Hanover is that when Hanover sold him that year for $105,000, its 128 other yearlings brought a total of $789,500.

Dancer the trainer took Dancer the pacer back to his farm in New Egypt, New Jersey and immediately discovered that he'd paid a record price for a colt that didn't want to pace.

"He was tough," recalls Dancer. "He was good mannered, but he just didn't hit the pace too good. He would go so crooked, in and out. In spots he would be good-gaited, but not always."

During the winter Stanley Dancer feared that the colt would never develop into the kind of performer he was supposed to be for such a record price. In the early summer of 1959, he took his stable to the old Good Time Park mile track in Goshen for some final prep miles.

In seeking a solution for Dancer Hanover's weaving on the track, Stanley asked Delvin Miller to train the colt a few times at Goshen. Miller liked the youngster, sensed his extreme speed, and told Lawrence Sheppard as much. Sheppard knew that Dancer wasn't thrilled with the colt, so he called the young trainer.

Dancer Hanover with driver Delvin Miller on Jug day
(*Photo courtesy of the U.S. Trotting Association*)

"Say, son, I know you've had a lot of trouble with getting that colt gaited and going, but I'm interested buying him," said Sheppard. Dancer was practically rubbing his hands his hands in glee.

"I'll make you one offer," said Sheppard. "It may not be what you want, but it's a real good offer in my mind. I'll give you $200,000. I don't want to dicker on him. Just let me know in a few days."

Dancer recalled many years later, "That sounded awful good to me."

One of Dancer's partners balked, and said that the colt was worth more. Dancer countered by saying Sheppard had made one offer and wouldn't go any higher. If this man thought he was worth more than $200,000, then he could simply buy the partners out at that price.

The man decided not to do that, and Dancer Hanover was sold back to Hanover. Delvin Miller took over his training and the colt developed into an extremely fast but often unpredictable pacer. He got a 1:56.4 mark as a four-year-old and earned $87, 746. So he never actually paid for himself on the track, but his pedigree and speed earned him a spot in Hanover's stud barn.

From his first crop, Dancer Hanover sired a Triple Crown winner in Romeo Hanover, and he sired other fast pacers from the mare Romola Hanover. They were the exception rather than the rule in his stud career, and when Dancer Hanover later experienced fertility problems he was leased to a Canadian breeder.

Stanley Dancer remembers Lawrence Sheppard warmly, recalling how helpful he was to the ambitious young trainer. He knew that Sheppard could be a tough businessman, but he also knew how intensely interested he was in the game. Sheppard was knowledgeable enough about horses and driving that he could speak on equal terms with the trainers he encountered.

In the summer of 1958, young Dancer had a talented and fast Tar Heel filly named Honick Rainbow. She had lots of pluses and one major minus: she could kick like a mule and was never hesitant to use her hind feet.

In fact, Dancer recalls that Honick Rainbow once kicked him and fell down while winning a race. The filly became known as much for her kicking as she did for her pacing.

That fall Dancer recalls that he and Sheppard hitched a ride on Max Hempt's private airplane to the Tattersalls Winter Sale in Lexington. Hempt and his farm manager, Jimmy Rue, completed the four passengers.

After the sale, as they were getting airborne out of Lexington, Sheppard, Hempt, and Rue were laughing and enjoying a libation. Suddenly Dancer heard a crash, boom, bang and the small plane shook.

That got everyone's immediate attention, and the pilot told them that they'd lost an engine. They would have to return to Lexington. He calmly radioed for clearance to make an emergency landing and then set the small plane and his passengers down safely.

Dancer recalls, "My hair was standing on end." He was so unnerved by the event that when he got off the small plane and onto terra firma that he proclaimed, "I'm never flying again."

Sheppard barked to him, "Son, would you rather be riding in this plane with only one engine, or driving that kickin' bitch?"

"Give me that kickin' bitch, Mr. Sheppard," Dancer managed to say.

Dancer Hanover as a stallion

Sheppard's 1955 investment in Adios quickly began to pay off handsomely. The first Little Brown Jug winner by Adios had been Adios Harry in 1954, but John Simpson won the Jug two years later with Harry's brother Noble Adios.

From 1958 through 1962, Adios sired five straight Little Brown Jug winners. And it wasn't unusual for many of the other colts in the Jug to be sons of Adios. Shadow Wave won the Jug in 1958, followed by Adios Butler in 1959.

Bullet Hanover took home the prize in 1960. Stanley Dancer won his first Jug in 1961 driving Henry T. Adios (named for Henry Thomas, Hanover's trainer in the late 1930s) and Dancer repeated the next year with Lehigh Hanover.

In 1961, Bullet started in the stud and Dancer Hanover joined him a year later. Lehigh Hanover gave the farm three sons of Adios when he began breeding service there in 1964. Dancer recalls how seamlessly the Lehigh Hanover deal went.

"If I remember correctly, Mr. Sheppard called and made me one offer on Lehigh Hanover," says Dancer. "I think it was $250,000. I didn't even bother to shop around with other farms. We just sold him to Hanover."

In the end, none of Hanover's sons of Adios was able to sustain the male line of Adios.

Chapter 10

Winning The Classics

In 1956, trainer John Simpson won the Little Brown Jug with Noble Adios, reaching the highest pinnacle in the pacing world. That kicked off an eight-year period that would see Simpson win the Jug two more times and get to the winner's circle twice in the Hambletonian. Four of Simpson's five classic winners in that period would wind up in the stud barn at Hanover.

As Dwight D. Eisenhower began preparing for his second term in the White House early in 1957, John Simpson was a man on a mission. Two missions, to be exact. The first mission was to be holding the trophy after the first Hambletonian to be raced at DuQuoin, Illinois. The second was to make a return visit to the Little Brown Jug winner's circle.

Winning the Jug seemed more likely because Simpson was the pilot behind a whiz-bang son of Knight Dream named Torpid. He had blazed onto the Standardbred scene in 1956 and put all his rivals to shame, winning his stakes with ease.

Winning the Hambletonian would be a much higher mountain to climb, Simpson knew, and he wasn't sure he had the horsepower to get there. His best chance rested with a colt called Hickory Smoke.

Hickory Smoke was a son of Hambletonian winner Titan Hanover and out of Misty Hanover by Dean Hanover, so he had the Hanover brand stamped all over him. Sheppard's good friend Bowman Brown had bred him, and in 1956 Sheppard called Brown in an attempt to buy the promising two-year-old.

Paul Spears remembers that he was in Sheppard's office when his boss was negotiating with Brown, and the happy-go-lucky Archie Mudge, an executive with the Hanover Shoe Co., burst in, sized up the conversation, and proclaimed loudly, "I'm in!"

When Sheppard hung up the phone, he turned to Mudge and asked, "You're in? What the hell does that mean? In what?"

"In the deal you just made," said Mudge, not knowing the horse or the price.

So Sheppard took Mudge in as a partner on Hickory Smoke, and that's how Archie Mudge bought half-interest in a future Hambletonian winner for $7,500.

The Hambletonian was particularly important to Hickory Smoke because he was not eligible to all the top stakes. John Simpson knew he would have to make hay on Hambo Day.

Simpson set forth a schedule that he felt would have Hickory Smoke at his peak by the first of September. The season started in the Reynolds Stake at Buffalo. Hickory Smoke broke stride and finished back, but Simpson shrugged that off.

Hickory Smoke was up and down in his next few starts, but he was moving in the right direction. Then the son of Titan Hanover was involved in a mix-up at Grandview Raceway in Cleveland and came out of the skirmish with a swollen and lacerated knee and a battered ankle.

Simpson refused to panic. In fact, when he didn't like the looks of the colt's knee before his next start, Hickory Smoke was scratched. Such patience required a trainer to have extraordinary confidence in both himself and his colt; John Simpson had both.

Even when Hickory Smoke was rained out of his final prep, Simpson didn't waver. He sent Hickory Smoke to DuQuoin and instructed an assistant exactly how to train him.

The Jenneys, Lawrence Sheppard, John Simpson and Hickory Smoke
at Lexington in 1956

John Simpson races Hickory Smoke to a win in the Hambletonian race-off

On Hambletonian Day Hickory Smoke and his driver were letter-perfect and won in a three-heat struggle. The horse with the initials H.S. was headed for a stud career at a farm bearing the same initials. Horsemen lauded Simpson for his precision in honing Hickory Smoke to a razor's edge on the one day when it mattered most.

Getting Torpid to the winner's circle in the Jug was far easier, although Simpson got a mudbath in the final heat, which was contested over a sloppy and sticky clay track at Delaware. The heavy footing didn't stop Torpid from continuing his dominance over his contemporaries.

Simpson took a three-year vacation from the winner's circle at Delaware, but he found his way back in 1960 courtesy of Bullet Hanover, his favorite pacer. Bullet Hanover astonished the Standardbred world as a juvenile when he won the Fox Stake with a heat in 1:57 despite starting from the second tier. It was a full second faster than any two-year-old had ever gone.

*Torpid winning
at Yonkers*

*(Photo courtesy
of Michael Cipriani,
Yonkers Raceway)*

In the first heat of the 1960 Jug, Simpson fired Bullet Hanover into the first turn at Delaware and the colt suddenly jumped.

"I drove him off his feet," Simpson admitted later. Having made one error, Simpson wasn't about to make another error. He got Bullet back pacing, but cleverly counted his rivals to make sure he finished ninth.

Finishing ninth assured Simpson of a starting position in the second heat directly behind the first-heat winner Muncy Hanover. If Bullet Hanover had finished eighth, he would have started on the extreme outside in the first tier.

Bullet Hanover followed Muncy away from the gate in the second heat, but once Simpson nursed him around the first turn, everyone was soon following Bullet. He won the second and third heats and established a world record for a three-heat race.

Again, the 40-year-old Simpson had kept his cool and overcame the first-heat crisis to walk away with the silverware. It was clear that he was one of the greatest horsemen the sport had ever seen.

Simpson relished taking a plunge at the pari-mutuel windows when the price was right. There is no rule in racing that prohibits a trainer or driver from betting on a horse that he trains or drives, and no one knew when Simpson's stock was ready to win better than he did.

One veteran horseman remembered Simpson racing the talented trotting filly Anna Dares in the late 1950s. She was entered in a race in which the local newspaper handicappers gave her little chance of winning.

*Bullet Hanover
and John Simpson
at Lexington*

"They apparently don't think much of your chances tonight," a friend said to Simpson before the races.

"Well, here is what I think of her chances," said Simpson, as he calmly peeled $200 in bills from his wallet. "Bet this on her to win."

And win Anna Dares did.

Perhaps Simpson's most celebrated betting score came in the 1962 Messenger Stakes. With its purse of $169,403, it was the richest race in harness racing history.

Lawrence Sheppard was in New York that day and he planned to return to Hanover. Simpson asked, "Are you going to stay for the Messenger?"

"Hell, no, you'll be lucky to get a check," said Sheppard.

"I don't know, Mr. Sheppard, maybe you ought to stay and watch," said Simpson.

Rich purses draw a crowd and a field of 10 three-year-old pacers were dropped into the box to take a shot at the bonanza. Simpson's horse was Thor Hanover, a chestnut son of Adios who had high speed but was a bit faint of heart. The public debated the merits of Adora's Dream, unbeaten in 13 lifetime starts, as well as Coffee Break and Lehigh Hanover. The bettors relegated Simpson and his chestnut flyer to the ranks of the also-rans.

When Thor Hanover drew post 10 in the second tier of starters, any chance of victory seemed to fade from sight. He couldn't beat this group of horses under the best of circumstances, and he surely couldn't beat them if he had to weave his way through traffic.

John Simpson didn't quite see it that way. He knew that Thor Hanover had the high turn of speed so often found in the sons of Adios, but he also knew he had to be careful how to use it. If Thor were used too hard too soon, he would fold up like an accordion.

As the race went off, Adora's Dream forged his way to the front after being stung hard in the opening quarter. He got no breather because soon Stanley Dancer had Lehigh Hanover right at his throatlatch.

That's the way the race developed into the stretch. Suddenly there was a streak of red in the middle of the track. It was the chestnut Thor Hanover and Simpson. The canny driver had spotted an opening and he was using Thor's burst of speed, carefully conserved earlier in the race, to wedge through the crowd.

At the wire Thor Hanover had a half-length on a wave of pacers.

The crowd at Roosevelt Raceway roared as the $2 win payoff flashed on the tote board. $144! John Simpson just smiled. Not only had Thor Hanover won $84,715 in purse money, but Simpson himself had pocketed some long green after he had bet on the colt.

The same year that Simpson won the Messenger with Thor Hanover, he won a heat of the Little Brown Jug with Gamecock, a Tar Heel colt co-owned by Lawrence Sheppard. The youngster's name was significant because both Simpson

Thor Hanover winning at the Messenger

and Sheppard attended cockfights on occasion. The tradition of fighting roosters runs deep in Simpson's native state of South Carolina where the state university's athletic teams are known as the "Fighting Gamecocks."

In 1963 Simpson brought out a small son of Star's Pride that could be a handful at times, but Simpson knew he possessed wicked speed. The rest of the world knew that, too, when this colt called Ayres won as a two-year-old at Delaware in 2:00.1.

Horsemen and spectators must have thought the teletimer was broken, or had been tripped early. A two-year-old colt trotting in 2:00.1 on a half-mile track? Impossible! The world record was 2:03-1/2 and horses simply didn't break a world record by more than three seconds. But Ayres did.

Ayres lost the second heat, and that necessitated a raceoff between the heat winners. Simpson got Ayres around the first turn and then suddenly the colt made an abrupt right turn for the paddock.

"He was bulling. He just pulled himself up and wheeled around," said Simpson many years later. "He'd had enough. He was just mad. It had been building up in him. He was smarter than his trainer. In that third heat, Ayres said, 'I've had enough, you SOB. What do you want me to do now?'"

Simpson admitted that he had let Ayres get away with too much misbehavior at times. The colt had so much speed and his rivals would practically fall down trying to trot with him. Ayres needed to go to reform school to improve his manners.

Ayres was an ideal pupil for a man of John Simpson's skills. The trainer was smarter than the horse, and Ayres would soon learn that. Simpson knew that the speed was there, but Ayres had to be made into a manageable racehorse. He was putty in the hands of the sculptor John Simpson.

In his training miles, Ayres was required to follow another horse endlessly. He balked at this restraint initially, but soon he accepted it as his lot in life and learned to relax. Ayres didn't realize it, but John Simpson was teaching him the manners he would need as a three-year-old. And since Ayres was bred and owned by Charlotte Sheppard, you can be sure Simpson wanted to make the most of his ability.

Those manners were very much in evidence as Ayres swept through the Triple Crown that year, winning the Yonkers Futurity, Hambletonian, and the Kentucky Futurity.

The only real anxious moment of the season came in the opening round of the Hambletonian when the Star's Pride colt skipped over the shadow of the television cable at the start. Ayres momentarily lost his feet, but John Simpson never lost his cool. Ayres was back trotting in the blink of an eye.

Ayres rolled on relentlessly in that heat to scorch the DuQuoin oval in 1:56.4, the fastest mile ever in Hambletonian history. He took the second heat handily.

*John Simpson
driving Ayres
in the Kentucky
Futurity*

That year Ayres might have swept Horse of the Year honors had it not been for a two-year-old pacer whose exploits left horsemen and observers astonished.

His name was Bret Hanover and all he did is start in 24 races in 1964 and win each and every one of them. The sport had never seen anything quite like Bret, and he was the overwhelming choice as Horse of the Year.

Lawrence and Charlotte Sheppard and John Simpson were partial to Ayres, of course, but if they had to yield Horse of the Year honors, it wasn't so bad to play second fiddle to a colt bred and raised at Hanover. Bret had sold for $50,000 as a yearling in 1963, making him the highest-priced baby in the breed that year.

In 1965, Bret picked up where he left off the previous season, rolling along like Old Man River. He didn't stop until he had won 35 straight races. Another son of Adios knocked him off, this one named Adios Vic, but his three defeats were just bumps along the road to the Triple Crown of pacing and repeat honors as Horse of the Year.

In 1966 as a four-year-old, Bret Hanover proved to be harness racing's greatest box office attraction. He paced his way into history that October at The Red Mile when he looped the famous track in 1:53.3 in a time trial, making him the fastest Standardbred ever.

Even though Bret Hanover went to Castleton Farm in Kentucky to begin stallion service in 1967, Hanover had the honor of breeding and raising this extraordinary pacer, who was later voted as the Pacer of the Century in several polls.

Adios died in the summer of 1965, but he did so without owing anyone ever associated with him a penny. Certainly Lawrence Sheppard's investment in Adios had paid dividends. Besides, he had two aces in the stud barn that made it very easy to forget Adios.

On the pacing front, Tar Heel had proven to be a remarkably prolific sire and a perfect cross for all the Adios mares that Hanover had assembled. He was a workhorse stallion for Hanover with his first babies arriving in 1954 and his final crop being foals of 1981.

Some of the early standout winners for Tar Heel that gave promise of things to come were O'Brien Hanover, Thorpe Hanover, Tar Boy, and Tarquinius.

They were followed by an endless wave of stakes winners such as Gamecock, Bengazi Hanover, and Zip Tar.

To achieve his lofty status, Tar Heel had to overcome the aversion that many trainers had to them. Charles Keller III, squire of Yankeeland Farms in Frederick, Maryland, recalls that his father bred to Tar Heel early in the stallion's career, then stopped using him.

Sheppard confronted the senior Keller, a famed major league baseball player in his younger days, and asked, "Charlie, why did you quit breeding to Tar Heel?"

"Well, Shep, a lot of the trainers don't like the Tar Heels," countered Keller.

"Oh, hell, you don't ever want to listen to those damn trainers," retorted Sheppard.

Keller went back to breeding to Tar Heel, and two of the best performers ever sired by the pacing monarch were Tempered Yankee and Sly Yankee, both from Keller's mare Sue Adios.

The yearlings by Tar Heel were not always the most attractive individuals at the sale. In fact, you could often easily pick them out because of their large heads and Roman noses. Their hocks were often a little coarse and their pasterns tended to be straight and stubby. Those were all qualities they got from their sire.

They also inherited a big motor from Tar Heel and the rugged constitution to hold up to the rigors of racing. Oh, the Tar Heel fillies could be harridans, kicking a bit too often like Honick Rainbow, but they were soon to find a special niche in the breed.

Tar Heel was overshadowed by Adios during the early stages of his stud career, but the final crop of Adios was born in 1966. That summer a Tar Heel colt frolicked in the fields of Hanover next to his dam, a young Adios mare. This colt was named Laverne Hanover, a name that often caused him to be mistaken for a filly. There was nothing feminine about the way that Laverne Hanover destroyed his rivals on the track, however, and he gave Tar Heel his first Little Brown Jug winner in 1969.

Two years later, another son of Tar Heel, also from an Adios mare, was back in the winner's circle after the Little Brown Jug. His name was Nansemond and he had stunned the harness racing world by upsetting the seemingly invincible Albatross.

Wherever you looked during this era, you found pacers by Tar Heel winning in the top classes. Otaro Hanover, Kentucky, Penn Hanover, Isle Of Wight, and Keystone Pat were just a few of the Tar Heel standouts in the United States and Canada.

Those Tar Heel fillies weren't exactly welcomed by trainers, who found them sour and uncooperative all too often, but you won't find many better fillies than Sunnie Tar and Hazel Hanover, two distaffers sired by Tar Heel.

The daughters of Tar Heel were ultimately to fill a special role in the breed as fountains of pacing speed. Bret Hanover was one of the first of a long line of brilliant pacers from Tar Heel mares, but some other champions from daughters of Tar Heel were Romeo Hanover, Ralph Hanover, Silk Stockings, Armbro Omaha, Tyler B, Tarport Hap, and Silent Majority.

Tar Heel soon acquired the nicknames as the "King of Queens" and Hanover's "Chairman of the Brood." The farm crew always held him in great affection. Even as he aged and his back swayed dramatically, he was a favorite for many. He lived to the advanced age of 34 before quietly easing into eternity in the summer of 1982.

Hanover placed an ad in the trade journals with a photo showing Tar Heel in his paddock. The ad contained these words:

May his spirit, gentleness, intelligence, and courage
Live along with Tar Heel's name
And his greatness in descendants
Burn with an eternal flame
For without the mighty King of Queens
Racing would never have been the same.

Tar Heel sired 1,368 foals, a total that is particularly remarkable because most of his breeding career preceded the widespread use of artificial insemination in Standardbreds. His offspring earned over $39 million.

While Tar Heel was proving to be a cash cow for the farm's pacing ledgers, Star's Pride was his counterpart on the trotting side. Star's Pride was at first a consolation prize when Demon Hanover proved unattainable, and Sheppard surely took great consolation when Star's Pride became a far greater sire than Demon Hanover. In fact, after being syndicated for $500,000, Demon Hanover spent one year in the Bluegrass before dying suddenly in 1958.

After Emily's Pride, Diller Hanover, and Ayres came more Hambletonian winners. In the darkness of the 1965 Hambletonian final, the colt Egyptian Candor upset the filly Armbro Flight; both were by Star's Pride. The following year the Star's Pride filly Kerry Way won the classic at DuQuoin.

Two years later, Nevele Pride won the Hambletonian as easily as he won virtually everything else in his career. What Bret Hanover was to pacing in 1964-66, Nevele Pride was to trotting in 1967-69. The Triple Crown was child's play for the Star's Pride colt from the Hoot Mon mare Thankful, and he closed out his career as a four-year-old by becoming the fastest trotter in history with a 1:54.4 effort.

Star's Pride wasn't done siring Hambletonian winners, and the final two were especially meaningful to the Hanover team, but Lawrence Sheppard wouldn't live to see them. Hanover-bred Lindy's Pride, sold as a yearling with the name Galahad Hanover, won the Hambletonian in 1969. The final Hambo winner by Star's Pride was Super Bowl, later a stallion of monumental influence at Hanover.

Since the mid-1960s, it was apparent that Lawrence Sheppard was failing physically. The signs weren't dramatic, but he no longer had the energy or strength to manage a dozen different enterprises and spread himself so thin. The years of hard living, hard work, and non-stop smoking were catching up to him. He knew it.

He could still summon plenty of strength to teach a youngster on the payroll a few lessons when the occasion warranted it.

In April of 1967, a young Canadian whiz kid named Murray Brown started to work at Hanover Shoe Farms after a brief stint at nearby Lana Lobell Farm. He was a native of Montreal and harness racing took hold of him as a teenager and never let go.

Brown and some of his buddies spent much of their spare time — too much, he might admit — going to the races and watching such legends as Keith Waples, John Hayes, Roger White, Jack Kopas, and others.

Along with five friends, Brown formed the Valiant Six Stable and campaigned a pony-sized pacer named Auction Time. He considered himself the number one harness racing fan in Montreal, although his interest in betting was soon augmented by a fascination with pedigrees.

Brown began doing pedigree charts for horsemen and owners in the Montreal area. That led to a job with the Miron Brothers, then a major racing and breeding operation in Quebec. After Adrian and Gerard Miron decided to cut back, Brown went to Lana Lobell Farms where he stayed for seven months.

That's when Lawrence Sheppard entered the picture, telling Brown that he saw a future for him at Hanover, but only after he gained some experience working at *The Harness Horse* magazine in nearby Harrisburg. After a few months learning about publications, Brown was ready to wear the orange and blue colors of Hanover and settled in on the farm staff.

Young Murray Brown joins the Hanover staff

One of his first assignments in his new job was to travel to Roosevelt Raceway on Long Island to see the Messenger Stakes. It was won by Romulus Hanover, a chestnut son of the farm's stallion Dancer Hanover from the wonderful matron Romola Hanover.

Soon after Brown returned, Lawrence Sheppard summoned him with a question about his travel expenses. "Where did you stay, boy?" asked Sheppard bluntly.

"At the YMCA," said Brown. The room cost was eight dollars.

"Hey, you're with Hanover Shoe Farms now," said Sheppard. "This is a high-class outfit. We go first class."

That summer of 1967 the first crop by Lehigh Hanover began racing, and one of Brown's jobs was to handle the Hanover advertising and promote its stallions. When a few of the first starters by Lehigh Hanover won races, albeit in slow times, he drew up an ad and placed it in the June 14 issue of *The Harness Horse* magazine.

The ad copy saluted the accomplishments of Nevele Romeo p,2,2:04.2h, Lehigh Boy p, 2, 2:08.4h, Instamatic p,2, 2:11h, and Perky Hanover p,2, 2:15.2h.

Once again, Sheppard summoned Brown to teach him a lesson.

"Why would you put this out?" asked Sheppard. "It's premature. Who's looking for horses like this?"

"And he was right," admitted Brown many years later.

Since that call from Lawrence Sheppard at the end of 1966, Murray Brown has become so closely identified with Hanover Shoe Farms that his friends say, "he bleeds orange and blue." Brown has amassed an incredible range of contacts within the sport and truly found his niche in doing public relations for the farm and managing the Standardbred Horse Sale Co.

As the end of his life neared, Lawrence Sheppard felt that Hanover was well set for the future. He had recruited Don Millar from the USTA to manage matters on the farm, John Simpson would train and campaign the racing stable, and Paul Spears was there to control the purse strings.

He told his wife Charlotte, "Things are in good hands. They'll do what is right for the farm."

Even though Sheppard's health was precarious in the fall of 1967, Brown remembers that he fought his way through the Harrisburg sale and kept a watchful eye on everything, including his young public relations director.

"Boy, I was watching you from the auction stand," Sheppard told Brown after the sale. "You did a great job. Tell people what we have to sell. Don't tell them what to buy, but just expose them."

Brown remembers that Sheppard instructed him that if a buyer ever asked about a Hanover yearling, he should be completely honest in giving his opinion.

"But if they don't ask, just keep your mouth shut," said Sheppard.

In 1967, the 876 horses sold at Harrisburg fetched over $4.9 million and the Hanover yearlings brought a total of $2,281,800 in bids. The top dog was Bart Hanover, a brother to Bret, who was hammered down for $105,000.

Lawrence Sheppard, John Simpson, Paul Spears, Murray Brown, and the entire Hanover team had reason to smile when the last horse was sold. It was a record-breaking year for both Hanover and the sale company.

Paul Spears remembers how Sheppard never lost his stubborn attitude even as he lost his health.

"He had a great affinity for the Catholic school here in Hanover," says Spears. "He liked the kids there. He got the priest in and said he wanted those kids to have a gymnasium, and that he'd give $750,000 to build it."

The priest was overjoyed, and working with his superiors and an architect he developed an ambitious set of drawings for the addition to the school. Sheppard then had a heart attack and the priest rushed to the hospital to show Sheppard the realization of his wish.

"He was lying there in an oxygen tent gasping for breath," recalls Spears, "but he said that he still wanted to see the plans."

When Sheppard noticed some adjacent rooms, he asked the priest what they were. He was told one was a kitchen, and another one was a meeting room for the nuns.

"I didn't tell you I wanted to build a damn kitchen or meeting room," gasped Sheppard. "I wanted a gymnasium. Get your drawing and get the hell out of here."

The priest pleaded for him to sign off on the plans, and even blessed the ailing man, but Sheppard was adamant. He pointed toward the door, and the priest exited.

After Sheppard was released from the hospital and was convalescing at home, he summoned Spears to revive the gymnasium plans. He still wanted to see those youngsters have a gymnasium, but he knew this strength and his days were limited. He asked Spears to work with the church hierarchy to fulfill his wishes.

"I'll put up $750,000 and not another damn cent," said Sheppard. "I'll do what I said I would do."

Spears set up a meeting with the church officials and a contractor to discuss what could be done. They were still hopeful of including a kitchen and meeting room, but Spears simply drew a red line through those sections of the drawing.

The contractor figured the final cost to be $780,000, and Spears said he'd go back to Sheppard and see if he could cover the extra $30,000. Sheppard agreed, and the work began.

The gymnasium was finished in January 1968, and Spears recalls taking a very sick Lawrence Sheppard and his wife Charlotte for the grand opening.

"He wanted to see it, and they had a big thing at the school," recalls Spears. "All the children were there and so were the church officials. We took him all through it."

For Lawrence Sheppard, it was his last hurrah. His health deteriorated and on Feb. 26, 1968, he died at Hanover Hospital.

Writing in *Hoof Beats*, former Hanover manager Jim Harrison concluded, "In my opinion, Lawrence B. Sheppard exercised a greater influence on the improvement of the harness horse breed than any man who ever lived."

He got no argument.

After Sheppard's death, John Simpson, acting in his new capacity as president and general manager of Hanover Shoe Farms, announced the farm would "continue to function, guided by the same high standards which he [Lawrence Sheppard] represented."

Simpson wrote with pride about the Hanover personnel, facilities, and its band of broodmares and stallions.

"We pledge to maintain the same principles and high standards, which for the last forty-two years, have made the name HANOVER the GREATEST NAME IN HARNESS RACING," he wrote in an open letter published as an advertisement.

Charlotte Sheppard became the chairman of Hanover Shoe Farms after her husband's death. She may have been raised to be a housewife and mother, but she was a strong-willed woman who loved horses and whose own success as a breeder should not be overlooked.

Dale Welk certainly won't forget Mrs. Sheppard. When he was a small boy riding in his father's pick-up truck, he dreaded the visits to the Sheppard home because she was always so demonstrative in her affections.

"Does that woman have to kiss me again?" young Dale would ask his father.

"Mrs. Sheppard was a real sweetheart," laughs Welk. "She always wanted to give me a hug and a kiss. She was just that kind of person. When I was a teenager, I remember her riding around the farm on her golf cart. And she'd stop and speak to every person on the farm."

The first job that Clyde Sterner, then the maintenance supervisor, assigned to Welk was to scrub the Sheppards' swimming pool with wire brushes, a chore necessary before the pool was filled and opened for the summer.

"Mrs. Sheppard had the housekeeper bring me and the other guys drinks and snacks, and sat with us for a while as we filled the pool," he recalls. "We all wanted to get in the pool, but we couldn't do that as long as she was there."

Finally Mrs. Sheppard read their adolescent minds, and said, "Why don't you boys get in the water and play a while? Clyde's not going to catch you."

Despite his youth, Welk could see the Mrs. Sheppard had an inner toughness, too, that "iron fist in a velvet glove" character that some women possess.

Although she certainly was not equal to her husband in the affairs of the farm, Charlotte Sheppard was not without experience in handling horses. One keepsake that Russell Williams cherishes dearly is an old black-and-white photo of Charlotte Sheppard driving Peter Manning in the 1920s.

When Sonny Sheppard died in a plane crash, he had owned a half-interest in Goddess Hanover and that passed to his mother. She bought out Sonny's partner and in 1953 Charlotte bred Goddess Hanover to Hoot Mon.

From that mating came Cassin Hanover, a wonderful stakes filly who gave Mrs. Sheppard a triumph in the 1957 Kentucky Futurity, America's oldest trotting stake.

Goddess Hanover also gave her a filly named Arpege who later produced the Triple Crown winner Ayres.

From Cassin Hanover Mrs. Sheppard bred a Hickory Smoke filly in 1961 named Elma. She was not only a superior stakes filly on the Grand Circuit, but she also competed with distinction against the best in Europe as an older mare.

When older horsemen recall the best trotting mares of the 1960s, Elma invariably ranks among the best. In turn, by breeding Elma to Super Bowl, Mrs. Sheppard got a 1974 colt she simply named Texas after her native state.

In the 1977 Kentucky Futurity, Texas was truly the lone star as he sprinted home with a straight-heat win. It was exactly 20 years after his granddam Cassin Hanover had won the same event.

"She didn't try to compete with her husband, but she did like having a good horse," says Williams.

Although she never meddled in business affairs, Charlotte Sheppard wasn't reluctant to interject herself in matters relating to the farm. Russell Williams recalls that when a large piece of land became available near Hanover, Lawrence Sheppard wanted to grab hold of it but felt the price was a bit too dear.

"He never liked to pay more than about 50 cents an acre," laughs Russell. "So it was a hard thing for him to buy land. He agonized over paying the going price and he talked it over with his wife. So she bought the land herself. That piece of land was the Appler Farm in Bonneauville and it became our yearling farm."

With John Simpson to race the horses, Don Millar to manage the farm, and Paul Spears to watch over money matters, Hanover seemed assured of continuity. Unforeseen factors, however, altered the management structure within a few years.

Cassin Hanover wins the 1957 Kentucky Futurity.

Cassin Hanover after her 1957 win at the Kentucky Futurity. Driver Fred Egan, 78, retired after this win. Pictured next to Cassin are Clarence Gaines, Fred van Lennep, Egan in the sulky, Katherine H.E. Nichols (behind Egan), K.D. Owen, Charlotte N. Sheppard (owner), Octave Blake, E. Roland Harriman (behind Blake), H. Willis Nichols, and L.B. Sheppard. Every person identified is a Hall of Fame Immortal.

Elma winning at Hollywood Park in 1964 over Porterhouse, Express Rodney and Speedy Count

Best Of All at DuQuoin in 1966

Chapter 11

Simpson Takes The Reins

After Lawrence Sheppard's death, John Simpson began turning more and more of his stable responsibilities over to son John, Jr. Serving as president of the world's largest breeding farm was not a part-time job.

With the same boldness that characterized Lawrence Sheppard's modus operandi, John Simpson acted quickly to move some fresh faces into the Hanover stallion barn.

From the time that John Simpson won his first Little Brown Jug with Noble Adios in 1956 through 1966, the winner of each Delaware classic had been either Hanover-sired or Hanover-bred. In 1967 that 11-year streak was broken by a Kentucky-bred son of Good Time named Best Of All.

A year later, Hanover announced that Best Of All was joining its stallion ranks. The lithe, leggy pacer was a perfect fit for the brawny Tar Heel mares found in such abundance at Hanover. Besides, Hanover was missing a stallion from the Good Time male line and that would add a new dimension to the farms' stallion lineup and yearling offerings.

Best Of All had been the champion two-year-old of his season, pacing more 2:00 miles than any freshman in history. He fought valiantly in the sophomore classics against an entry from the Billy Haughton Stable that included Romulus Hanover, Nardin's Byrd, and Meadow Paige and was the most consistent colt in the class.

As a four-year-old, Best Of All was virtually unbeatable once catch-driver Bobby Williams took over the driving assignment behind him. He was named Pacer of the Year in voting at the end of the season.

Two years later, another son of Good Time was headed to Hanover. His name was Columbia George, and he was widely admired by horsemen for his tenacity in completing two tough seasons on front tendons that looked very suspicious. Columbia George fought many battles in 1970 against Most Happy Fella and whenever they appeared on the track, the fans got their money's worth.

Breeder George Smith, Jr. named Columbia George after his father, who had been a star on the Columbia University baseball team. Columbia George was trained and driven by veteran Roland Beaulieu, who was often at a disadvantage when competing against the top Grand Circuit regulars.

Columbia George at the fifth race of LBP on Oct. 10, 1969
(Photo courtesy of Harness Horse)

In the fall of 1971, a free-legged bay named Steady Star from the hills of Tennessee astonished the sport by breaking Bret Hanover's 1:53.3 world record in a time trial at Lexington. He wasn't content with merely breaking it — he put it into oblivion.

With Joe O'Brien in the sulky, Steady Star roared around the historic mile oval in 1:52, a time that left some old timers wondering if that record would last forever.

Steady Star didn't have fashionable breeding; he was a grandson of Tar Heel from a mare by Averill, but you couldn't deny that he was a picture-perfect pacer when he put his mind to it. His performances were often compromised by the fact that he fought his driver behind the starting gate, forfeiting needed energy before the race started.

To the Hanover team, Steady Star evoked memories of Billy Direct, another free-legged pacer that had been foaled in Tennessee a few decades earlier.

In fact, Billy Direct was the great-grandsire of Steady Star and Billy didn't have much pedigree on his female side either. Steady Star was a horse that Hanover clearly needed to have and he started his breeding career there in the spring of 1972.

A muddy race at Vernon Downs for Steady Star and driver Joe O'Brien
(Photo courtesy of Bill Taylor, Vernon Downs)

As he was grabbing the reins at Hanover, Simpson was fighting a battle far more difficult than any he had ever faced on the racetrack. His eyesight was deteriorating, slowly but surely. He could still function, still drive a horse, and still drive a car, but his visual acuity wasn't the same as it had been. And it was far more serious than normal aging that forces bifocals upon many people past age 40.

Simpson spent more and more time at Hanover and less time with the horses in training. It wasn't an easy decision for him, but the darkness that was creeping into his world left him with no other choice.

"Dad always felt that his problems were caused by a racing accident at Delaware, Ohio," says his son Jim Simpson. "He hit the hub rail with his head. It was never proven for sure, but that's what he always thought."

The senior Simpson drove in the Hambletonian for the final time in 1969, finishing up the track with Bonfire Hanover while another Hanover product, Lindy's Pride scampered to an easy victory.

From 1949 through 1969, there had been only three years when John Simpson was not in the Hambletonian. It's ironic then that his final drive was behind a future Hambletonian winner. In 1969, Simpson steered Timothy T in the Hoosier Futurity at Indianapolis. The colt finished second in the first heat, but came back to take the second dash in 2:04. Simpson, who owned the colt himself, accepted the trophy, took the colt back to the stable, and hung up the lines forever. He would never again drive a horse competitively. He was 49 years old.

John F. Simpson Sr. and Timothy T

Best Of All, Columbia George, and Steady Star were all superior horses, the kind that Hanover wanted in its stud barn, the kind that had the potential to become successful sires. But while the Hanover team was excited about their potential, they lamented the big fish that got away.

The big fish wasn't actually so big. He was a smallish, compact colt named Albatross, but he was a whale of a pacer on the track and he swallowed up all of his foes in 1970 and 1971.

On the eve of his sophomore season, Albatross was syndicated by Alan J. Leavitt of Lana Lobell Farms, which was located just a few miles away in Hanover. Part of the syndication agreement was that the colt would be transferred from his developer Harry Harvey and given to Stanley Dancer to train and race as a three-year-old.

Dancer knew that he was getting a gold mine when Albatross arrived in his stable and nothing that the colt did during the 1971 season convinced him otherwise. The only dark moment in a season full of highlights was the shocking upset by the Tar Heel colt Nansemond in the Little Brown Jug. Dancer took much of the blame for that defeat upon himself, realizing afterwards that he had raced Albatross too hard in the weeks prior to the Jug.

Albatross as a young stallion

It was the bitterest disappointment in Stanley Dancer's career. Albatross was the greatest pacer he'd ever driven, and he was beaten in the race that mattered most. It was a heartbreak that Dancer would nurse for decades.

After the Jug, Albatross was shipped to Lexington for the Tattersalls Pace and Dancer saw this as a chance for the colt to redeem himself. He hadn't deserved to lose the Jug. Albatross was the best colt in his class, and now Dancer was out to dispel any doubts.

In the first heat, Albatross started from the second tier in the field of 12, but Dancer threaded him through traffic in the first turn and he grabbed control on the backstretch. After that it was merely a matter of how far he would win by and how fast he would pace.

Or was it? Coming off final turn, some leaves blew across the track and Albatross was so startled that he jumped as they blew under his feet, causing Dancer and the spectators some anxious moments.

He lit back pacing, however, and charged down the stretch under a head of steam. He hit the wire in 1:54.4 and the aficionados roared their approval. They had just witnessed the fastest race mile in Standardbred history, and it was by a mere three-year-old. And a three-year-old who started in the second tier and then lost momentum with his missteps in the final quarter.

It was almost incomprehensible. The crowd rose to its feet to salute the new world champion.

The Tattersalls Pace, like so many major stakes of that era, was a two-heat event, and Albatross had to come back for a second mile. This time he started from the rail by virtue of winning the first heat. Just prior to the start, something spooked Albatross and he almost went to his knees. Dancer had a tight hold on his colt and prevented him from going down, but Albatross again lost momentum, this time at the start.

That made little difference once he found his gait and found room. The others were racing for second place as he whirled around The Red Mile again in 1:54.4, now establishing a new two-heat world record.

Everyone at The Red Mile that day was positively giddy after seeing history made. Everyone, that is, except John Simpson and Murray Brown. They could only think of what a great stallion Albatross could be.

"Damn! Leavitt's got him tied up," said Simpson to Brown as they left the track.

Albatross ended the season by whipping the best older pacers in training in the American Pacing Classic in California and wound up with $558,009 in the bank. No Standardbred had ever earned more in a single season. Albatross was easily voted Horse of the Year.

Racing fans were thrilled to hear that Albatross was coming back as a four-year-old to cover himself with more glory. But things didn't go exactly as planned. In fact, they didn't go well at all. Albatross was beaten in his first three starts by the five-year-old Isle Of Wight, a brother to Nansemond, the colt that had upset Albatross in the Jug.

Albatross and Stanley Dancer beat Nansemond and Herve Filion
in the Canadian Pacing Derby

Every horseman knows that starting a four-year-old against toughened older campaigners is a dicey proposition, one fraught with the potential for failure. It was no disgrace that horses in better form beat Albatross, but this was a horse that wasn't supposed to lose.

Members of the syndicate that owned Albatross weren't happy. They voted to dump Dancer as the horse's trainer, and replace him with Lee Broglio. They would use catch-drivers to race him.

One dissenting member of the syndicate was Louis Silverstein, a longtime patron of the Dancer Stable along with his wife Hilda. He decided that the only way to prevent the horse from leaving the stable was to buy Albatross himself.

"Mrs. Silverstein was always very nice to me, and she didn't want me losing that horse," recalled Dancer many years later. "I knew that Mr. Silverstein could afford to buy the horse, but he didn't have a breeding farm and couldn't keep him in his back yard."

Silverstein understood that he needed some allies in his endeavor and he suggested that Dancer try to enlist the support of a breeding farm in purchasing Albatross. Dancer picked up the phone and called John Simpson at Hanover.

Simpson simply couldn't believe that the owners would fire Dancer so quickly and so unreasonably, but Dancer admitted that was the situation. He then asked Simpson if Hanover might want to buy a chunk of Albatross.

"Absolutely!" said Simpson without a moment's hesitation.

The syndicate members who wanted to replace Dancer agreed that they'd sell their 70 percent interest for $1,750,000, making the whole horse worth $2.5 million.

Murray Brown recalls being with Simpson when Stanley Dancer called Hanover to discuss the Albatross deal. Simpson knew all he needed to know about the pacer's prowess on the track, but there was one X factor he didn't know about.

"How big are his testicles?" Simpson asked Dancer.

"Bigger than average," was the answer. That was all Simpson needed to know.

"That was the only question he asked," says Brown years later. Albatross was being sold without any guarantees of fertility, and Simpson knew that testicle size is a good indicator of a horse's fertility.

Albatross was then resyndicated with John Simpson and Hanover Shoe Farms in the controlling position. Of the 50 shares, Hanover took 27, Hilda Silverstein took eight shares, John Rollins and Hazel Shriner each bought five. Stanley Dancer and John Simpson each bought two shares and Hal Jones, Hanover's superintendent, picked up the final share.

"Louis Silverstein got all the credit for putting the deal together to get Albatross, and he certainly deserved some of it, but it was Simpson's courage and Hanover's money that did it," emphasizes Murray Brown.

The new ownership must have breathed confidence into Albatross because he won his next 10 races and was virtually unbeatable that year. In June, he lowered his own world race mark by pacing in 1:54.3 around the tight turns of the 5/8-mile track at Sportsman's Park in suburban Chicago.

Speaking for Hanover Shoe Farms and the new owners of Albatross, John Simpson said that they had never considered replacing Dancer with another trainer and had faith in the ability of the horse and his trainer.

That fall at Delaware, Ohio, Dancer brought Albatross back to settle a score. He knew that Delaware racing fans hadn't seen Albatross at his best in the Jug, so he took aim at the world record on a half-mile track. At that time, the fastest performance ever on a half had been by the trotter Nevele Pride — driven by Stanley Dancer — when he circled the Saratoga twice-around in 1:56.4.

No pacer had ever raced faster, but Dancer put Albatross into a $2,000 Free-For-All that was really a time trial sans prompters because none of the other three horses in the race could force Albatross to work hard.

Dancer understood how to light a speed spark in his son of Meadow Skipper, however, and he kept it lit for the entire mile as Albatross paced in 1:55.3, shattering the world race record on a half-mile track.

No one was more enthusiastic about the performance than John Simpson. After the race, he stood in the middle of the track past the finish line. When Dancer pulled Albatross up after accepting the plaudits of the crowd, Simpson grabbed his future stallion by the bridle and proudly led him into the winner's circle.

Perhaps the greatest tribute to Albatross was when Dancer said, "he was never better" after he won his final start of his career in the American Pacing Classic at Hollywood Park.

Albatross was retired in a ceremony at Dover Downs in Delaware, and John Simpson took the lines and jogged Albatross around the track with Murray Brown's four-year-old son Andrew sitting in his lap.

Once again that year Albatross was the overwhelming choice for Horse of the Year and he entered the stud at Hanover with a $5,000 stud fee. From that point forward, everything was wine and roses in his life, and the acquisition of Albatross was one of the greatest blessings ever to befall Hanover Shoe Farms.

Albatross wasn't the only brilliant performer that Stanley Dancer campaigned in 1972. In fact, Dancer dominated the sport in that era, and his trotting king that season was Super Bowl, a son of Star's Pride.

Super Bowl racing in California

As a two-year-old, Super Bowl had been slow to mature and Dancer thought he had other freshman trotters in his shed row with more talent. His brother Vernon often drove Super Bowl while Stanley handled the lines on stablemate Star's Chip, but as the summer turned to fall, it was obvious that Super Bowl had a big motor inside his lanky frame. At the end of the year, he was picked as the champion of his class.

Super Bowl as a young stallion

By the start of the 1972 season, Super Bowl was a trotting machine who could be driven with two fingers. He could leave the starting gate at top speed and finish the same way. That combination made him hard to beat, although a talented group of rivals, including Delmonica Hanover, Songcan, and Spartan Hanover took their best shots at him.

Before the Hambletonian, Dancer was being courted by several breeding farms interested in Super Bowl, who was owned by his wife Rachel and the Silversteins' Rose Hild Breeding Farm. Max Hempt was interested for his Pennsylvania farm, as was John Cashman, then operating Buttonwood Tree Farm in New York. John Simpson asked Dancer if he would give Hanover the first chance at Super Bowl when he put a price on him, and Dancer agreed.

The price that Dancer quoted to Simpson that summer was a cool million bucks, and Simpson snapped up Super Bowl quickly, feeling certain that he would finish out the season strong and make an appealing stud candidate.

The Hambletonian that summer was a mere cakewalk for Super Bowl. He was a bully merely toying with his pursuers. Glen Garnsey driving Flush made a run at Super Bowl down the backstretch, all to no avail. When Super Bowl hit the wire, he was still under wraps and the timer read 1:56.2, the fastest mile ever by a three-year-old trotter. The second heat was a mere formality.

Super Bowl's future as a stallion was a mere formality, too, and after the race it was announced that Hanover had purchased the tall son of Star's Pride. He would enter the stud there the next season.

Dancer recalls that when he made the deal with Hanover for Super Bowl, his partner Louis Silverstein went along only reluctantly. The businessman felt that a million dollars was too cheap for a horse like Super Bowl. After all, the price on Albatross had been $2.5 million.

Dancer then offered, "Well, you can buy out our half of the horse for a half-million and I'll race him for you whenever you want."

"No, now you're not talking sensibly," lectured Silverstein.

A few days later Silverstein called Dancer and said, "I don't think it's enough, but you go ahead and sell him."

When they later went to Hanover to formalize the agreement, Silverstein still wasn't happy with the price.

"I'm not saying you took advantage of the boy," he told Simpson and the others from Hanover, "but, you know, this horse is worth a lot more money. I'm not going to back out on the deal, but he's worth more."

A deal was a deal, however, and a million bucks was a million bucks. Super Bowl was sold to Hanover. He was then syndicated among a group of leading breeders.

Super Bowl also won the Yonkers Trot and shipped to Lexington in an effort to complete the Triple Crown by winning the Kentucky Futurity. It was destined to be one of the most bizarre and memorable renewals of America's oldest trotting stake.

Archrival Songcan had not been eligible to the Hambletonian, so the Kentucky Futurity would be his chance to show up Super Bowl. Songcan was coming off a world record performance over the twice-around track at Delaware, Ohio, and the Kentucky Futurity shaped up as a two-horse race.

That is how it developed in the first heat with Super Bowl taking the lead, as expected, and driver George Sholty tucking Songcan in neatly on Super Bowl's back. The two leaders stayed that way until deep into the stretch, but a funny thing happened on the way to the finish line. As they near the famed tunnel at The Red Mile, Sholty gave Songcan his head and the son of Florican exploded out of the hole.

He exploded so fast, however, that one of his front hooves hit Super Bowl's right sulky tire, flattening it. The tire acted as a brake, slowing Super Bowl in the final hundred yards to the wire. Songcan was gaining, and Super Bowl was fighting back. Dancer was urging him on, but the drag was slowing them.

The wire came up just in time, and Super Bowl won by a neck in 2:00.

"Two minutes flat," said one wag, referring to Super Bowl's tire. "Really flat."

In the second heat, Dancer again sent Super Bowl to the front and once again one of Songcan's errant front hooves struck Super Bowl's right tire, flattening it again.

This time Super Bowl had to pull his sulky 1200 yards, not merely a hundred yards. And Dancer knew that if the tire slipped off the rim and wrapped around the axle Super Bowl would stop abruptly and the entire field might go piling into him.

Dancer adroitly shifted his weight to the left side of his sulky seat, trying to ease the pressure on the flattened right tire. He rode on a wing and a prayer the remainder of the mile and Super Bowl did his part, ignoring the flopping tire and going on to win in 1:59 over Spartan Hanover. Songcan finished third, but was placed fifth and last for interference.

The famous Kentucky Futurity race in which Super Bowl and driver Stanley Dancer raced with a flat tire — and still won by a neck in 2:00. The same thing happened in the second heat, and Super Bowl won again in 1:59.

Super Bowl was not only voted the champion three-year-old, but also named Trotter of the Year over Speedy Crown, Fresh Yankee, Flower Child, and many other stars.

John Simpson relished the victories of Albatross and Super Bowl in 1972, and when they came to the farm he was proud to pose for photos with them. He knew, however, that his days of handling horses were coming to a close as his vision continued to fail.

Murray Brown recalls driving with Simpson to Brandywine Raceway in Wilmington, Delaware. Simpson had two fillies to drive in qualifiers and he won with both of them.

"He was happy after the races," recalls Brown. "Then he asked me if I'd drop him off in Baltimore on my way back to Hanover. I dropped him off at Johns Hopkins University and they operated on his skull the next day."

Brown was stunned. "I never even knew he had an eye problem. He had done a marvelous job of concealing it."

Son Jim Simpson says, "He was actually able to drive a car a little in 1972, but then he had to quit driving." For the next 23 years of his life, the fiercely proud John Simpson, who had been in absolute control of his life to that point, depended on others for transportation and guidance.

Understandably, accepting such a fate wasn't easy. He was still in the prime of life, and the rewards that come to those successful in their careers were coming to Simpson, but he was robbed of his most precious sense.

In the coming years, Simpson would see many specialists and yet none of them could prevent his gradual spiral into blindness. He endured test after test, but the prognosis was grim: his eyesight would steadily diminish to the point where he would become totally blind.

At first there was rage, anger, frustration.

"He initially referred to himself as sightless," says Jim. "He didn't like to use the word blind. I guess that the word 'sightless' was more palatable to him while it was happening."

It was a curious bit of quibbling for Simpson, who preferred blunt talk to euphemisms all his life. His refusal to accept blindness is hardly unusual, as many people consigned to such a fate go through a period of denial at first. It would be a long time, Jim says, before his father could refer to himself as a "blind old bastard."

John Simpson's world was shrinking, and getting darker day by day.

"It was a real tough time for him," says Jim. "He enjoyed being the captain of his own ship."

In his younger days, Simpson had spent many hours in tackrooms playing gin rummy and other card games with fellow horsemen, and he knew that in life, as in cards, you played the hand you were dealt. If he were fated to be blind, he would simply adjust and try to make the best of a bad situation.

Since his own eyes had failed him, Simpson had to rely on the eyes of others to help him. And he had spent a lifetime building contacts within the sport to help him visualize the horses that he needed to know about, both on the farm and on the tracks of North America.

On the farm, he came to rely extensively on Murray Brown, Hanover's public relations ace, and Peter Boyce, the tall, taciturn Canadian veterinarian who was to spend a quarter-century at Hanover.

Beyond the boundaries of the farm, the telephone served John Simpson well.

"He listened to a lot of people, a lot of trainers who he respected," son Jim says. "He asked a lot of people questions. He had people calling him, giving him their opinions, and he also called others."

The one person that Simpson respected and admired above all others was Delvin Miller. They had prospered in the sport after World War II and Simpson recognized that Miller had extraordinary insight in anything related to harness racing. He also knew that the Midas of Meadow Lands wasn't perfect, and he would often dismiss Miller's foibles by saying, "Oh, that's just Delvin."

Jim says that his father found a way to weave his interrogations into routine conversations.

"He might be talking to a horseman about an issue related to The Hambletonian Society, and he would ask what a certain filly looked like," says Jim. "He never forgot things either. He knew female families and their traits, so he really knew about the conformation of sires and broodmares."

One trait that Lawrence Sheppard and John Simpson shared was their disdain for many of the major breeders in Kentucky. The rivalry between Hanover and the old-line breeders in the Bluegrass colored their perception of the racing world.

"Mr. Sheppard and Simpson often said that the only thing that Kentucky breeders agreed upon was their hatred of Hanover," says Brown. "I don't know if that hatred really existed or not, but they thought it did.

"I think he tried to be a lot like Mr. Sheppard," says Brown of Simpson. "Some of it was natural, and some of it was added by being in touch with Mr. Sheppard for so long."

Many people who knew John Simpson superficially never saw through the gruff exterior he showed to the world. Murray Brown knew the man behind the mask exceedingly well.

In September 1967, Simpson drove from Hanover to Liberty Bell Park, the Philadelphia 5/8-mile track that had opened just a few seasons earlier. He was driving an unheralded colt named Aztec against a field that included Hambletonian winner Speedy Streak and the filly champion Flamboyant.

Fitted with plastic shoes for the first time, Aztec was a two-length winner with Simpson just joy riding in the sulky. Aztec paid $16.40 to win.

The next morning at the Hanover fairgrounds Simpson handed an envelope to Brown.

"What's this?" asked Brown.

"You had a bet last night," said Simpson.

"I didn't know anything about making a bet," said the perplexed PR man. He then opened the envelope and counted out $1,300.

"I was then making about $7,000 a year and my wife and I had a child," recalls Brown. "I loved my job, but we were living more or less hand-to-mouth. That was almost 20 percent of what I was making as an annual salary."

Brown says that Simpson handed him many such envelopes over the years they worked closely together at Hanover. Finally, he confronted Simpson and asked, "You've never, ever told me that I lost a bet and that I owe you a hundred bucks."

Simpson just laughed off that idea.

Another surprise that Brown recalls occurred when The Meadows Racing Network became available on satellite. Simpson had a dish installed in his home and could listen to the races. He enjoyed following the nightly results.

"One afternoon I came home and there were construction people in my yard," says Brown, who was befuddled by the scene. "I didn't know anything about it, but they were putting up a dish. Simpson had ordered one for me. I think it cost $8,000 at the time."

Once when artist Bill Orr was photographing horses to use as references for his paintings, all his camera equipment was stolen. It was a devastating blow to Orr, and almost robbed him of his livelihood. When Simpson heard about that, he simply found out what kind of equipment Orr needed, bought it for the struggling artist, and paid for it. It was a kindness that Bill Orr never forgot.

When it came to money, Simpson prided himself on being the "fastest pen in the East" in paying bills. No one was ever going to say that Hanover Shoe Farms was a deadbeat. Just as John Simpson paid his bills promptly, he expected others to do the same and woe to the person who consistently fell behind in meeting his obligations. John Simpson's wrath could be as memorable as Lawrence Sheppard's.

Although Simpson could be harsh on the deadbeats in the business and could be brutally objective and honest in appraising a horse, he kept a soft spot for a few select horses, most notably Star's Pride and Tar Heel.

"When one of the offspring of these stallions would win a big race, it would literally bring him to tears," says Brown. "He loved that whole female family from Elma, too."

Simpson's love for Elma was so apparent that Charlotte Sheppard gave him a half-interest in the many-splendored mare. After Mrs. Sheppard's death, she willed her interest to Simpson. If Dean Hanover was the apple of Lawrence Sheppard's eye, Elma was the girl with everything to John Simpson.

Like Sheppard, Simpson had a sandpaper exterior, but he also had a soft spot for the horses and people who meant the most to him.

Chapter 12

Simpson's Folly

By the end of the 1970s, the stallion Meadow Skipper practically owned the world of pacing. Those races not won by sons and daughters of Meadow Skipper were won by the offspring of his sons. It wasn't unusual for the entire field in a pacing stake to trace its male line to Meadow Skipper.

Foaled in 1960, Meadow Skipper was one of those rare horses — Adios was one, and Star's Pride was surely another — that could so dominate his era that other male lines were quickly chased into the shadows. The lines of Good Time, Knight Dream, and Tar Heel, successful in previous decades, ultimately could not withstand the onslaught of Meadow Skipper and his sons.

The two best sons of Meadow Skipper were Most Happy Fella, a foal of 1967, and Albatross, foaled a year later. Both horses got off to sensational starts in the stud and promised to extend the Meadow Skipper dynasty.

There were exceptions to that Meadow Skipper dominance, of course. The offspring of Bret Hanover and his sons won some stakes of that era. There was a good pacer developed at a county fairgrounds in Indiana named Abercrombie. In New York, there was a solid free-for-aller appropriately named Big Towner.

If Meadow Skipper and his sons represented the future of pacing pedigrees, Big Towner seemed to represent the past. His sire, Gene Abbe, was 30 years old when Big Towner was foaled. Gene Abbe's grandsire, The Abbe, was foaled in 1903, making Big Towner only three generations removed from the 1800s.

Big Towner's mother had never been harnessed, much less raced, and while she was sired by the Little Brown Jug winner Shadow Wave, the rest of her pedigree seemed like leafing through a sepia-toned scrapbook of harness racing history.

Names like Guinea Gold, Protector and Guy Axworthy all showed up in the maternal pedigree of Big Towner. They were good horses in their day, but by the 1970s their day had come and gone decades earlier.

Big Towner (left) and John Chapman winning the Cory Pace at Yonkers in 2:00.4 by two and a half lengths

(Photo courtesy of Michael Cipriani, Yonkers Raceway)

Yet no one could deny that Big Towner was a good pacer. He'd proven that time and time again over the twice-around tracks in New York. He was a mightily successful star in the New York Sires Stakes and in 1977 he won the $254,200 OTB Classic at Monticello Raceway.

Old-fashioned pedigree or not, there was no doubt that Big Towner was a legitimate race horse.

In 1978, Big Towner jumped into the ranks of free-for-allers. While others had wilted before such a difficult challenge, he thrived. He didn't win every race, but when Big Towner didn't win he made the winner work hard.

Big Towner could get away from the starting gate like a jackrabbit, an invaluable asset when racing on a half-mile track. But he finished his races every bit as fast as he started them.

One person who watched Big Towner week after week and came to love the horse was John Simpson, Jr. When he wasn't at the track himself, the young Simpson could watch the races on television. With each race, he became more and more convinced that Big Towner was a very special horse.

John Simpson, Jr.'s affinity for Big Towner was ironic because most of his greatest wins in the sport had come behind trotters. When he won the Hambletonian with Timothy T in 1970, he was the youngest driver ever to score a victory in America's greatest trotting classic. He won the Kentucky Futurity four times.

Yet John Simpson, Jr. knew a good horse, trotter or pacer, when he saw one, and Big Towner was a good one. Good enough for Hanover Shoe Farms, he thought, and he called his father.

"Dad, you've got to bring Big Towner to Hanover," he pleaded. His father listened, but didn't leap.

In fact, the father would reply, "Why in the hell would I want to stand a son of Gene Abbe?"

The son wasn't about to be rebuffed. Week after week the calls came to Hanover.

"Big Towner is a horse you've got to have," he told his father.

While Simpson worked over his father from the outside, Murray Brown worked on the boss from the inside.

"I was a big fan of Big Towner," says Brown. "He was a prototype of a great race horse. I believed in him. I thought he would be a great sire. Johnny and I just kept after him."

John Simpson, Sr. knew that horse racing periodically produced freaks — horses that seemed to be far ahead of their contemporaries or to excel far beyond the benchmarks of their breeding.

"Dan Patch was a freak," said Simpson. "He was way ahead of his time."

Simpson knew that these freaks could become the people's choice on the track, but they weren't the kind you wanted to build a stock farm. After all, Dan Patch had enjoyed precious little success as a stallion.

Still his son and Murray Brown pressed him. Big Towner would be an outcross for all the Meadow Skipper blood, they argued. But Hanover Shoe Farms was a business, and it stayed profitable by giving its customers what they wanted. In that era, what the customers wanted was Meadow Skipper blood.

Finally, Simpson relented. Big Towner would come to Hanover.

"I think he finally got Big Towner just to get me and Johnny off his back," recalls Brown.

The industry was amazed. Big Towner at Hanover? While the waves of Meadow Skippers were washing away all pacing records, to get a stallion by Gene Abbe seemed like taking several steps backward. Would the NBA go back to center-jump rules? Would John Travolta give up his dancing shoes for high-button boots?

Immediately Big Towner was dubbed "Simpson's Folly" by one prominent owner. It was a term of derision that wouldn't last very long.

While Big Towner may have seemed like a retro choice for the stud barn, there was nothing old-fashioned about the way that Hanover was marketing its

Big Towner at Hanover

stallions and yearlings in the late 1970s. In a brief window of time, some of the most creative ads ever seen in harness racing were produced under the Hanover banner.

Certainly the most memorable of them was created in one summer day when Simpson met with Murray Brown and Ken Heineken, the ad man from Salisbury, Maryland, whose agency handled the farm's advertising.

"We need to get more trainers to come to Hanover to see the yearlings at the fairgrounds," Simpson told Heineken. "They're missing out on a chance to see these yearlings lead, to find out which ones show the best. One guy who comes every year is Billy Haughton. He'll spend three or four days here. He'll buy several of our yearlings, and they're not necessarily the highest priced ones. But Haughton's done his homework. Next year those yearlings will probably be damn good two-year-olds."

Simpson, Brown, and Heineken talked over other matters that day, as they often did, but Heineken's mind kept going back to the need to write an ad targeting trainers, convincing them to appraise Hanover's yearlings in action.

Heineken drove back to his office in Salisbury. Creating an advertisement that read, "Come see the Hanover yearlings this fall" would have been direct and informative. It also would have been almost instantly forgettable. Heineken wanted something more creative, and he knew that Hanover did, too. And when he sat down with copywriter Paul Kratzer, a masterpiece resulted.

The ad that Heineken and Kratzer created was one of the most unusual and effective ads ever to grace the pages of harness racing's trade journals. It showed a photo of Billy Haughton holding a sale catalog and watching yearlings lead at the Hanover fairgrounds. Above the photo ran this riveting headline:

This man is about to steal a horse.

Then the body copy read:

And we help him. In fact, we actually encourage this kind of behavior.

Every year this man visits Hanover Shoe Farms to look over our yearlings. He spends a few days, maybe even a week, studying our colts and fillies, planning his strategy.

Often he asks our people for inside information, "How's that colt's brother training?," "Has his dam thrown any other foals this big?," "His dam had a colt by Tar Heel last year, didn't she?"

Our people answer his questions as well as they can. And for every answer he puts a mark in his book.

He's measuring, scheming, and learning.

He'll be out at dawn to watch us lead the yearlings. He studies their conformation and watches them in action. He can judge their temperaments, reflexes, and racing potential.

He isn't necessarily after the top priced Hanover yearling. He's interested in the first, second, or third foal, the yearling no one had really noticed because he has! He spotted something in that colt or filly that will make it a champion, a big money winner.

He has an edge on the other bidders.

And he'll steal that champion yearling for much less than he's really worth at our November Harrisburg Auction.

He's one of the few horsemen who have learned that the greatest and biggest stake winners do not always bring the highest prices.

They go to the man who does his homework best, our horse thief.

If you'd like to steal a horse, send for our yearling catalog. Then plan to spend some time here at Hanover — studying.

We'll help you learn.

After all, we've made successful horse thieves out of a lot of people like you.

"You know the most amazing thing about that ad?" asks Murray Brown. "Billy Haughton's name isn't mentioned once."

A rereading of the copy verifies that. Haughton's stature in the Standardbred world and his reputation for selecting yearlings were such that he

This man is about to steal a horse

And we help him. In fact, we actually encourage this kind of behavior.

Every year this man visits Hanover Shoe Farms to look over our yearlings. He spends a few days, maybe even a week, studying our colts and fillies, planning his strategy.

Often he asks our people for inside information, "How's that colt's brother training?", "Has his dam thrown any other foals this big?", "His dam had a colt by Tar Heel last year didn't she?"...

Our people answer his questions as well as they can. And for every answer he puts a mark in his book.

He's measuring, scheming, and learning.

He'll be out at dawn to watch us lead the yearlings. He studies their conformation and watches them in action. He can judge their temperaments, reflexes, and racing potential.

He isn't necessarily after the top priced Hanover yearling. He's interested in the first, second or third foal, the yearling no one has really noticed, because he has! He spotted something in that colt or filly that will make it a champion, a big money winner.

He has an edge on the other bidders.

And he'll steal that champion yearling for much less than he's really worth at our November Harrisburg Auction.

He's one of a few horsemen who have learned that the greatest and biggest stake winners do not always bring the highest prices.

They go to the man who does his homework best, our horse thief.

If you'd like to steal a horse, send for our yearling catalog. Then plan to spend some time here at Hanover - Studying.

We'll help you learn.

After all, we've made successful horse thieves out of a lot of people like you.

Hanover
The Greatest Name In Harness Racing

When understatement works: The effective Hanover ad created by Heineken and Kratzer that showed a photo of Billy Haughton holding a sale catalog and watching yearlings being shown at the Hanover fairgrounds.

didn't need to be identified. Everyone knew Billy Haughton. In that respect, the ad was a masterpiece of understatement.

For decades, advertisements in Standardbred trade journals were straightforward and utterly without any creativity. They were slapped together by magazine staffs that were harried and hurried and unable to give each ad more than cursory attention.

When Murray Brown came to Hanover in 1967, he created a series of ads that were unlike others in the magazines. Instead of selling a specific stallion or yearlings, the ads sold the Hanover name. In the trade, such ads are called institutional ads because they sell a concept rather than a product.

In one memorable ad, he showed a group of men in a spartan office at the farm. They were dressed in the plaids and denims that so often characterize the clothing of the working farmer. These men were obviously not Wall Street brokers. Instead, they were the foremen at Hanover Shoe Farms.

In the copy, written by Murray Brown, each man was identified and his decades of experience with horses were detailed. By the time you finished the copy, while you might not want these men to buy your stocks and bonds, you surely would entrust them to care for your horses.

It was an advertisement that didn't promote a single yearling or stallion; it promoted Hanover Shoe Farms. And it made you feel good about having horses at Hanover.

Brown wasn't afraid to promote specific yearlings. In the winter of 1968, he ran a photo of two furry yearlings looking at the camera under the headline, "Handsome, Aren't They?"

One was Romunda Hanover, a brother to Romeo and Romulus Hanover, the fastest full brothers in the sport's history. The other was Magnum Hanover, a Bullet Hanover colt from the six-time 2:00 matron Maggie Counsel.

It was a sneak preview of the farm's 1968 yearling consignment. Someone must have been reading because Romunda Hanover became the highest-priced yearling in Standardbred history that fall at $115,000. He raced briefly under the name of Nevele Bigshot.

Romunda Hanover, who fetched $115,000 in Hanover's
1968 yearling consignment
(Photo courtesy of Winants Brothers Inc.)

Another memorable ad devised by Brown showed that only 36 broodmares had produced the winners of $500,000 or more, and 23 of those mares were sired or bred at Hanover or owned by Hanover.

This group included such modern foundation mares as Romola Hanover, Brenna Hanover, Greer Hanover, Duke's Dutchess, Besta Hanover, Lura Hanover, Treasure, Thankful, The Old Maid, Evalina Hanover, Lucine Hanover and others.

Murray Brown confesses that he "knew nothing" about advertising copywriting when he began doing the Hanover ads, but he did have a good understanding of the breeders and owners in the sport. He also knew that Hanover had plenty to promote. While he wrote the copy, he was still dependent on the trade journals to create the designs for his ads. Brown was far too busy with his responsibilities to become a one-man advertising agency.

In the 1970s, more creative advertising began to appear in the harness journals. The Lipman agency in New York was retained to create ads for Monticello Raceway and later for Pine Hollow Stud.

In 1976, Ken Heineken was casting about for clients for his small agency in Maryland, and since he knew a little about harness racing, he thought he would try to land the biggest advertiser in that game.

"I knew very little about the horse business then," admits Heineken. "I subscribed to *The Harness Horse* because I owned a race horse. I got an appointment with John Simpson at Hanover, then I read everything I could about Tar Heel and Star's Pride, and put it on a tape recorder."

Heineken got to Hanover the night before his meeting, and found a room above a gas station in town.

"I went to sleep that night listening to the tape I'd made," says Heineken.

The next morning he met Simpson for the first time and found him cordial and cooperative. Heineken explained how his agency operated and what he could do for Hanover, and Simpson ended the conversation by saying, "I'll get back to you."

Heineken took a liking to Simpson. While some saw him as a tyrant, Heineken simply saw a "nice guy." He had hopes he would land the Hanover account.

When Simpson failed to call back, Heineken pitched Max Hempt at Hempt Farms. They reached an agreement that resulted in Heineken's agency taking over the farm's advertising.

"Right after the Harrisburg sale in 1976," recalls Heineken, "I got a call from Murray Brown. They wanted to meet with me again. That's when I started to work for Hanover."

When Hanover wanted to emphasize the value of Tar Heel fillies as potential broodmares, it was Heineken who gave the aging stallion the title of "Chairman of the Brood."

Heineken's agency also created an extensive marketing campaign for the Standardbred Horse Sale Co., renaming its catalog "The Black Book" and giving the weighty volume great recognition in the sport.

Heineken relished Simpson's company, and freely admitted "he did a lot for me." He speaks with great fondness of being Simpson's guest one year at the Hambletonian and also at Simpson's fabled hunting camp in Florida. He even asked for advice from the master.

"I had a Speedy Count trotter called Count Statis and he'd hit his shins and make breaks," recalls Heineken. "So I called Mr. Simpson up, told him the situation, and asked for his advice."

Simpson told Heineken to take a metal sweat scraper and hammer it down so that it was thin and flat. Then, the horseman told the ad man, tear up the horse's leather shin boots and slip that flat metal piece between the layers of leather. Then sew them back up again.

"Count Statis still hit his shins, but he never made a break after that because he couldn't feel it," explains Heineken.

Hanover and Heineken parted ways in the 1980s, but they left a legacy of enduring classics in Standardbred advertising.

Chapter 13

The Price Of Poker Goes Up

Two dramatic changes came to harness racing in America's Bicentennial year.

A new style of sulky, featured bent shafts, was introduced and it immediately found favor among horsemen. They felt that its design created more "lift" for the horse and enabled it to carry its speed much further.

Horsemen soon believed that you couldn't win if you didn't switch to the so-called "modified" sulky. Canadian legend Joe O'Brien was one of the final holdouts for the conventional style of sulky, but the proof was in the statistics. In 1975, there had been 714 miles in 2:00 or faster. By 1977, with the new bikes in widespread use, there were 2,355 2:00 miles. The era of extreme speed had arrived, and where it would stop nobody knew.

An even more dramatic change in the sport was the opening of the Meadowlands, a one-mile track built on reclaimed New Jersey swampland just west of Manhattan. It was hailed as the super track of harness racing, and it quickly lived up to its billing.

Standardbreds racing at the Meadowlands were going miles faster than most horsemen would have dreamed possible a few years earlier, and the purses there were going through the roof.

With the new track came new races. The New Jersey oval needed a signature event, so it created the Meadowlands Pace for three-year-olds and kicked it off in 1977 with a stunning $425,000 purse.

That caused credibility problems for the Little Brown Jug, traditionally the target for any trainer with a top sophomore pacer. Its purse was $150,000 in 1977, about one-third of the jackpot offered in the Meadowlands Pace. Sure, the Jug had tradition and its Americana setting, but in horse racing money talks, and the money offered by the Meadowlands was practically screaming.

By 1980, the Jug purse was up to $207,361 and it was taken by Niatross, but when that great pacer won the Meadowlands Pace two months earlier, the purse

141

was a cool million dollars. A county fair in Ohio couldn't keep pace with the Meadowlands.

Times were changing. That was even more evident in the bounty offered for freshmen pacers. For a half-century since its advent in 1927, the Fox Stake had been the definitive event for two-year-old pacers. John Simpson had been proud to win it with Torpid and Bullet Hanover in the 1950s. The Fox Stake was raced at the Indiana State Fair, and without pari-mutuel wagering to augment the purse, the Fox Stake was funded almost entirely by owners staking their colts. In 1977, the Fox Stake purse was $100,000.

That same year the Meadowlands started a rival race for first-season pacers named after Woodrow Wilson, the New Jersey governor who later became President. The purse for the first Woodrow Wilson was $280,000.

Again, the rules of the game were changing. The proud sponsors of the Fox Stake managed to get its purse up to $171,416 by 1980, but such efforts were futile when pitted against the money machine of the Meadowlands. That year the Woodrow Wilson was contested for a purse of more than $2 million.

Increased purses were good for the sport, and yearling prices reacted accordingly.

In 1974, the average yearling price in the United States had been $6,903 and by 1980 it had risen to $18,754, an increase of 172 percent. Optimism was abundant.

For breeding farms like Hanover, the increase in yearling prices was the good news. The bad news was that breeding stock was now becoming a lot more expensive to acquire, particularly stallions.

A new breed of owners was entering the sport. They didn't always know horses, but they knew a good investment when they saw one and racehorses, with all their opportunities to shelter income from taxes, were now deemed a good investment. Money poured into stallion syndicates from people who had no intention of ever breeding mares to the stallion, but simply wanted a chance to make a profit or write off their losses.

This was a new way of doing business to John Simpson, and he didn't like it. He didn't think it would last, but it was sure playing hell with his chances of landing the stallions he wanted.

"He liked to be proactive in getting the best stallions and mares," says Murray Brown. "In the 1980s, he got incredibly frustrated when stallions were priced way out of the range of being reasonable. He just couldn't force himself to compete at that level because it made no financial sense. He could get very obstreperous and nasty during that time. It was all born out of his frustrations.

When Albatross became such a smashing success, Simpson cast about for a suitable son to join his sire at Hanover. The first one he coveted was Sonsam, the quicksilver colt whose sweeping move on the backstretch in the Meadowlands Pace is the stuff of legends.

Simpson had long known Sonsam's trainer and driver George Sholty, but Sonsam was already betrothed to the new wave partnership of syndicators Morty Finder and Lou Guida. After the colt broke a bone in a routine training mile at Roosevelt Raceway in 1979, Sonsam was retired to Finder's Pine Hollow Stud in New York.

That same year, however, another Albatross colt, this one only a two-year-old, was causing horsemen to talk about him in hushed tones. His name was Niatross and no one could figure out how to beat him. He ended the season with 13 wins in 13 starts and he'd never really been asked to pace.

John Simpson's spotters told him that Niatross was something special, even more so than Sonsam. They were right on the money, as Niatross proved during his memorable sophomore season. He ushered in the era of sub-1:50 speed with an epochal 1:49.1 time trial for trainer-driver Clint Galbraith at Lexington.

Niatross had been sired at Hanover, foaled at Hanover, and raised at Hanover, but he wasn't coming home. Super syndicator Lou Guida had staked his claim in Niatross when he was a two-year-old and he controlled the horse's breeding career.

"Simpson really wanted Niatross," recalls Brown. "He'd known Clint [Galbraith] for a long time, and he talked to him, but there was no chance of getting Niatross."

Often the closest pursuer of Niatross was Storm Damage, a royally-bred Bret Hanover colt. Hanover had no chance to land Storm Damage, either, because he was owned in part by Castleton Farm. He would stand at Castleton's New York facility.

Simpson didn't like settling for a consolation prize, but in this case he had to. He knew, however, that often the best horse on the track was not the best horse in the stud barn. Tyler B may have been the third-best colt in this class, but he was good enough to be the best in many other classes and Simpson secured his services at the end of the 1980 season.

Everyone at Hanover watched the homegrown products with special interest and when a colt proved to be exceptional on the track, Simpson began evaluating that horse as a candidate for the Hanover stallion barn. Their performance might later prove disappointing, but Simpson sized up many stallion prospects each season in hopes of finding one with the right stuff.

A colt that intrigued him in 1983 was Ralph Hanover, a son of Meadow Skipper from the Tar Heel mare Ravina Hanover. The smallish colt swept the Little Brown Jug, Cane Pace, and Messenger Stake to win the Triple Crown that year.

Simpson, of course, wasn't the only one perceptive enough to think that Ralph Hanover would appeal to breeders, and the price on the brown colt escalated to the point where Almahurst Farm of Kentucky was the winning suitor with a $7 million bid.

Simpson liked Ralph Hanover, but he thought that price was beyond reason, so he retreated from Ralph Hanover and waited for another candidate.

He didn't have to wait long. That same year John, Jr. was campaigning a beautifully-made son of Big Towner named Walton Hanover. He got beat a few times, but he never went a bad race and by the end of the year he was voted champion two-year-old pacer of his class.

Triple Crown winner Ralph Hanover and co-owner Ron Waples
pace to a 1:57 victory in the Messenger Stakes at Roosevelt
(Photo by Bert Meurer, Roosevelt Raceway)

*Walton Hanover
driven by
John F. Simpson Jr.*

The head man at Hanover knew that he had the inside track to Walton Hanover's stud services through his son, but he also knew that the market was still clamoring for Meadow Skipper-line stallions in that era. A son of Big Towner wouldn't suffice.

In 1984, a lightly-raced son of Albatross named Colt Forty Six burst into national prominence when he won the Review Stake at the Illinois State Fair in Springfield with a mile in 1:50.3, the fastest race ever by a Standardbred.

Simpson knew this colt and his maternal family well because Colt Forty Six had gone through the Harrisburg sale ring as part of the Hanover consignment. He was out of the aging Tar Heel mare Hoopla. Now Simpson had the youngster in his sights as a stallion candidate. Still, while the fast record was important, Colt Forty Six had to do more.

He did a lot more about five weeks after his record mile by winning the '84 Little Brown Jug in straight heats for his popular trainer-driver Chris Boring. Here was a horse that John Simpson was now quietly coveting. At the same time, he made sure that Walton Hanover had a spot in the stud barn at Hanover.

"We had heard that fall that Blue Chip Farm had Colt Forty Six locked up," recalls Murray Brown. "He was to be syndicated and stand in New York State. Andy Grant was the agent on both Walton Hanover and Colt Forty Six, but somehow the deal at Blue Chip fell through."

After the Harrisburg sale in 1984, Brown distinctly recalls telling Simpson, "We're going to run an introductory stallion ad on Walton Hanover."

"What about the other horse?" asked Simpson.

"What other horse?" replied Brown.

"Colt Forty Six," said Simpson. It was the first time that the farm's public relations director knew about the new stallion. Simpson and Grant had worked out the details alone.

"That was the only time we'd ever got a new stallion and there was no conversation with myself or Peter Boyce," says Brown. "I was astounded."

There were dissenting voices that were not so sure Colt Forty Six had the makings of a desirable breeding horse. True, he was a son of Albatross, and undoubtedly a fast one, but he didn't have the prettiest set of hocks in the world. If John Simpson could see, some people felt, he would have passed on Colt Forty Six.

Simpson already knew from his sources that Colt Forty Six didn't have flawless hocks and he also knew exactly how the horse had inherited those hocks.

"We've had to live with those Billy Direct hocks," he said, referring to the sire of Tar Heel. "Thank God we didn't discard Billy Direct because of his hocks and thank God didn't discard Tar Heel because of his hocks. And Tar Heel had a sway back and short pasterns to boot. Curby hocks don't concern me as much with a pacing stallion as they would with a trotting stallion."

Colt Forty Six and driver Chris Boring winning the 1984 Little Brown Jug

(Photo by Steven Smith)

Murray Brown shook his head in disbelief at the way that Colt Forty Six had come to Hanover through the back door. He didn't feel he was the horse that Hanover needed, but he knew all too well that predicting success or failure with stallions is a tricky business.

Colt Forty Six wasn't by any means the most exciting pacing prospect in the sport at that time. While Murray Brown was making arrangements to run ads on Colt Forty Six, Lou Guida was in the process of syndicating Nihilator, a son of Niatross, in cooperation with P.J. Baugh of Almahurst Farm. This was the same Almahurst that had snared Ralph Hanover just a year previously.

The price for Nihilator shocked the sport: his syndication was valued at $19.2 million. Hanover Shoe Farms wasn't a player in this deal. The farm took no shares in the champion colt.

The comments were muttered under the breath, not for public consumption, but the word was out: Hanover was no longer playing in the major leagues. Simpson was blind, was living in the past, and wasn't willing to ante up the money to get the headliners coming off the track.

The value of well-bred fillies was skyrocketing, too, along with stallion values. Replenishing the broodmare band was much easier and far more affordable since breeders could simply retain yearling fillies as future broodmares. And no one at Hanover ever forgot the importance of broodmares.

After all, it had once been John Simpson's task to break and train most of the fillies that eventually found their way into the Hanover broodmare band. Although he might not have been at Hanover when Miss Bertha Dillon was the most revered broodmare in the world, he understood what broodmares meant to a farm.

Some extraordinary producers were graduates of the Simpson stable. One exemplary alumna was Romola Hanover, the nonpareil pacing mare who was the hottest mama in the sport in the 1960s.

Her first son Romeo Hanover won the Triple Crown for pacers in 1966 and his kid brother Romulus Hanover was voted the sophomore pacing king the following year. A few years later, Romola's daughter Romalie Hanover was one of the most admired fillies in the sport.

This trio had been sired by Dancer Hanover, but Romola Hanover also had exceptional performers by Lehigh Hanover, Torpid, and later even Albatross.

Another pacing matron whose offspring were big-ticket items at Harrisburg each fall was Maggie Counsel, the dam of six three-year-olds with 2:00 records by the early 1960s.

No farm could long endure without replenishing its broodmare band. Retaining yearlings fillies was deemed the best way to do that. Each year Hanover published a list of the fillies it kept to train in the front of its catalog. The retained fillies were selected for pedigree and conformation.

Peter Boyce, Murray Brown, and Simpson would confer on the fillies best suited for future broodmares. Conformation was important, but so was how their pedigrees fit the Hanover stallions.

"I don't like to keep a filly that I can breed to only one horse," said Simpson.

Like most major farms, Hanover followed this practice for decades. It was prudent. There were no secrets about the policy. Still, there was that nagging notion among yearling filly buyers that they were looking at merchandise that had been rejected by the farm.

In the 1980s, Murray Brown noticed that prominent Canadian Thoroughbred breeder E.P. Taylor, faced with the same skepticism from buyers, found a unique way to solve it. He offered his yearlings for sale at a set price, but when half of his crop was sold, he retained the remainder.

That sparked an idea for Murray Brown, and he took his plan to the boss. He suggested pairing select yearling fillies of comparable value and selling them at same time. The successful buyer would then have the chance to pick which one of the fillies he wanted; Hanover would retain the other one.

"Simpson's lost his mind," one prominent breeder grumbled. "When he leads those fillies into the ring, they'll be kicking each other."

Except that John Simpson and the Hanover horse crew knew horses. The fillies that were paired together were stabled next to each other at the Hanover fairgrounds prior to the sale and also at the sale arena itself.

"The only time that they fussed is when you led one away from the other," said Simpson at the time. "As long as they were together, they didn't even switch their tails. And we had no real problem with them at sale time."

This practice was continued for several years.

Simpson was naturally partial to his own yearlings, but he knew that a broodmare band the size of Hanover's needed regular infusions of fresh blood. The farm had to look at other sources for future broodmares, and he often deputized sons John and Jim and Murray Brown to cast about for a useful yearling filly from Castleton, Lana Lobell, Walnut Hall, or another major breeder.

Many of Hanover's mares came to the farm after their racing days were done, either through private sales or public auction.

"I get letters and calls all the time from people wanting to sell Hanover mares," said Simpson in 1985.

The sport seemed awash in a flood of new money. The stock market had blasted off in the summer of 1982 and was getting stronger. The million-dollar purses that had once shocked people in the sport were now routine.

The price of poker was going up, thanks in some measure to the prevalence of limited partnerships that were giving well-heeled individuals a chance to invest in horseflesh and reap all the tax benefits associated with it. The fact that these people knew or cared little about horses often made little difference; there were managing partners who handled the details and distributed the profits, if any.

The bandwagon was rolling and yet John Simpson had his feet firmly planted on the ground and refused to get swept away. When asked about limited partnerships at the height of their popularity, Simpson was the contrarian.

"I think that they're detrimental to the business, and that they are robbing the investor in the long run," he said.

"The reason I say that is because if you take people — monied people — and get them into one of these limited partnerships, and maybe they have a very bad experience because of mismanagement or someone using bad judgment. They lose money and say, 'What the hell kind of business is this?' and they get out.

"If these same people had gotten in the business and been handled a little better, they might have made good owners. But too many of them get a sour taste in their mouth from one of these partnership deals and away they go."

Simpson not only felt that that deals were bad for investors, but he also felt that some deals were so blatantly outrageous that they were sitting ducks for investigation by the Securities and Exchange Commission.

His, alas, was a voice in the wilderness. The deals continued to flourish until the Tax Reform Act of 1986 helped burst the bubble. The new law imposed participation guidelines for investors in the horse business. No longer would wealthy businessmen be able to make an initial investment in a limited partnership, and enjoy the rewards while not participating in managing the investment.

The value of horses — not just Standardbreds — plummeted. The impact on the Standardbred yearling market, however, was almost immediate. The average Standardbred yearling had sold for $16,167 in 1988 and by 1992 the average had dropped to $12,129.

Things didn't look too promising for the horse business.

Florida Pro racing at Vernon Downs in 1978
(Photo by Mike Taylor, Vernon Downs)

Florida Pro

*(Photo by
Monica Thors)*

Chapter 14

Trotting Peaks And Valleys

Although John Simpson had an extraordinary grasp of what made a superior Standardbred, he didn't possess a crystal ball for seeing which stallions would fail and which ones would rise to the top. He wasn't alone; every major breeding farm has had more than its share of duds at stud.

In fact, one of the more famous anecdotes about Lawrence Sheppard involved someone who praised the Hanover stallions just a little too loud and long, and finally Sheppard had to interject a dose of realism.

"There has never been a time in the history of Hanover Shoe Farms that there hasn't been at least one failure in the stallion barn," Sheppard said.

One horse that came to Hanover heralded as a can't-miss stallion was Florida Pro, a robust son of Arnie Almahurst. The big brown colt had been a standout on the track for trainer-driver George Sholty, winning a heat of the epic 1978 Hambletonian over Speedy Somolli before dropping the decision in the third heat.

Sholty always contended that it was his driving, not Speedy Somolli's speed, that beat Florida Pro that day. He could be excused for covering for the burly colt, which went forward virtually every time Sholty asked him.

Florida Pro was an outcross to many of the Star's Pride and young Super Bowl mares in the Hanover broodmare band and Simpson saw him as the right horse at the right time. When his breeding book was opened the first season, it was quickly filled by knowledgeable breeders.

The Florida Pro bandwagon never got very far. He sired some promising youngsters in his first crop, which hit the races in 1982, but he failed to follow up with the precocious speed that was so necessary in American trotting. The sons and daughters of Florida Pro were often clumsy, awkward, and slow to find themselves. That was a formula for disaster.

Like every other Hanover stallion before him, Florida Pro had no excuse. He was given the best mares a stallion could ever want, and his offspring got into

The long and short of it —
trainer/driver George Sholty and Max Hempt
(Photo by George Smallsreed, Jr., USTA)

the hands of the best trainers. They simply couldn't compete on equal terms with the Speedy Crowns, Super Bowls, and Speedy Somollis.

By the mid-1980s, it was obvious that Florida Pro wasn't the horse to follow up on Super Bowl's success. He was skating on thin ice.

Another horse appeared on the horizon that commanded Simpson's attention — and the attention of everyone else in harness racing. His name was Prakas and he was a lithe son of Speedy Crown from a Star's Pride mare.

Prakas had been a respectable juvenile, but it was as a three-year-old in 1985 that he blossomed into a world champion by showing speed never before seen in a trotter. When he won the Hambletonian, he trotted the first sub-1:55 mile ever in that classic, taking the final heat in 1:54.3.

A month after the Hambletonian, Prakas had a large field in the World Trotting Derby seemingly at his mercy, so his connections decided to cut him loose and find out just how fast he could trot.

When Prakas got to the front, driver Bill O'Donnell let him keep on rolling and he opened up ground on his adversaries. Once he turned into the stretch, Prakas was prone to drift out from the rail, but he kept trotting at full speed. Faster and faster he trotted, and further and further out into the track he drifted.

When he hit the wire, he was in the middle of the track, but it made no difference because the timer flashed 1:53.3. No trotter had ever gone faster, even in a time trial.

John Simpson had been following Prakas closely and now he struck faster than a coiled cobra. Prakas was coming to Hanover, make no mistake about it.

Speedy Crown was all the rage on the trotting scene then, and Simpson needed a Speedy Crown stallion at Hanover if he wanted to stay competitive.

Prakas, winner of the 1985 Hambletonian

By the end of the 1985 season, Prakas had earned $1,610,608, more money than any trotter in a single season. There was no question he'd be in great demand as a stallion.

Along with his habit of drifting out, however, Prakas had a few other quirks. He often refused to go to the starting gate unless the parade marshall escorted him. He was not the soundest horse in the world, and trainer Per Eriksson allowed Prakas to get his exercise by walking in a "power cart" designed to build strength.

Still, Prakas was enormously appealing to breeders, who lavished their best mares on him. But the results were much the same as Florida Pro's less than a decade earlier.

The offspring of Prakas didn't want to be racehorses. Not all of them, but enough of them balked and battled their human handlers that they quickly got a bad rap among horsemen. They showed some speed, but they also showed a surly attitude and some of their sire's unsoundness. When trainers begin knocking a sire, you can usually write his epitaph. That was the case with Prakas.

Thank God for Super Bowl. While Florida Pro and Prakas were floundering, Super Bowl just kept cranking out high-class stakes winners.

The double whammy of failures by Florida Pro and Prakas had an impact on Hanover Shoe Farms that went far beyond creating a revolving door in the stud barn. Hanover had committed many of its best trotting mares to these stallions, mares from the deepest families in the breed. If these mares had been mated to other stallions, they could have been expected to produce their share of stakes winners, but being bred to two unsuccessful stallions was a one-two punch that many could not overcome.

For example, Florida Pro and Prakas served many daughters and granddaughters of Elma, John Simpson's all-time favorite mare, but these matings yielded little of consequence.

During her days on the track, Elma gave Lawrence Sheppard and John Simpson many thrills, but she also turned them into art connoisseurs in a roundabout way. It all began in 1965 when the men from Hanover took Elma on a European vacation.

She was prepped for a tour of Europe's greatest trotting classics. The men from Hanover went along to watch her race, to have a little fun, to drink a little whiskey perhaps, and to learn more about the world of trotting.

They'd heard that old saying, "When in Rome, do as the Romans do," so perhaps Sheppard and Simpson switched to wine when in Italy. They also knew that when racing a horse in Europe, you'd better have a European driver. That's why they contracted with Hans Fromming, the legendary German reinsman. Simpson supervised Elma's conditioning, but it was Fromming who took the lines when the contestants were called to the track.

Lawrence Sheppard and John Simpson were famous in Europe, and they were greeted hospitably by the leading breeders, owners, and horsemen in every country they visited. They inspected the facilities, admired the horses, and noticed that something was quite different in Europe.

Everywhere they went they saw artwork of famous trotters. Paintings hung on office walls, on living room walls, and in the stables. It became apparent to Sheppard and Simpson that the great horsemen of Europe honored their most beloved trotters by immortalizing them on canvas.

As they flew back across the Atlantic, Sheppard told Simpson with typical bluntness, "We need to get some class. We need to get some paintings of our horses."

John Simpson had an artist in mind, a Floridian he'd known for a few years. The man lived in his neighborhood in Maitland, a suburb of Orlando. His name was Bill Orr.

"John Simpson lived near me, but so did Delvin Miller, Billy Haughton, and Jimmy Arthur," recalls Orr. "They all lived within two blocks. So I started going out to watch them train at Ben White Raceway."

Orr was no stranger to horses. He had grown up in Michigan and worked an entire summer as a 14-year-old to earn the money to buy his first horse. During World War II, Orr served in the Remount Corps in the U.S. Army and earned his stripes breaking horses for service to Uncle Sam.

He was also no stranger to art as he had started classes at the Detroit Art Institute at the tender age of eight. He had been trained as a portrait artist, and had all but forgotten horses after the war until he moved into a horse milieu in Maitland.

"John and Billy Haughton told me that if I wanted to get started painting harness horses, I had to paint the best," recalls Orr. "They told me that I ought to paint Countess Adios."

Countess Adios was a free-legged beauty that had beaten colts in winning the 1960 Messenger Stake and Cane Pace, but was not eligible to the Little Brown Jug. She was thus was denied the chance to sweep the Triple Crown. Delvin Miller and his assistant Jimmy Arthur trained the fabulous mare, and Arthur's father was her caretaker.

"Jimmy's father brought her out of the stall and would stand holding Countess Adios for me for hours," says Orr. "I took some Polaroid shots of her, and I also had time to draw her."

Simpson admired Orr's artistic talent and eye and soon had him painting members of his family. One painting that Simpson particularly appreciated showed his daughter Charlotte with a horse that her namesake Charlotte Sheppard had given her.

"It was a beautiful red hunter-jumper," recalls Orr. "I presented the painting to John and he hung it right on his living room wall."

Not long after Sheppard and Simpson toured Europe and saw stunning artwork everywhere, Sheppard visited Simpson's home in Orlando saw the painting of Charlotte Simpson and her horse. He appraised the painting with the critical eye of a man now interested in art.

"That," Sheppard told Simpson emphatically, "is the best painting of a horse's eye I've ever seen."

Hanover Shoe Farms had found its artist.

The first horses that Orr painted for Hanover were the Triple Crown winner Ayres and European tourist Elma.

To get adequate reference for his paintings, Orr would travel to Hanover and photograph the horses, then work from his pictures to complete the painting.

He quickly learned that doing the painting once didn't necessarily mean that the commission was completed.

Ayres portrait by Bill Orr

"Sheppard was tough," Orr says. "Every time I brought a painting to him he would find something wrong with it. He liked to be combative and point out an error."

John Simpson realized that the artistic temperament didn't take kindly to criticism from an aging businessman, so he pulled Orr aside and quietly advised him. "He always does that," Simpson said. "Just paint in a mistake and give him something to find. Then he'll get over it."

Orr remembers painting Tar Heel in front of a red silo at Hanover with the farm's breeding shed in the background. When Sheppard saw the "maison d'amour" in the background, he exploded and told Orr, "I don't want Tar Heel painted standing in front of [the breeding shed]," he said, using a blunt term for the facility.

After Sheppard's death, Simpson continued the tradition of having Orr paint the Hanover stallions and select mares. Though Simpson's eyesight dimmed, his commitment to the artwork never diminished. His failing vision forced Orr to adjust his artwork to accommodate his friend and patron.

"I had to rethink how John could best see these images," explains Orr. "He was paying for them, and I wanted him to see them."

One painting that Orr recalls manipulating because of Simpson's failing eyesight was an action study of Japa, the daughter of Star's Pride and Elma that raced so brilliantly in the mid-1970s.

"I got photos of Japa at DuQuoin when Billy Herman scored her down," he says. "She was way up off the ground and looked beautiful. When I did the painting, I simplified the background. I underpainted it. I took color out of the background, but tried to keep it realistic."

Orr took the painting of Japa to Simpson's house in Orlando. He left it in his car on purpose, hoping to lure Simpson out into the sunlight for the initial viewing.

"I leaned it against the back wheel of my car," says Orr. "The rest of the yard was in shadow from the trees, and the sunlight hit that painting like a spotlight. That meant that the pupil of John's eye was wide open."

Simpson studied the painting for several minutes without uttering a word, then said softly, "Wow! She was really flying!"

Japa driven by Jim Simpson in 1977 at Vernon Downs,
coming in at 1:59
(Photo by Mike Taylor, Vernon Downs)

Tar Heel portrait by Bill Orr

Certainly the most famous piece that Orr did for Simpson was a portrait of the great horseman flanked by Tar Heel and Star's Pride, two of his all-time favorites.

To the casual viewer, it is an unusual painting of dark horses against a dark background.

"His sight had deteriorated a lot by then," continues Orr. "The background looks as black as night, but it's really a deep, deep olive green. I wanted to give John an image simple enough that his eye was not distracted. I painted the horses by painting the highlights. The eyes of the horses were the most powerful part."

Simpson's hands were shown out of proportion in the painting as a tribute to his horsemanship.

"I never saw him drive a race," admits Orr, "but I saw him train at Ben White. The secret of horsemanship is great hands, and John Simpson had the touch."

Simpson's hands are positioned as if he were holding the lines while driving a horse, and Tar Heel and Star's Pride were two horses that had benefited from his masterful touch.

Orr will never forget Simpson's reaction when he first saw the life-size canvas. The master horseman asked Orr to bring it into the huge bathroom in his Florida home. The room had banks of fluorescent lights in the ceiling. Orr propped it up for inspection, then Simpson instructed him, "Lay it down."

"He went over every inch of that painting," says Orr. "I don't know how long he was down there. I got nervous. I had no idea what was going through his mind, but I felt sure that he was doing far more than looking at the painting. The painting was touching something inside him, and he was remembering these horses that he loved. I'd never had that experience with a painting before."

Simpson liked the painting enough to authorize limited edition prints to be made from the original, and he distributed the prints to his many friends in the sport.

The fact that Simpson commissioned paintings after he could not see them was a trait, Orr feels, in character with that generation of horsemen.

"The owners and breeders today just don't have the same feel for a horse that those men had," Orr emphasizes.

John Simpson certainly had a feel for a horse when he was holding the lines, but when blindness robbed him of the chance to train and drive, he still could indulge his passion by owning a few horses.

Sugarcane Hanover and Jim Simpson at DuQuoin in 1986

In 1984, there was a trotting yearling in the Hanover consignment that caught the eye of both Jim Simpson and Dr. Peter Boyce. His name was Sugarcane Hanover and he was a Florida Pro colt, the first foal of the Super Bowl mare Sugar Hanover.

Jim Simpson and Boyce fell in love with the effortless gait that this colt showed as a yearling next to the lead pony at the Hanover fairgrounds. They

Hanover Farms president John Simpson Jr. and farm superintendent Dr. Peter Boyce

(Photo courtesy of Allied Pix Service Inc.)

None of the other bidders at the Harrisburg sale seemed too interested in Sugarcane Hanover, and he was hammered down at a price of $15,000 to the account of John F. Simpson, Sr.

The shrewd horseman knew that many people looked askance upon him buying a colt from the Hanover consignment, feeling it was a buy-back or a pre-arranged deal. Superficially, it just didn't seem right, but that didn't deter Simpson for a moment.

"Hanover Shoe Farms does not bid any of the yearlings in," insisted Simpson in an interview at that time. "Hanover Shoe Farms is a corporation. If John Simpson, Sr. buys a yearling from Hanover Shoe Farms, he pays for it out of his own pocket. It's the same way with Paul Spears or any other buyer. Paul and I are stockholders. Why shouldn't the stockholders of a company be entitled to buy that company's product?

"These people who knock us and say that Hanover Shoe Farms bids in its yearlings, they're full of crap," said Simpson with typical bluntness. "I'm telling the truth."

Jim Simpson and Peter Boyce were telling the truth, too, when they said that there was something special about Sugarcane Hanover. It took a while for that special ability to surface, however, because Sugarcane did nothing initially to stand out from the crowd.

"You would hardly even know he was in the barn," explained trainer Jim Simpson. "When we would go over the horses with problems and we'd come to his name, we'd just say, 'Yeah, he's okay' and go on to the next horse."

160

One trait that Sugarcane shared with his mother is that "they both hit the ground very lightly, just like a cat," according to his trainer.

Quick like a cat, perhaps, but also occasionally as stubborn as a mule. He didn't care to work unless he had to.

"If you turned him behind the starting gate with other horses and didn't chirp to him, Sugarcane would just stand there and watch them leave," Jim Simpson said.

The young Simpson brought him along carefully, skipping the big-money early stakes and pointing him for the clay tracks of the Midwest. It was at the Indiana State Fairgrounds oval in Indianapolis that he first popped into the headlines by beating Royal Prestige and Express Ride — the first two finishers in the Peter Haughton Memorial a month earlier — with a 1:58.3 mile.

Then disaster struck. Sugarcane made breaks at DuQuoin, something that many young trotters will often do, but one of Sugarcane's hind hooves struck the rear quarter of a front hoof. A week later he broke stride again at Garden State Park and he came back from the track with blood on a hoof, a telltale sign of a quarter crack.

Quarter cracks are not death warrants for horses, but John Simpson trusted Mother Nature more than man in healing horse injuries. He told his son simply to turn Sugarcane out for the season and let time heal him.

In the early spring of 1986, Sugarcane seemed ready to start a full season, but things changed quickly when the quarter cracks reappeared after his first race in May.

A month-long layoff ensued and Sugarcane wasn't tight enough to ask him to start in the Hambletonian. So while the Hambletonian horses were enjoyed their moments of glory fighting for a $1,172,082 purse, Sugarcane Hanover was racing at Pocono Downs for $5,500.

The Simpsons, father and son, also didn't feel that Sugarcane was ready for the next big payday looming for sophomore trotters, the World Trotting Derby, in early September. Soon, however, the pendulum would shift to Sugarcane's side. By October he was ready.

In the first heat of the time-honored Kentucky Futurity, catch-driver Ron Waples sent Sugarcane Hanover to the front and the colt won under wraps in 1:56. Royal Prestige took the other elimination.

Tension mounted before the final to see if Sugarcane could claim the title of class leader. Would Royal Prestige find a way to win, as he so often did? Or would a third heat win to force the event into a raceoff?

Waples drove Sugarcane with confidence, allowing Royal Prestige to set moderate fractions in front. When Waples pulled on his right line and eased Sugarcane into the clear, the race was on! It was over sooner than everyone expected as Sugarcane simply cruised past Royal Prestige, Waples still clutching the handholds on his lines.

Jim Simpson and Ron Waples at the Kentucky Futurity
(Photo courtesy of Monica Thors)

Later that season, Sugarcane Hanover and Royal Prestige met again in the Breeders Crown and the Shamrock, both at Garden State, and by now the son of Florida Pro had his rival's number and won both events.

Sugarcane Hanover's accomplishments had earned him a spot in the stud at Hanover Shoe Farms, but Simpson was having too much fun racing his prize trotter. Besides, he thought that perhaps Sugarcane's best days lay ahead of him since he was finally sound.

In 1987, Sugarcane was given a slow and deliberate prep, but when the Breeders Crown was held at the Meadowlands in early August, Sugarcane was unstoppable as he blasted past Express Ride to win in 1:54.3. He ended his season by winning the 1-1/4-mile Van Lennep Memorial Trot at Pompano Park in a world record 2:27.4.

Sugarcane's apparent soundness, and his record in the extra-distance event, caused the Simpsons to think about sending Sugarcane to Europe in 1988. But Europe came to Sugarcane before Sugarcane ever got to Europe.

162

In the late 1980s, trotting was booming in Scandinavia and the most coveted status symbol among the monied crowd in the Nordic countries seemed to be an American-bred trotter.

Owners and their agents scoured the tracks and training centers, inquiring about horses available, getting prices, seeking vet exams, and making irresistible offers.

One horse high on the most wanted list was Sugarcane Hanover, but John Simpson didn't really want to sell.

Norwegian Helmer Strombo tried to get Simpson's attention when he offered him a flat million dollars for Sugarcane. Simpson declined.

Strombo wasn't dissuaded. He upped the ante. The response was the same. Simpson then told him that $2 million would get the job done. Strombo considered the asking price, then came back and said, "Sold!"

Sugarcane Hanover crossed the Atlantic and wasted no time in dazzling horsemen in his adopted country by winning the Oslo Grand Prix in record time. He then went to the Elitlopp in Sweden and won a heat despite breaking stride at the start.

He dropped the final to the American-owned meteor Mack Lobell.

In November 1988 Sugarcane Hanover and Mack Lobell met again, this time at Garden State Park, one of Sugarcane's favorite haunts. The occasion was the $600,000 March of Dimes Trot, and when the French hero Ourasi crossed the Atlantic, the race became one of the greatest international events in North America.

So much attention was focused on the duel between Mack Lobell and Ourasi that many bettors forgot Sugarcane's past heroics over the same Garden State track. They were reminded when Sugarcane burst from behind Ourasi in the final yards to cruise to an easy win.

He was retired to stud after that race, and became an enormously popular stallion in Europe.

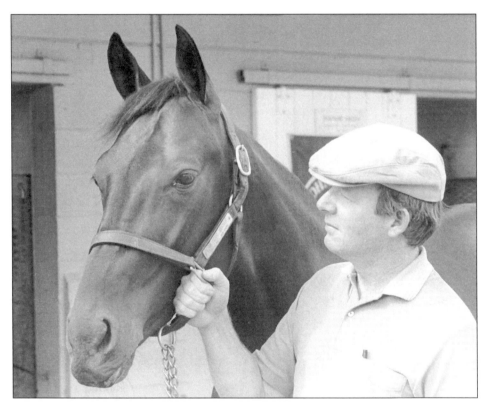

Sugarcane Hanover and Jim Simpson
(Photo courtesy of the U.S. Trotting Association)

Chapter 15

A New Team Takes The Field

In April 1987, Charlotte Newton Sheppard slipped away peacefully after 88 years of a full and vibrant life. Her death sparked a contest for control of Hanover Shoe Farms that was conducted behind the scenes, away from the sport's trade journals. To the outsider, the transition was so seamless as to be invisible, but those closest to it recall how tense and unpleasant the drama was.

Many businesses flourish for decades as long as the founder remains at the helm, but when the inevitable time comes for the torch to be passed to a new generation, internal struggles often occur.

Numerous horse farms had fallen victim to such woes. Walnut Hall Farm, the colossal farm in Kentucky that dominated the sport in the first 50 years of the 20th century, has been divided several times after deaths or disagreements in the family.

Castleton Farm ceased its operations as a Standardbred farm in December 2000, when it dispersed its horses. Barely a month later, the sport was shocked when the dissolution of the Armstrong Brothers breeding and racing operation, Canada's largest, was announced.

The history of harness racing is replete with dispersal sales that occur when the owner of a breeding farm dies and the heirs are unable to agree on control or a future course. Would that happen at Hanover? How would the three daughters of Charlotte Sheppard decide the future of the farm? Would harness racing be treated to the spectacle of the farm's 400 mares going onto the market at one time? What would that do to prices in a market already depressed?

Everyone associated with Hanover Shoe Farms knew that they would go through trial by fire in settling the estate of Charlotte N. Sheppard. And they knew it wouldn't happen overnight. The farm was only one of many assets that she owned at her death. (The shoe company and over 250 retail stores had been sold to an English firm in late December 1977.)

A confidentiality agreement that was part of settling the estate precludes those involved from discussing the details of what happened after Charlotte Sheppard's death. Those interested in harness racing, however, were concerned only with the fate of the breed's largest farm.

Charlotte Sheppard often repeated what her late husband had told her. "These guys [meaning Simpson, Spears, and Smith] will help you," Lawrence Sheppard often said. "Listen to them."

"My grandmother had been very skillful in maintaining things after L.B. died," says her grandson Russell Williams. "She did that for almost 20 years. She kept everything going. She worked with John Simpson and Paul Spears from time to time, but usually only when there was a problem. Otherwise they ran the farm."

Estates the size of Charlotte Sheppard's move through the courts at an exceedingly slow tempo. Matters were complicated by the fact that daughter Pat Winder wanted to see the existing team headed by John Simpson to maintain management of the farm. Sisters Alma and Charlotte felt that the Sheppard family should reassert its control of the farm.

Patricia Sheppard Winder never sought a high profile role in harness racing, but the stand that she and her son made after her mother's death was critical to the farm's continuity.

She had grown up at Hanover and loved to ride horses with her sister Alma when they got home from school each afternoon. When it came time for her to go to college, she weighed the merits of Sweet Briar, Radcliffe, and Rollins. Since Rollins College is in Winter Park, Florida, not far from where her father's horses wintered, it was not a hard decision for her to make.

She stayed in the Orlando area after graduating from college, got married, and Russell arrived in 1954. His parents were divorced when he was a young boy and Patricia raised Russell and her other children as a single mother.

She never lost her interest in horses, and always kept a few of her own.

"Her horses were strictly a hobby," Russell admits. "She was not interested in world domination."

Another factor that governed the limited role of the Sheppard daughters in Hanover Shoe Farms, says Russell, is that Lawrence Sheppard didn't see them as assuming a position of authority. He lived and did business in a man's world.

"It was fine for his daughters to own horses and follow them, but he didn't discuss business with them," says Russell. "I think that was exacerbated by the loss of Sonny. He didn't have the energy to transfer his business hopes to his daughters."

("His own wife was an exception to that," chuckles Williams, noting how strong-willed Charlotte Sheppard could be. "Maybe it was because he had no choice.")

After her mother's death, Pat Winder's sisters were trying to lure her into their camp with arguments of family loyalty, but Winder had so much faith in John Simpson that she decided to bet her money on him in this race.

That conflict spawned a legal battle that ultimately resulted in Pat Winder and son Russell Williams, along with John Simpson and Paul Spears, buying out the shares in the farm held by Alma and Charlotte. It was a momentous change in the farm's history. Instead of being owned almost entirely by the Sheppard family, ownership now rested with the Winder/Williams family and the families of John Simpson, and Paul Spears.

"If a corporation is to continue, it will eventually be run by someone other than the original owner," notes Williams. "Very few families can persist in supplying the talent to run a major business generation after generation. In order to keep the Hanover Shoe Farms at the top of the game, it was necessary to have people like John Simpson in the commanding role."

When Charlotte Sheppard died, John Simpson was 67 years old. He was past normal retirement age in the ordinary working world, but John Simpson was anything but ordinary and he didn't buy into that rocking-chair lifestyle. Besides, he knew that he had to see the farm through the transitional stage after Mrs. Sheppard's death.

By this time, Simpson had adjusted to the darkness that enveloped his world, and he wasn't about to let his disability undermine his intention to keep Hanover first in harness racing. Simpson had carried on many of the policies that Lawrence Sheppard had used to build Hanover, and wanted to see those policies continued.

To be sure, life had changed for John Simpson. Blindness robbed him of his beloved pastime of quail hunting, and he supplanted that with an interest in sports in his later years.

"He would listen to football games often," says son Jim, "but mostly that was to enjoy the camaraderie of his friends. He loved to sit around at his hunting camp and shoot the breeze with his buddies."

Because he had spent so many years in Orlando, Simpson had a wide circle of friends in the community. The Simpsons' family doctor, Russell Douglas, was a close friend, as were John Taylor, a central Florida rancher, and John Booth, a judge.

Simpson had amassed a considerable bank account as a result of his professional success and acumen in buying and selling horses, and while he reinvested some in horses, he plunked a lot into Wall Street.

"He was a great disciple of John Templeton, the money manager," says son Jim. "He bought the Templeton mutual funds, then he would find out what individual stocks the funds were holding and invest some more directly into those stocks. He was a buy-and-hold type of investor."

In the final years of his life, John Simpson particularly enjoyed each autumn when horsemen would find their way to Hanover to watch the yearling colts and fillies display their gait and speed next to a lead pony at the Hanover fairgrounds.

"He really looked forward to that," says Jim. "There was a time when trainers would spend a day or two at the farm. I remember Billy Haughton and Joe O'Brien staying over for a few days. Dad loved to quiz them and to talk about horses with them. He always liked talking to Howard Beissinger, too. He thought a lot of his ability."

By the end of 1991, Hanover Shoe Farm was through the transition to the new ownership. Simpson was comfortable giving up daily management duties. He was past 70 and the signs of advancing age were becoming evident. Simpson knew damn well he wasn't immortal, and that he couldn't run Hanover forever.

He took great pride in being at the helm of Hanover for almost a quarter-century. Through the high-flying '70s and '80s, with the limited partnerships mania and the pie-in-the-sky prices, Hanover had stayed the course. Hanover had survived while many of the high-flyers had fallen.

He took particular pride in the accomplishments of Albatross and Super Bowl, the two aces he had held in his hand during his years running the farm. Albatross was the reigning sovereign of pacing stallions. Sons like Niatross, Sonsam, Jaguar Spur, Tucson Hanover, Simcoe Hanover, Kiev Hanover, Fame, Coal Harbor, Merger, and Royce had carried the Albatross name to the top of the stallion list several times.

Albatross was also the sire of the only filly, Fan Hanover, ever to win the Little Brown Jug. She wasn't the only resplendent filly ever sired by Albatross. Three Diamonds never took a back seat to any other filly on the track, and produced a Jug winner herself in Life Sign. Cheery Hello, Turn The Tide, Halcyon, Keystone Wallis, Jefs Eternity, and Albaquel were all outstanding fillies by Albatross, too.

At one point in his career, Albatross's stud fee was $75,000, the highest ever for a Standardbred.

Super Bowl dueled Speedy Crown for supremacy among trotters during the same period, ultimately besting his rival in Hambletonian winners. Super Bowl got his first Hambletonian winner in 1979 when Legend Hanover took home the trophy and added another winner three years later when Speed Bowl was triumphant.

One of Super Bowl's sons, Probe, was a co-winner in the controversial 1989 Hambletonian and Giant Victory claimed sole possession of the trophy two years later. That gave Super Bowl a quartet of Hambletonian winners.

When Simpson retired, he could reflect on dozens of outstanding trotters sired by Super Bowl. The stallion's best sons included Napoletano, Sandy Bowl, Express Ride, Joie De Vie, Royal Troubador, Manfred Hanover, Supergill, and Final Score.

Super Bowl demonstrated that he was a superior sire of fillies when the champion Superlou appeared in his first crop. Later came a horde of stakes-winning fillies such as Armbro Keepsake, Davidia Hanover, Jef's Spice, Stage Entrance, Jean Bi, and Delmegan.

Yes, John Simpson had reason to take pride in Super Bowl's accomplishments as he prepared to step down. And Super Bowl's best son was yet to appear.

Simpson even had the last laugh on those who had dubbed Big Towner as "Simpson's Folly." The son of Gene Abbe fought his way into acceptance by the mainstream trainers and his offspring were admired for the same traits their sire displayed: quick speed, versatility, and enduring soundness.

The Big Towner fillies were especially successful and especially coveted. He sired a pair of millionaire pacing mares in Town Pro and Sweet Reflection, but his list of top fillies didn't stop with those two. He also sired Uptown Swell, Hardie Hanover, Towner's Image, Brees Brief, Central Park West, Headline Hanover, Maudlin Hanover, and many others.

Reflecting on his father's years at the helm of Hanover, Jim Simpson said that one of his father's greatest assets was his memory.

"In his prime, he never forgot anything that he heard, and he filed it all away," he says. "He had great intuition, a great feeling for the business as a whole."

The son looks back on the number of high-priced stallions that Simpson deftly avoided in the early 1980s when the business was booming and even the second-tier of colts in a season were syndicated for amounts in the millions.

"He was the subject of a lot of criticism then," admits Jim. "He kept saying that the value simply wasn't there. He felt that the bubble was going to burst. And it did."

Simpson was very proud of the team that he built to manage Hanover. Paul Spears had been an officer of Hanover Shoe Farms for decades and he knew the operation inside and out, especially from the financial perspective. Murray Brown could handle the sale, advertising, and public relations. Peter Boyce made sure the horses on the farm stayed fertile and healthy. And his son Jim and Russell Williams, Lawrence Sheppard's grandson, were waiting in the wings.

Yes, the time was right, thought Simpson, to pass the torch to the team he had so carefully built.

The first quarterback of the new team was a familiar face on the Hanover scene. Paul Spears had been president of the Standardbred Horse Sale Co. since 1968 and he knew all the prominent players in harness racing.

Born in 1924, just before Lawrence Sheppard had started Hanover Shoe Farms, Paul Spears grew up on the other end of the Keystone State and admits that he knew little about harness horses as a youngster.

"My father had an old pacer he used for delivering groceries, and he'd race him around the fairs once in a while," he says.

When Uncle Sam beckoned during World War II, Spears was shipped off to Europe, but arrived just as the Germans were waving the white flag of surrender. He was then shipped stateside en route to action in the Pacific, but the hostilities ceased there, too, before he saw combat.

Spears saw plenty of combat on the gridiron at Indiana University in Pennsylvania as he played both fullback on offense and middle guard on defense.

"That was common back then," he says. "You played all 60 minutes of the game."

When Spears wasn't hitting his opponents hard, he was hitting the books hard in pursuit of a business degree. He graduated in 1949.

Spears taught school for a year while waiting for the girl who became his wife, Josephine, to earn her permanent teaching certificate. Although he coached the school football team to one of its best seasons ever, the business world held more allure for Spears than the academic world.

He heard through the grapevine that Ford Motor Co. was recruiting educated young men anxious to make a mark in the auto industry. That appealed to Spears, so he and Josephine moved to Michigan. He was among a wave of young bucks such as Lee Iacocca and Robert McNamara who were known as the "whiz kids" and who modernized Ford's management practices.

America was in love with the automobiles, and the interstate highway system then under development would make it easier than ever for people to travel.

Spears saw a bright future at Ford, but he didn't see a bright future for him and his wife in the Motor City.

"I didn't like the traffic and the hassle of the city, so my wife and I just got an apartment, not a house," says Spears. "We didn't intend to stay there forever."

Josephine Spears had grown up in Hanover and in early 1953 she heard through her father that the Hanover Shoe Co. was looking for an ambitious young replacement for a retiring executive. Paul Spears learned more about the opening, liked what he heard, and applied for the job.

He was granted an interview, and he wisely did some homework about the company and its president Lawrence Sheppard.

"I'd read everything I could about him," says Spears. "I was in awe of the man."

Another Hanover executive conducted most of the interview with Spears, but Sheppard decided to sit in at the end, making the nervous young job applicant sweat.

Sheppard interrupted to add that he had just one question to ask. Spears knew that how he answered that question would probably determine whether he would get the job, but he had no idea what the question was. Sheppard took a long drag on his ubiquitous cigarette and asked, "Can you separate the [crap] from the pumpkin?"

Spears was flabbergasted by the blunt question, but he managed to blurt out, "Yes, Mr. Sheppard. I think I can."

He was hired.

He went to work as Controller of Hanover Shoe Co. and various other Sheppard enterprises on May 1, 1953. Every pair of Hanover Shoes then sold for $8.45 a pair and they were known as an excellent value that wore well and would last virtually forever. The leather and the workmanship used in making Hanover shoes were the best in the industry and the product inspired incredible customer loyalty.

Spears hadn't been on the job many weeks when Sheppard told him, "Before long I'm going to make you into a halfway lawyer, a halfway shoe salesman, and a halfway horseman."

Like Lawrence Sheppard, Paul Spears didn't like doing things halfway.

During the next 25 years, Spears learned a lot about legal matters and making shoes. Immersed in the Hanover environment, it was impossible for him not to also learn that Lawrence Sheppard's greatest love was breeding harness horses.

Although Spears was employed by the Hanover Shoe Co., he immediately began handling the accounting duties for the farm, too. Sheppard soon elevated the young man to the position of vice president of the farm.

"When you worked for Lawrence Sheppard, you worked on anything he wanted you to, whether you got paid by that company or not," says Spears. "The first job he gave me was at the bank in Hanover shuffling tax-exempt bonds and trying to straighten out a mess they had."

Spears threw himself into his work for decades and earned Sheppard's respect. He worked long hours religiously and served his employer well, but by the time he was in his 50s he was looking for some diversion. He was a trifle too old to return to his gridiron days, but the competitive fires still burned. Instead, he decided to learn to drive horses.

No one ever learned to drive horses overnight, so Spears spent countless hours going slow jogging and training miles before he was ready to race. And his first starts came far from the bright lights of the Meadowlands and other pari-mutuel palaces. His first efforts came at county fairs in Pennsylvania with names like Hughesville and Troy.

His initial partner on the track was a mare named Graceful Lass, who hardly lived up to her name.

"She was a terrible kicker," recalls Spears with a laugh. "I think people figured that if I could keep my interest in driving with her, I'd be okay."

His other partner, wife Josephine, wasn't so sure about this risky business her husband was trying, but she tried to hide her anxiety and support her husband.

Like any new driver, Spears made his share of mistakes. His biggest problem at first was getting horses away on gait at the start of a race. He wasn't getting the easiest horses to drive, and the combination of an inexperienced horse and a green-as-grass driver usually doesn't make for a pretty picture.

Spears also knew that the hard-bitten veterans of the sulky sport probably looked askance at him, wondering, "What in the hell is that guy doing out there?"

Spears had excellent tutors available in the Simpsons, and he relied on the expertise that was so accessible to him. When a horse jumped off at the start, Jim Simpson would ask, "Did you have a good hold of him?"

"Well, I thought I did," said Spears, quietly resolving to take firmer grip next time.

Although John Simpson was blind and unable to see Spears drive, he, too, provided counseling. After a race, Spears would describe a situation that occurred during a race to Simpson and ask what he would have done.

"John is one of the greatest horsemen we've ever had," said Spears when he was driving regularly. "He's accomplished everything a person could in this business, and I'm one of his greatest admirers. It was great for me to have the benefit of his experience."

When Paul Spears was named president of Hanover Shoe Farms, Jim Simpson and Russell Williams were named vice presidents. They are some three decades younger than Spears, so it was obvious that they would soon play a major role in the farm's future.

*Paul Spears
in his office
at Hanover*

Jim Simpson grew up not only in the shadow of his father, but also in that cast by his brother, John, Jr., who is seven years older.

As the eldest son and bearer of the famous name, young John Simpson was guided toward a career in harness racing. His father may have been able to open doors for him, but it took ability and horsemanship to walk through the doors and hold his own in the rough and tumble world of Grand Circuit competition.

John Simpson, Jr. excelled from the start. When he won the Hambletonian in 1970 with Timothy T, he was just 25 and the youngest driver ever to win the sport's greatest classic. By that time, however, he was already established as a regular on the Grand Circuit, and more honors come his way during the ensuing decade.

*(From left) Jim Simpson, Paul Spears and Russell Williams
confer in the office at Hanover Shoe Farms*

While his older brother was winning the Hambletonian, Jim was an undergraduate student at the University of New Mexico, far from the world of harness racing. He majored in biology, but admits that he had no real idea what he wanted to do when he graduated.

"I didn't show much interest in harness racing when I was young," he concedes. "My brother had more interest, so my father fostered that."

Jim says that his father never steered him toward a career in harness racing, but he also didn't discourage it. The younger son was so argumentative around the household, however, that everyone told him he should go to law school. Lawyers, his siblings and parents told Jim, get paid to argue.

"I enrolled in a law school in Delaware, but never attended," says Simpson. "Being a lawyer was never a very serious ambition for me."

If you grew up in the Simpson family, it was impossible not to absorb some horsemanship from the people who surrounded John Simpson. As a youngster, Jim knew Frank Ervin, Delvin Miller, Clarence Gaines, and many other people steeped in Standardbred lore.

Once he was out of college, Jim began to take a greater interest in the racing world. His father forced him to learn the hard way, making sure that his surname didn't isolate him from the hard work that all horsemen must endure.

Jim apprenticed with some of the best horsemen in the business until he was ready to take over training the Hanover Shoe Farms stock. During the winter they were based at Ben White Raceway in Orlando, Florida, and in the spring they would ship north to a base at a pari-mutuel track.

Jim Simpson not only developed and trained Sugarcane Hanover, but also Sven Hanover, winner of the first heat ever contested in Breeders Crown competition. He also campaigned Chickadee Newton, Burnell Newton, and other many stakes stars.

As a trainer, Jim Simpson tried to blend traditional horsemanship with an avid interest in any new tool that would help him. For example, he embraced computers long before many others in the Standardbred world and quickly realized their value to a racing stable and breeding operation.

It was Jim Simpson who later spearheaded Hanover's move into the computer age, not only using computers as record-keeping tools on the farm, but also for the farm's Internet site.

The website contains information on the farm's stallions, of course, including photos and an updated list of performers. It also contains a section of farm history, yearlings sales, staff, and board rates.

Simpson has made certain that the farm's staff is computer literate because he understands how the Internet has changed the way that information is transmitted in the world, and especially in the world of harness racing. He's made Hanover the vanguard of this important trend.

Russell Williams was virtually a non-entity in harness racing, a name unknown to most people, until his grandmother's death in 1987. When the squabbling over her estate threatened the future of Hanover Shoe Farms, however, he stepped into a more visible and more vibrant role.

Growing up in Orlando, Florida, Russell was certainly aware of his family's horses. He respected — and feared — his grandfather Sheppard and made periodic visits to Ben White Raceway during the winter to see the racing stable managed by John Simpson. Unwittingly, young Russell displayed a preference for quality even in his limited contacts with horses.

"Romola Hanover is the one horse I remember most," he says of the filly who later became the greatest broodmare of her day. "She was racing when I was a kid. I've heard that she was tough to be around, but she seemed to like little kids.

Sierra Kosmos led by Russell Williams

From my point of view, she was the friendliest horse in the barn. I used to go straight to her stall."

His contacts with horses were limited to the winter, however, and otherwise Russell was a typical city boy with little chance to develop his skill with them.

His mother Pat Winder often told him that there were only two truly honorable professions, practicing law or training horses. After all, her father Lawrence Sheppard had been trained as a lawyer, but loved his horses far more than he loved the law.

"I didn't have much aptitude with horses," Russell admits. "I liked them. I could ride. But I didn't have that special affinity for them. Since I wasn't cut out to be a horseman, it seemed that I should be a lawyer."

He went off to law school at the University of Richmond, and after graduation he clerked for a federal judge.

"That was the best job I ever had or ever will have," he says. "It was very demanding. I did better work than I realized that I could. It taught me a lot. After that, I wasn't afraid to go into federal court."

Williams relished the opportunities to practice law in Richmond. Replete with various courts, Richmond presented a young lawyer with a cornucopia of career options once he nailed up his shingle.

"My goal was to put together a small but excellent litigation practice," he explains. "I saw myself working with four or five other lawyers doing both plaintiff and defense work."

Williams opted to forsake his law practice when the future of Hanover Shoe Farms seemed uncertain, and devote his time to the farm and the Standardbred Horse Sale Co.

"You have to give law 110 percent," he says. "I can't practice law on the side, so when I came to Hanover, I had to stop."

Williams is also involved in a number of philanthropic organizations, most notably the Hanover Shoe Farms Foundation, which he chairs. Serving with him are Jim Simpson and Pat Eisenhauer (daughter of farm chairman Paul Spears). It's an offshoot of the L.B. Sheppard Foundation, which had been established in the 1940s.

"We give money to charities in the Hanover area and to selected organizations in harness racing," he says.

Today the L.B. Sheppard Foundation remains an active contributor to both the Hanover community and harness racing. Charlotte Sheppard DeVan and her family preside over this foundation. In the 1990s, the L.B. Sheppard Foundation made a substantial contribution to the Harness Racing Museum in Goshen, New York, and which resulted in the Founders Room being renamed the L.B. Sheppard Room. In addition to Sheppard, several other giants in 20th century harness racing are honored in the room.

Beyond the world of horses, Williams has a passion for antiques and skiing. It's not easy to indulge a love of skiing in southern Pennsylvania, so he has to head to the hills periodically to sate his skiing lust.

"I'll ski any hill with snow on it," he says, pointing out that there's a slope within a half-hour of Hanover that keeps him in practice. Curiously, this pastime grabbed hold of him at age 40. ("It was a mid-life crisis sort of thing," he laughs.) He knew little about skiing until then. Certainly growing up in Orlando the only kind of skiing he knew about was done on water behind an outboard motor.

Williams also has the largest collection of Standardbred books and art in the world. The books do far more than fill shelves in his home; they provide him with a window on the history of harness racing and he periodically pores over them.

He is particularly interested in learning more of the history of Hanover Shoe Farms, but his grasp of the sport's past certainly doesn't stop there. He relishes the opportunity to read about the great horses of the past, the kind of horse described by author Dwight Akers at the beginning of his 1938 volume *Drivers Up*:

"That horse is noblest, on whatever pasture bred, whose rush outstrips the rest and whose dust is foremost upon the plain."

Much like his grandfather, Russell Williams is intent on having Hanover Shoe Farms breed horses whose dust is foremost.

No Nukes and driver Glen Garnsey at Delaware
(Photo courtesy of the U.S. Trotting Association)

Chapter 16

Young Turks In The Stud Barn

When Paul Spears became president of Hanover, he was eager to find some fresh faces for the stallion barn. It was similar to the approach John Simpson had taken in his first few years at the helm.

Spears knew it was time to upgrade, both stallions and mares. The Hanover yearlings weren't capturing the fancy of the buying public the way they had in previous years.

In 1991, a trio of sophomore pacing colts swept across the land, dominating their rivals and dazzling their admirers wherever they raced. Alphabetically, they were Artsplace, Die Laughing, and Precious Bunny.

Precious Bunny and Die Laughing rose to the top of the class that year while Artsplace struggled with various maladies. The picture-perfect Die Laughing was a hot commodity as a stallion candidate and that didn't escape anyone's notice at Hanover. At the end of the year it was announced that Die Laughing would go to stud at Hanover. No Nukes was the cock of the walk among pacing stallions then, and now Hanover had one of his best sons.

But the deal between Hanover and the colt's owners blew up, and Die Laughing was placed at another farm. Hanover was left empty-handed. Fortunately, Paul Spears already had set his sights on the father.

No Nukes had been the leading sire in the sport in 1991. His offspring earned over $12 million that year, a record sum for any Standardbred stallion in a single season. The son of Oil Burner had started his career at Lana Lobell Farms in New Jersey, but when that farm went bankrupt he was moved to the farm of his trainer Steve Demas.

Spears talked to Demas about making No Nukes a member of the Hanover team, and Demas agreed. The stallion had become unruly and dangerous; some changes were needed.

The Hanover team could see that Hanover also needed a facility in New Jersey since the sires stakes races there were going for lucrative sums. Jim

Simpson scouted out property and found that the former Almahurst Farm stallion station was almost perfect for Hanover's needs.

"I liked it right away," says Spears. "I contacted the realtor and negotiated on the property. A bank in Lexington then owned it. We built a nice house there, too. It's a lovely farm, and a nice set-up."

"I remember the first day we brought No Nukes to the breeding shed," says Spears. "I've never seen a horse carry on the way he did. He knocked the mare down. It was awful. I made a hard and fast rule that No Nukes was never to be handled by one person again. There would have to be two people, one on each side of him."

On Little Brown Jug Day, the third Thursday in September of 1992, the Hanover team was in Delaware, Ohio, on business. The first order of business was to devote their attention to a trotter, an activity that isn't exactly frowned upon on Jug Day, but it is highly irregular. Jug Day belongs to the pacers.

The Hanover crew had some business to conduct in the morning before the afternoon's races began. They went straight to the stall of Sierra Kosmos, the flashy-gaited son of Nearly Perfect who had set a world record for three-year-old trotters on a half-mile track the previous day.

Sierra Kosmos trotting in 1:56.2 at Delaware

Sierra Kosmos trotted in 1:56.2 easily, too, in a typical performance by the high-stepping colt. Trainer-driver-owner Rick Beinhauer sent him right to the front at the start and the others were gasping for air in their futile attempts to keep up.

The performance wasn't a surprise because anyone who watched the three-year-old trotting crop closely in 1992 could tell you that Sierra Kosmos was the fastest one of the bunch. Unfortunately, he was not eligible to many of the major stakes and he sat on the sidelines while others had a chance to shine.

After his record performance at Delaware, Sierra Kosmos had great marketability as a stallion prospect. Not only was he extremely fast, but he was an outcross stallion in a breed that was inundated with Speedy Crown and Super Bowl blood in trotting pedigrees.

So when the Hanover team got to the stable area to see Sierra Kosmos, they wanted to make sure he passed physical muster. What they saw was a slender brown colt, liberally splashed with white markings on his feet.

They could see how well he would fit, both physically and genetically, to the statuesque Super Bowl mares and others in their broodmare band. Once they had made a decision, it was only a matter of working out the details with Beinhauer.

Sierra Kosmos would race once more, taking a 1:53.4 mark in his final start at Lexington, before it was announced that he would begin breeding service at Hanover in 1993 at a fee of $6,000.

With the inspection of Sierra Kosmos behind them, the Hanover team could look forward to the big show on Jug Day. Western Hanover, a colt bred and raised at the farm, was on the brink of making history. He was heavily favored to win the Little Brown Jug, the final leg of the Triple Crown for pacers.

The team from Hanover was proud not only because they had raised and sold him, but also because it seemed sure that Western Hanover was "coming home" to Hanover as a stallion. Nothing had been announced yet, but Paul Spears and Murray Brown had met with Western Hanover's owner George Segal over lunch at the Union Square Café in New York the day before Alf Palema won the Hambletonian.

"George told us what he wanted to do with Western Hanover, and we agreed to it," says Brown, recalling that luncheon. "The business end of it might have taken five minutes."

Admittedly, the Triple Crown had lost much of its luster for both pacers and trotters by the 1990s. When the Triple Crown was initiated in the mid-1950s, the Little Brown Jug, Messenger Stakes, and Cane Pace were truly the three biggest tests for a sophomore pacer. Similarly, the Hambletonian, Kentucky Futurity, and Yonkers Futurity (later the Yonkers Trot) were the big ones for trotting sophomores.

181

*Western
Hanover in
training with
Gene Riegle*

A major shift in pacing priorities occurred when the Meadowlands Pace was started in 1977. The money offered in that race was impossible to ignore. Almost overnight the Meadowlands Pace and the Jug became the twin targets for three-year-old pacers.

In 1984, the Ontario Jockey Club inaugurated the North America Cup to showcase the best sophomore pacers on the continent. By 1987, it too had a $1 million purse. Even though that purse was paid in Canadian dollars, it was too tempting for trainers to resist.

Suddenly the Messenger Stakes and Cane Pace were overshadowed by the megabucks events in New Jersey and Ontario. Concurrently, half-mile tracks were falling out of favor with trainers and owners, and some of the better three-year-old pacers began skipping the Messenger and Cane. In the first 25 years of the Triple Crown, that was virtually unimaginable.

In 1984, the Breeders Crown series was started, giving three-year-olds, as well as juveniles and older horses, another jackpot.

While the Triple Crown wasn't what it used to be in harness racing, it would still give Western Hanover bragging rights as the first pacer to sweep the trio since Ralph Hanover in 1983. So the Jug victory was very important to Western Hanover, as well as to his breeder.

It was even more important to Western Hanover's trainer Gene Riegle and owner George Segal. They had brought out the gifted Artsplace just one year before Western Hanover and he was one of the most unstoppable pacers in the sport's history. His sophomore season, however, was strewn with hurdles and he sat out the Jug that year because of sickness. The Riegle/Segal combo really wanted to win the Jug.

Funny things can happen in the Little Brown Jug. Western Hanover was a son of No Nukes from an Albatross mare. Both No Nukes and Albatross had been brilliant pacers, but neither of them had a Jug victory to crow about.

Western Hanover had swept the Cane Pace at Yonkers Raceway, the first leg of the Triple Crown, in effortless style, going wire-to-wire despite being parked out for the first half. In the stretch, he sprinted away from his rivals to win by three lengths.

It was much the same in the Messenger Stakes a few weeks later. A fixture at Roosevelt Raceway on Long Island for decades, the Messenger was contested that year at Rosecroft Raceway in the Washington, D.C., metro area. The change of locale made no difference to Western Hanover as he worked his way to the front before a half-mile had been covered and once again drew off to win handily, this time by 2-1/4 lengths.

The next stop on his schedule was the Jug. Post position can be a killer at Delaware and on other half-mile tracks, so when Western Hanover drew post two in his elimination heat, owner Segal, trainer Riegle, and driver Bill Fahy breathed a sigh of relief.

The bettors at Delaware didn't see how anyone could best Western Hanover and sent him off at state-minimum odds of 1-5. Fahy rocketed his colt to the lead, but soon found himself challenged by outsider Fake Left. He yielded the lead to driver Ron Waples and Fake Left, then came back on the outside to retake control.

For Ron Waples, it was working out to be the perfect trip, a chance to yield to the heavy favorite and follow his cover the rest of the way. There was, however, one problem: Fake Left wasn't buying into the plan. When Western Hanover came along on the outside, Fake Left took such a strong hold of Waples that Western Hanover was unable to get past the leader.

Fahy accepted his fate, hoping that he had enough horse to forge his way past Fake Left in the stretch. Western rallied in the final quarter, but Fake Left held firm and won the heat by a neck.

That changed the complexion of the Jug. Crouch and Caprock had taken the two other eliminations. Nine pacers would return for a raceoff. If any of the heat winners repeated, the race was over.

This time, however, Fahy was not hung out to dry in a death duel for the lead. He was able to work out a perfect second-over trip. When it came time to get serious in the final quarter, he tipped Western Hanover three wide and the willing colt responded by nailing Fake Left at the wire.

That sent the Jug into a four-horse raceoff. After watching the preliminaries, everyone assumed it would really be a two-horse raceoff between Western Hanover and Fake Left. What they didn't know, however, is just how exciting this duel would be.

Fake Left again took the lead, but Western was never far off the pace. Again he launched his attack in the final quarter. By the time they turned into the stretch, Western was within a half-length of Fake Left and gaining with every stride.

But Fake Left wasn't relenting. He, too, was fighting with undaunted courage. The two drivers asked their colts for every ounce of effort. Ironically, Waples and Fahy had been involved in the most dramatic raceoff in harness racing history just three years earlier when Park Avenue Joe and Probe had dead-heated in the Hambletonian raceoff. Was history about to repeat itself?

The two pacers hit the wire as a team and it was impossible to separate them. The judges ordered a finish print. To fill time while the judges reached a decision, track announcer Roger Huston asked the crowd to cheer if they thought Western Hanover had won. A roar went up from the grandstand and bleachers. Then Huston asked how many people thought Fake Left had won. An equal roar was heard.

If the crowd wasn't sure, owner George Segal was. He was standing near the finish line when the two pacers went past the wire. Immediately he turned and walked toward the backstretch. He knew that there would be no Jug or no Triple Crown for Western Hanover. Fake Left had won.

What there would be for Western Hanover was a place in the stud barn at Hanover when he retired at the end of 1992. Murray Brown looks back on the chain of events as proof that "it's better to be lucky than smart."

"If we had been able to get Die Laughing, there is no way we'd ever have considered another son of No Nukes such as Western Hanover," he says. "Die Laughing came to be considered a failure and Western became a great success."

Western Hanover began serving mares at Hanover in 1993, a season that was to be a fateful year in the sport's history. The three-year-olds, both trotters and pacers, of that season put on shows that racing fans wouldn't soon forget.

The dominant two-year-old trotter of the previous season had been Giant Chill. He had not only won the early-season bonanza in the Peter Haughton Memorial, but he had held his form into the fall and took the Breeders Crown. Giant Chill, however, had to take a back seat the following season.

Two colts that were virtually unknown at the start of the season would transform this season into one of the most memorable. One colt was lightly raced at two and the other was unraced. Their names were American Winner and Pine Chip.

American Winner had every right to be a superstar because he was a son of Super Bowl and the third foal from BJ's Pleasure. Her first two foals had been Super Pleasure and BJ's Mac. The latter had won the Peter Haughton Memorial while the former had just missed winning that event after recovering from a break at the start.

By contrast, Pine Chip was a son of Arndon, who had lowered the speed standard for trotters to 1:54 in 1982 as a three-year-old. A decade later, however, Arndon had fallen out of favor as a sire and had been exported to Italy.

American Winner and Pine Chip hooked up early in the '93 season in a Pennsylvania Sires Stakes at The Meadows. It was the first of several such encounters and by the time the Hambletonian rolled around in early August, trotting fans knew that there were giants abroad in the land.

Pine Chip had defeated American Winner in the Beacon Course, the prep race for the Hambletonian, but no horse was going to touch American Winner on Hambletonian Day as he floated over the Meadowlands track to win in two heats.

American Winner and Pine Chip at Lexington in 1993

American Winner repeated his triumph in a remarkably courageous performance winning the Zweig Memorial at the New York State Fair, but it was a Pyrrhic victory because he came out of that race badly lame. The remainder of his season was compromised, and it was Pine Chip who moved to the fore.

Pine Chip whipped American Winner at The Red Mile that fall, trotting powerfully to win the Kentucky Futurity in record time. He did much the same in annexing the Breeders Crown later at Pompano.

While racing fans saw American Winner and Pine Chip as a pair of wonderful performers on the track, the Hanover team saw them as a pair of nonpareil stallion prospects with wonderful potential.

Hanover president Paul Spears pursued both horses aggressively, knowing that trotters like this didn't come along every year. Both of them could become dominant stallions, and he wanted to get at least one for Hanover. It would be almost too good to get both of them.

It certainly wouldn't be the first time in the breed's history that two superior stallions were foaled in the same crop. Scotland and Spencer were both born in 1925, King's Counsel and Adios were foals of 1940, Star's Pride and Florican came along in 1947, and No Nukes and Cam Fella were both foals of 1979.

In a stunning announcement in the fall of 1993, Hanover proclaimed its success by telling the racing world that both American Winner and Pine Chip were coming to stud at the historic Pennsylvania nursery.

Then a complication arose. Pine Chip, who had been shipped to Europe to compete in the classic Orsi Mangelli in Milan, Italy, in November, failed his fertility test. Hanover has traditionally used the services of the University of Pennsylvania's New Bolton Center, and the staff there sets rigorous fertility standards. Pine Chip simply didn't meet them. The deal was off. Pine Chip was placed back in training.

The loss of Pine Chip underscored the wisdom of going after both horses because American Winner was certainly a very desirable addition. Horsemen who saw him marveled at how light on his feet he was and how he seemed to float across the track so easily.

The arrangement that Spears negotiated with co-owner Robert J. Key gave Hanover breeding rights to American Winner, but no ownership interest. Key and partner John Glesmann retained full ownership of the stallion.

That year Pine Chip wasn't the only horse that was announced as coming to Hanover but never arrived. The other was Cambest, a durable free-for-aller. He stunned the sport with a 1:46.1 time trial in the summer of 1993, but a month later he was tested positive for a "milkshake," a performance-enhancing concoction, before a race at Delaware, Ohio.

Hanover released a statement which noted its high regard and respect for Cambest's owner and trainer, but said "due to the circumstances involved and in consideration of the negative public perceptions surrounding the incident . . . Hanover Shoe Farms has decided not to stand Cambest."

Cambest went to Walnut Hall Ltd. in Kentucky where he proved to be an extremely popular stallion, siring 312 foals in his first two crops.

Hanover Shoe Farms had to wait only one more year to get a son of Cam Fella, and he was a better racehorse than Cambest. His name was Cam's Card Shark and all that he did in 1994 was win 15 of his 18 starts and pocket $2,264,714, more than any harness horse had ever earned in a single season.

Along the way, Cam's Card Shark won the Meadowlands Pace and the North America Cup and virtually everything else. His season came to an unusual and premature halt when he was paraded for his elimination in the Little Brown Jug, then scratched due to lameness. He never raced again.

It didn't really matter because Cam's Card Shark had done enough to make himself appealing to breeders. He served 183 ladies in his first season and his books over the next five season ranged from 143-179, a perfect example of a stallion sustaining his popularity.

That same fateful 1993 season marked the racing debut of the foals by a young New Jersey-based stallion whose racing career consisted of only 14 starts. He was, however, a horse destined to alter the worldwide trotting scene. His name was Valley Victory.

Valley Victory was lucky to have a racing career at all or even live to breed a mare. His life was in jeopardy before many people even knew his name.

In early 1988, Swedish trainer Jan Johnson called New Yorker Arlene Traub to deliver some bad news about a two-year-old colt she had in training with Continental Farms Stable at Pompano Beach, Florida.

"Valley Victory is on the truck going to the University of Florida for surgery," Johnson said. "But don't expect to ever see him again."

The youngster

Cam's Card Shark at Adios

had been stricken with colic while in training at Pompano. The only hope was surgery at the University of Florida some 300 miles away.

Miraculously, Valley Victory pulled through the surgery and was sent to the training center at Hawkinsville, Georgia, to recover. Later he was shipped to New Jersey to resume training as a member of the Steve Elliott Stable.

Although he was delayed in getting to the races, once Valley Victory figured out what trotting was all about, he was a superstar on the rise. He won in the fall of 1988 at The Red Mile in 1:57.2, which was impressive enough, but the ease with which he stepped his final quarter in :27.2 astonished horsemen.

He finished off his season by going back to Pompano where he had first entered training and captured the Breeders Crown easily. At season's end he was named the champion colt of his class.

He took up as a three-year-old where he left off the previous season, winning everything in sight. He won his first six races as a three-year-old so impressively that he was clearly the dominant colt as Hambletonian time neared.

Dominant colt, yes, but what about that filly Peace Corps? Like Valley Victory, she was from the first crop by Baltic Speed, and she was sweeping through all of her stakes on the road to the Hambletonian.

It was a publicist's dream, and the Meadowlands staff capitalized on it. Thousands of buttons were printed for distribution to racing fans, half with the words "I Like The Colt" and the other half with "I Like The Filly."

The dream match never happened. Valley Victory fell ill prior to the Hambletonian and never raced again. Peace Corps was far from her best form on the big day and failed to win even a heat.

Initially it looked as if Valley Victory might be exported to Sweden for breeding purposes, but through the efforts of George Segal and Tony Pedone, he was saved for stud duty and placed at the upstart Southwind Farm in New Jersey.

When the offspring of Valley Victory hit the races as juveniles in 1993, knowing horsemen could sense that there was a change in the air. For years breeders and trainers had discussed what horse would lead trotting forward when Speedy Crown and Super Bowl finished the course. When the colts and fillies by Valley Victory continued to win, horsemen felt that they might have found the heir to the throne.

If they weren't convinced by the first season, the next season erased all doubt. The 1994 Hambletonian was won by Victory Dream, a son of Valley Victory. The other heat winner that day was Bullville Victory, also a son of Valley Victory. In fact, six of the 10 Hambletonian finalists that year were sons of Valley Victory. The new king had arrived.

While so much attention was focused on the Hambletonian that year, another son of Valley Victory making a big splash was an elegant two-year-old bay colt named Donerail. His name came from the hamlet in Kentucky where Walnut Hall Farm was located. Although he was foaled and raised in Kentucky, Donerail was to make 21 starts in his career, each one of them in New Jersey.

Donerail was selected and developed by Stanley Dancer, one of harness racing's true legends. As he neared age 70, Dancer had given up driving and turned those duties over to John Campbell.

Few horsemen could get a two-year-old trotter ready any better than Stanley Dancer and when Donerail won the E.H. Harriman Challenge Cup in 1994, it marked the 12th time that a Dancer pupil had won this early season test.

From that point, it was all easy money for Donerail as he rolled over his foes in the Peter Haughton Memorial. It was easy money for owner Robert Suslow to shop Donerail to prospective breeding farms, and Paul Spears was the first standing in line.

As pundits looked toward the 1995 Hambletonian, it seemed to fall into a pattern much like the build-up for the same event six years earlier. In 1989, Valley Victory had been the ascendant colt seeking trotting's Holy Grail; now it would be his son Donerail. In 1989 the lady in waiting for Valley Victory was Peace Corps; in 1995 the filly threatening the colts was CR Kay Suzie.

Alas, the outcome was much the same as in 1989. Donerail never made it to the Hambletonian and CR Kay Suzie, virtually conceded the race in advance, broke stride and failed to qualify for the final.

Donerail's abortive sophomore season was hardly disastrous, but the expectations had been so high that when he was merely winning — but not humiliating — his rivals, it was apparent that something was amiss. Rather than race a colt that seemed clearly off-form, trainer Dancer and owner Robert Suslow decided to retire Donerail.

Soon Suslow's phone was ringing

Stanley Dancer with Donerail

189

and Paul Spears was again on the phone. He was ready to welcome Donerail to Hanover and to handle the syndication.

"I previously had talked to Stanley Dancer about Donerail," recalls Spears. "I wanted the horse all along. I think he might have come along and won the Hambletonian, but I have tremendous respect for Stanley. He's one of the pillars of the industry. His word was good with me, and he didn't want to cheapen Donerail. I agreed with Stanley."

Donerail and his connections caught their share of criticism for quitting prematurely with Donerail, but Spears is still convinced it was the best decision.

"Maybe he would have won the Hambletonian, and maybe he wouldn't have," admits Spears. "Who knows? If he had kept on racing and started to lose races, he would not have been in the position he is today as a stallion."

By the end of that 1995 season, breeders recognized the influence that Valley Victory was having on the trotting picture, and they were quick to jump on the male line bandwagon. Donerail served a full book of 186 mares.

Paul Spears and the Hanover team recognized the emerging trend in trotting, too, and when another son of Valley Victory finished the season strong, Hanover was hot on his trail.

The colt's name was Lindy Lane and he was the antithesis of Donerail. While Donerail had been sensational from the get-go as a two-year-old, Lindy Lane was slower to develop. He was bred and owned by the Antonacci family's Lindy Farm of Connecticut and this operation doesn't aim at early stakes.

So while Dancer's Victory and Mr. Vic (also sons of Valley Victory) were grabbing the summer headlines in 1995, Lindy Lane was slowly being prepped for his racing career. He was so laid back in his work that he appeared to be a dud.

Once he began racing in late summer, however, Lindy Lane woke up. "He surprised the life out of me," admitted trainer Osvaldo Formia who hadn't cared much for the colt up to that point

Lindy Lane simply kept improving through September. He won the $100,000 Harold Dancer Memorial at Garden State in early October, defeating Dancer's Victory. He was not eligible to the Breeders Crown, so the only big race left for him was the $321,000 Valley Victory at Garden State in early November.

He won his elimination easily, but in the final he was parked to the half in 56.3 on a cold night. That's usually the death knell for a two-year-old trotter, but Lindy Lane was unperturbed. He just kept on rolling and hit the wire in 1:56 to win by open lengths.

The ease with which he won was enough to send breeders scurrying after his services and the farm with the most long green was Hanover. Just before Lindy

*Lindy Lane
driven by Mike
Lachance at the
Meadowlands*

Lane made his racing debut as a sophomore in 1996, it was announced that his future home would be Hanover Shoe Farms.

His debut had been delayed by some sickness, so Lindy Lane went into the Hambletonian with only three purse starts. In his final prep, however, he zoomed by the fillies Continentalvictory and Act Of Grace and the colt Mr. Vic to win the $334,500 Budweiser Beacon Course in stake record 1:53.

On Hambletonian Day, Lindy Lane easily won his elimination heat, and then hooked up in memorable duel against the filly Continentalvictory in the final. They trotted through the stretch together, but at the wire, the filly had the edge in 1:52.1, fastest mile ever in the Hambletonian.

Four weeks later Lindy Lane and Continentalvictory hooked up again and they turned the opening round of the World Trotting Derby into a duel to the death. Lindy Lane had drawn inside the filly and driver Bill O'Donnell sent his colt to the front. When Mike Lachance attacked with Continentalvictory, O'Donnell wouldn't let her go.

The two trotters by Valley Victory sailed down the backstretch at a frantic pace never before seen in a trotting race. The first quarter had been in 26 seconds and the half-mile marker was passed in 53.3 seconds.

Not even the two great trotters could withstand this punishment. Kramer Boy swept past them to win. The filly was fourth and Lindy Lane seventh.

Continentalvictory won the second heat and the raceoff while Lindy Lane managed a fourth place finish in the second heat.

After that day at DuQuoin, neither Lindy Lane nor Continentalvictory were ever the same again. The filly never won another race and Lindy Lane was only a shadow of the coming superstar he had been in early summer.

Still, when Lindy Lane went to stud in 1997, enough breeders recognized that he was a horse blessed with enormous potential and his first book reached a total of 182 mares.

Fortunately, both Donerail and Lindy Lane inherited the outstanding speed and desire that Valley Victory instilled in his offspring, but they were not plagued by the infertility problems that bedeviled Valley Victory and his first outstanding son Victory Dream.

Donerail and Lindy Lane were both fertile and that made them even more desirable with breeders. When their first crops hit the races and included many major stakes winners, their popularity, along with their stud fees, was on the way up.

Chapter 17

Changing Times, Changing Faces

By early 1995, John Simpson's health was failing fast. He was now confined to a wheelchair. His hair had long since gone gray and he had lost that ruddy complexion that came from a life spent outdoors.

He spent his time in Florida, living in Orlando and enjoying mornings at the idyllic training center he had developed north of Orlando near the community of Sorrento. His son Jim and daughter-in-law Georgia supervised construction and operation of the training center, but the aging horseman loved to visit and talk to trainers and visitors. It was one of the few pleasures left in his life.

John Simpson's mind remained sharp even as his body weakened. He never lost the intensity and drive that led him to greatness. Despite his blindness, he could spot the impostors in the horse industry and he railed at them and the damage they did to the sport he loved.

That self-assurance and determination was an innate part of Simpson's character. He was never tentative, never hesitant to speak his mind.

Neither did he lose time lamenting his blindness or wallowing in self-pity.

Simpson's approach to his fate was evocative of William Ernest Henley, a British poet who was afflicted with tuberculosis early in life. Henley's most enduring work was "Invictus" in which he celebrates his "unconquerable soul." The second stanza reads:

In the fell clutch of circumstance
I have not winced nor cried aloud
Under the bludgeoning of chance
My head is bloody but unbowed

Henley concludes his poem with two of most memorable lines from English literature, words that surely describe John Frazer Simpson well:

I am the master of my fate
I am the captain of my soul

In August of 1995, John Simpson went to bed one night and never woke up again. Sometime during the night his heart failed. He was 75 years old.

Because he had maintained a low profile in recent decades, seldom appearing at any public functions other than the Harrisburg sale, John Simpson was forgotten by many younger harness racing fans. After all, it had been almost 26 years to the day after he had driven his final horse.

Those deeply involved in the sport, however, knew what a towering figure he had been both on and off the track. It's perhaps the greatest compliment to John Simpson to say that that his fellow horsemen admired him most.

Stanley Dancer said, "John was a great, great horseman. Maybe he was the best of them all. The way he ran his stable, the way he had his horses rigged — he was a great horseman."

Dancer had admired Simpson for decades, and now he was gone. Soon Hanover, and the entire sport, would lose two more legends that were very near and dear to Stanley Dancer's heart.

Three summers later the 30-year-old Albatross was relaxing after a breeding season in which he served 61 mares, remarkable for a stallion of his age, but the smallest book he had enjoyed in his career.

Once he passed the age of 25, Albatross served fewer than 100 mares each season, but it might be said that he served them very well, stopping them at a rate that might make a younger stallion envious. His live foal rates always were 65 percent or higher. For the four previous seasons, his book had ranged from 84-99 mares

One day in early August Albatross exhibited distress associated with colic, an all-too-frequent malady in horses. The valiant warrior fought hard, but the prognosis for a 30-year-old horse with colic and a heart murmur is grim. No one at Hanover could stand to see Albatross suffer. He was allowed the blessing of a peaceful death. Many of the hardened horsemen at the farm, who had seen so much over the years and who knew this day was inevitable, found tears in their eyes.

When the final foal by Albatross was born the following year, his total contribution to the breed came to 2,642 colts and fillies. In 2001, his offspring passed the $140 million mark in overall earnings.

Little more than a year later, it was announced that Super Bowl had joined his illustrious studmate in that greener pasture in the sky. Super Bowl had been failing physically in the last years of his life, and he was retired from breeding service at the end of the 1997 season.

There was, however, nothing wrong with Super Bowl's fertility as he achieved a 75 percent live foal rate in his final two seasons. The infirmities of age simply caught up to him, and he was allowed to live out his life as an honored pensioner.

When Super Bowl passed from the scene, he left a legacy of 2,274 foals that had earned almost $80 million in North America and a considerable amount overseas.

Perhaps it was fitting that John Simpson, Albatross, and Super Bowl all left the scene in the last half of the 1990s. The extraordinary abilities of this man and these horses had helped reshape the breed and had sustained Hanover for decades.

Less than a year after John Simpson died, a 25-year-old veterinarian with the ink still wet on her University of Pennsylvania diploma walked onto Hanover Shoe Farms. Initially, Bridgette Jablonsky was a little overwhelmed. In fact, she felt a lot overwhelmed.

After all, she was a city kid from Long Island and now she found herself working on the world's largest Standardbred farm, a facility that sprawled for miles in every direction.

"It took me two weeks just to learn where everything is," she recalls.

Dr. Bridgette Jablonsky with (from left) Russell Williams, Jim Simpson and Murray Brown

Every college graduate marches into the working world with some intimidation, but for Bridgette Jablonsky that emotion was mixed with the excitement she felt at being part of Hanover Shoe Farms.

"Anybody growing up in the Standardbred business always associated the Hanover name with greatness," she says. "Being from New York, when I think baseball I think about the Yankees. When you think Standardbreds, you think Hanover. I knew it would be an extremely prestigious position."

Jablonsky had answered an ad that Hanover ran looking for a resident veterinarian. She was interviewed by Dr. Peter Boyce and was hired.

"I knew I was lucky to get this opportunity," she says.

Boyce is an expert in equine reproduction, so he started Dr. Jablonsky to work caring for sick and injured horses on the farm.

"At the same time, Dr. Boyce took me under his wing and tried to teach me about palpating mares," she recalls. "You don't do enough palpations in vet school to get good at it."

The chance to palpate mares and to learn more about the intricacies of equine reproduction was a real reward for Jablonsky, since that had long been her primary interest in veterinary medicine.

"I like neonatalogy, caring for sick foals, but I would rather palpate mares," she said.

While her primary responsibilities were the horses' medical needs, she took every opportunity to absorb whatever reproductive knowledge she could from Dr. Boyce.

The sheer size of Hanover kept Dr. Jablonsky busy, and she realized that as the new vet on the farm she was being watched closely by the farm's veteran employees.

"They had seen such excellence in veterinary work over the years," she says. "They could pick up immediately if you were doing something well or not. It was intimidating. It felt like being back in school and having a professor looking over your shoulder. But I wasn't a student any more."

Through her professionalism and hard work, Jablonsky gradually overcame the skepticism which greets any new professional. She recognized that Hanover had a nucleus of dedicated, knowledgeable horse people who had seen virtually everything possible on a horse farm.

At the end of the 1999 breeding season, Peter Boyce left Hanover after working at the farm for more than a quarter-century. He had served as both a veterinarian and farm manager at Hanover, and his departure left a huge void. How would Hanover fill it?

One of the most obvious candidates was David Helstowski, the manager of Hanover's facility in New Jersey. But when Helstowski was asked, he demurred, and said that the most logical choice was Bridgette Jablonsky.

Like Boyce, she was a veterinarian. Like Boyce, she saw the horses as individuals, not numbers. Unlike Boyce, she was still in her 20s. And unlike him she didn't have a Y chromosome.

Putting a woman, especially one so young, in charge of the world's largest breeding farm, seemed like an enormous risk.

While some people may have seen Bridgette Jablonsky's youth as a disadvantage, she sees it as a plus.

"This job is better suited to a young person," she says. "I know that at some farms the manager's position is more of an administrative or office position, but at Hanover it is very active job. It requires a lot of time."

The blonde veterinarian, who is single, says, "I joke with Jim Simpson that he should probably pay me not to get married. Because when I get married, there is no way I can do the job for Hanover and still have time for a husband and family. This job is all-encompassing."

Dr. Jablonsky lives in a house adjacent to the breeding shed. That is both good news and bad news for her. The good news is that she is never far from her work; the bad news is also that she is never far from her work. Her work is her life.

When she talks to friends who are married and starting families, Jablonsky tells them, "I have 350 babies to raise every year."

Perhaps the greatest asset that Dr. Jablonsky brings to her position is that she not only knows each of the Hanover mares and her offspring, but she sees the individual and not the herd.

"When I palpate a mare with the hip brand number 326, I don't think about her number," she explains. "I know that I am palpating Sara Loren Road. I know the mare, and I know how her estrus cycles were earlier this season and I know how they were last year. I know that she shows heat to the teaser for three days. When she produces a follicle, it's a big one, and you'd better breed her. That follicle won't be there in two days. I can guarantee you that because I've palpated her so often."

She also knows that Sara Loren Road earned almost a million dollars on the track and that her first foal was a stakes-winning colt with a 1:51.1 record at three.

"Then you get some of these old mares like Florie's Sister, who have been around a long time," she says. "She'll show heat to the teaser for two weeks. If you started breeding when she first started showing heat, it wouldn't do any good."

When Dr. Jablonsky was serving as the farm veterinarian, she paid scant attention to the fences and facilities on the farm; she was simply too busy tending to the horses to notice such things.

That changed, however, when she became the farm manager. She began to notice that some barns or fences needed painting.

"The barns are safe and comfortable and the stalls are certainly adequate," she explains. "When you manage something, you want it to look the very best. But it would take so much money and labor to make Hanover into a showplace."

She realized that the highest priority at Hanover Shoe Farms was breeding impressive horses, not building impressive barns. As long as the facilities at Hanover were safe, even if the farm was not a showplace, the farm would make its greatest investment in horses.

When she once mentioned to Jim Simpson that some maintenance work would help beautify Hanover, he asked pointedly, "What would you rather do: paint the barns and fences, or have a million dollars or more to spend on mares at the Harrisburg sale?"

She knew what the correct answer was.

Maintenance foreman Dale Welk recalls that near the end of John Simpson's tenure, the farm stepped up the spending for physical improvements on the farm, and the impetus was an anonymous letter published in the *Hanover Evening Sun* in 1988.

"What has happened to Hanover Shoe Farms?" the writer asked. "The fences and buildings are falling down and they're not being painted."

The letter went on to detail the farm's deterioration in detail that was agonizing for Welk, who was brand new in his job.

"I read that article and I didn't sleep that night," admits Welk. "I knew that I'd have to face Mr. Simpson the next day."

Simpson summoned Welk to the main office the next morning. As Welk walked toward Simpson's office, secretaries popped their heads out of doors as if to wish the condemned man a quick and painless execution.

"I sat down in front of Mr. Simpson and he just laughed," recalls Welk. "He wanted to know who wrote the letter. He joked a while and I was in a state of shock. I didn't know if the joking would end and he'd suddenly explode, so I just sat there. Then he told me that if I thought there were some things that needed to be done on the farm that we should talk about them."

Neither Simpson nor Welk ever learned who had written the anonymous letter.

"We started building some fences and got some new equipment after that," recalls Welk. He knew that Simpson was blind and had to rely on others to alert him to maintenance needs on the farm. Simpson also had to be mindful of the fact the maintaining Hanover's 3,000 acres is a never-ending expense.

"We've done a lot since then," says Welk. "We've put vinyl siding on the stallion and foaling barns. We've changed to a cream-and-green color scheme. We built 16 miles of fence in 1999 and 2000. We're trying to spruce up the farm a bit."

Hanover had used box wire fence for many years, but began replacing it with four-board fences painted white. Welk feels that wire fences can lead to puncture wounds easily if any of the strands of wire work loose.

At one time the farm whitewashed its fences instead of painting them, but when whitewash was deemed hazardous to the people working with it, Hanover opted for the traditional white paint.

"We can get six to eight years out of a painting job," says Welk, "and the fence is still white after all that time."

Neither Lawrence Sheppard nor John Simpson ever wanted to run the prettiest horse farm in the world; just the best horse farm.

Chapter 18

Replenishing The Pacing Ranks

With the changing times came changing stallions. Ball And Chain, one of the richest sons of Albatross, joined the Hanover stallion roster at the end of 1996. A year later the farm grabbed the first prominent son of Artsplace to enter the stud when it secured the services of Arturo. This consistent colt had pocketed almost $1.3 million in two seasons at the racing wars and breeders found him to be an irresistible bargain at a $4,000 fee.

Cam's Card Shark achieved success from the moment his first crop made it to the races. In 1999 he had a pair of heat winners in the Little Brown Jug in sons Royalflush Hanover and Mystical Shark. The following season he had the champion juvenile Bettor's Delight, winner of the Breeders Crown and Governor's Cup.

In 1997, just a few weeks prior to the Harrisburg sale, a gelded son of Western Hanover named Western Dreamer won the Messenger Stake, giving him the Triple Crown for pacers. It was a wonderful boost for his sire's career.

It also boosted the sale potential for the yearlings that Hanover had to sell by Western Hanover that fall. The Westerns were a nice lot, but there was one who stood out over the others. He was so exceptional that he would have stood out in any year, in any consignment.

There are many perfectly acceptable individuals in every yearling sale that become nice racehorses. In every sale, there are also a few exceptional individuals that draw crowds of admiring horsemen.

Rarely, however, is there a yearling that rises far above his contemporaries in conformation and that intangible quality of presence. In 1997, Hanover Shoe Farms had such a colt in Dead Eye Hanover.

He was a son of Western Hanover and the first foal from the Coal Harbor mare Daisy Harbor. Coal Harbor is not a name usually found in uptown pedigrees. He was a competitive Grand Circuit type during his years on the track, but as a stallion in Ontario he had little opportunity to prove his mettle.

His daughter Daisy Harbor was well remembered by horsemen. When they saw her son, they stopped in their tracks and let their eye savor every aspect of this exceptional individual. Dead Eye Hanover was a showstopper.

Many owners and trainers coveted the colt, and anyone who wanted to join in the bidding would need a strong seat belt and an even stronger checking account. The bidding was sure to be fast and furious.

Dead Eye Hanover walked into the sales ring and the onlookers lined the walls of the Pennsylvania Farm Show Arena, as often happens when a special horse sells. The pedigree reader touched on the highlights of the colt's pedigree while the colt stood majestically in the ring.

Then the bidding exploded. As expected, it shot past $100,000 quickly and headed for $200,000. It passed that mark and kept going. It didn't stop until a bid of $250,000 discouraged all others.

The winning bidder was Bob Glazer of Pepper Pike, Ohio. Doing business under the name of Peter Pan Stable, Glazer had become a major player in the sport during the 1990s, using a variety of trainers to condition his extensive array of colts and raceway stock.

Glazer's father Sam was a successful businessman, perfecting and then marketing the popular Mr. Coffee appliance that was found in millions of American homes and offices. He profited handsomely when he sold the business. Son Bob cultivated an interest in harness racing while in college, and began building his own racing stable when he was still in his 20s.

Continuing his stable policy, Glazer gave Dead Eye Hanover a new name, selecting The Panderosa as a play on the name of the western ranch (The Ponderosa) featured in the TV series *Bonanza*.

The Panderosa didn't make his racing debut as a two-year-old until early August, but he quickly demonstrated that his beauty was far more than skin deep. He was a high-priced baby who lived up to — and exceeded — expectations.

The Panderosa won in 1:51.3 at Lexington in his fifth purse start as a juvenile and was just beaten a nose by Island Fantasy in the $600,000 Governor's Cup at Garden State in late November.

Bob Glazer had every reason to be optimistic about The Panderosa's chances as a three-year-old, but he was experienced enough to understand that success as a two-year-old is no guarantee of the same as a sophomore. In this case, however, The Panderosa turned promise into performance.

In late June, the son of Western Hanover dazzled racing aficionados in Ontario when he swept the $1 million North America Cup with a 1:49.4 effort that was really no effort at all.

The Panderosa

He completely dominated the Meadowlands Pace, winning from post 10 in 1:49.3 despite racing outside the entire mile. Now pundits were beginning to talk of The Panderosa as one of the greatest ever, a colt worthy of discussion in the same breath with Bret Hanover, Niatross, and Albatross. They anxiously waited to see what further triumphs would come his way, and the folks from Hanover hoped that he would come their way when his racing days were done.

Everything had gone smoothly in the first half of the season for The Panderosa, but thereafter the 1999 season was a bumpy ride.

On Hambletonian Day in 1999, many people wanted to know just what The Panderosa could do on a hot afternoon in a division of the Oliver Wendell Holmes at the Meadowlands. The large crowd bet him down to 1-5, and fans were eager to see the superstar buzz a mile well below 1:50.

Driver John Campbell eased the colt away from the gate and let the field settle down. The Panderosa was gliding around the first turn. Suddenly he broke stride. Broke stride? That was totally out of character for a colt that had been perfect to that point in the season.

As the high-powered field of pacers rocketed down the backstretch, The Panderosa cantered in the middle of the track, falling hopelessly behind the pack.

Campbell knew it was futile to give chase and wisely allowed The Panderosa to finish the mile on his own.

That race was the beginning of a frustrating period that saw the colt break stride in the Cane Pace at Freehold and in the Little Brown Jug at Delaware. The Western Hanover colt rebounded to win impressively at The Red Mile, but he performed poorly in his final start in the Breeders Crown at Mohawk Raceway.

In October of 1999, owner Bob Glazer and his mother had dinner with Jim Simpson and Murray Brown. Earlier in the year, Hanover had been interested in The Panderosa as a stallion, but the $10 million price tag hanging from his halter was a bit too dear. Now the situation had changed considerably. One thing that hadn't altered was Hanover's interest in standing the horse. Glazer, too, was interested in having the horse at Hanover.

Over dinner they talked terms and negotiated on a few minor points. An agreement was reached. Glazer would retain full ownership in The Panderosa, but the horse was headed for Hanover. The farm's compensation would come in the form of breeding rights.

Glazer set the stud fee at $10,000. Murray Brown's sense of the market told him that was wrong. He even thought that $7,500 was too high.

"That could really hurt this horse," he told Glazer. "He isn't going to get the quality of mares or the number of mares he ordinarily would if you had priced him reasonably."

The phone at Hanover began ringing off the hook as breeders requested bookings to the prize pacer. Even his late season stumbles hadn't demitted the demand for his services, and the $10,000 stud fee was deemed a small price to pay by commercial breeders.

"I've never been more wrong," admitted Brown in short order.

The Panderosa received a bevy of 184 broodmares in his first book, and they were extraordinary by any standard.

The 2000 racing season was marked by the spectacular success of Gallo Blue Chip, a plain bay pacer who will never win any beauty contests. That mattered little since he won over $2.4 million in 2000 taking on all comers in his class.

Gallo Blue Chip was a gelding, however, and while his accomplishments made headlines throughout the year, he would be of value to the sport only on the track. Breeders look for horses with potential to contribute after their racing days are done and that year the two pacers breeders looked at most intently were Western Ideal and Dragon Again.

Both horses had been foaled in 1995 and had remarkable backgrounds.

Dragon Again was a son of Dragon's Lair, a colt sold by Hanover as a yearling under the name Santee Hanover. He was from the first crop by Tyler B, the stallion John Simpson secured when Niatross and Storm Damage were unavailable. Less than a year after being hammered down at auction, Dragon's Lair scored one of the sport's most memorable upsets when he defeated Nihilator in the Breeders Crown.

Dragon Again, who retired from pacing with earnings of $2,343,428.

Dragon Again won in 1:52.3 or faster in each of the four seasons he raced. He took his juvenile mark in 1997 at Lexington, and finished third in the Breeders Crown a few weeks later.

During his sophomore season Dragon Again added $793,803 to his bankroll while racing against the best. He was third in the Meadowlands Pace and fourth in the North America Cup.

Normally when a colt goes through 33 grueling starts in his first two years of racing, just about all the juice has been squeezed from him. Dragon Again defied that belief as he simply got better with age. As a four-year-old he dropped his mark to 1:49.1 and pocketed almost a half-million dollars in 13 starts. He won eight races, and was never worse than third.

Dragon Again saved his best year for his last year on the track. As a five-year-old he continued to crisscross North America, winning on every size track against the best pacers in training. For his labors, owner Ed Mullinax gained $891,740 and the pacers got a new record of 1:48.3.

He hung up his hobbles with earnings of $2,343,428. He had finished on the board in 60 of his 70 lifetime starts.

Western Ideal showed how gifted he was as a two-year-old when he won in 1:54.3f, but then he sat out the next season with an injury. Owner George Segal knew how much potential this pacer had and he was willing to wait for him. Returning to the races as a four-year-old, the son of Western Hanover won four of his 22 starts and $177,970.

Western Ideal, another successful pacer, who battled it out on the track with Dragon Again

Segal's patience was fully rewarded during the 2000 season when Western Ideal was the bully in the ranks of the aged pacers. He won 10 of 14 starts, finished second three times, and took home $1,220,000 in purse money. He won in a nifty 1:48 when he captured the Breeders Crown in late July.

Western Ideal and Dragon Again faced off several times during the season, and Dragon Again whipped his foe twice in July, but thereafter Western Ideal had the upper hand every time they met.

Jim Simpson watched the winnings of this pair of pacers pile up week after week and he began thinking that Hanover just might find a stall for one of them in the stallion barn. It helped, of course, that Hanover had a close relationship with the owners of both superstars — George Segal, the owner of Western Ideal, and Ed Mullinax, owner of Dragon Again.

But which one would make the best stallion? It was a question no one could answer with certainty. The situation was reminiscent of the plight facing Lawrence

Sheppard almost a half-century earlier when Tar Heel and Solicitor went up for auction as part of the W.N. Reynolds dispersal at Harrisburg.

Sheppard bought both. The Hanover team of 2000 took a similar approach to Western Ideal and Dragon Again. They welcomed both into the Hanover fold.

Western Ideal was ensconced at the New Jersey facility at a fee of $10,000 and his book filled quickly. Dragon Again moved into the historic stud barn in Pennsylvania at a $5,000 fee.

Tar Heel left an indelible imprint on the breed while Solicitor accomplished little. What will be the legacy of Western Ideal and Dragon Again? It's impossible to say, but in the year 2000 they were the best two pacing stallions in training and Hanover had to have them.

While Lawrence Sheppard simply bought Tar Heel and Solicitor, outright ownership of stallions is seldom wise for breeding farms today, so both Western Ideal and Dragon Again were syndicated with interests being sold to major breeders. Syndicated stallions were virtually unknown in 1951 when Sheppard bought the two big guns in the Reynolds dispersal.

Each stallion syndication is unique, depending on the circumstances. For example, the approach taken on Western Ideal was far different than that used with Dragon Again. George Segal's Brittany Farms owned Western Ideal when he retired and then entered the stud under the ownership of Brittany, Hanover, and Perretti Farms. Each partner, of course, has a large quantity of superior mares to send to the young stallion.

"George didn't want to syndicate Western Ideal until he had made it as a stallion, and George is in a position to do that," says Jim Simpson. "It was the same way with Western Hanover. George has proven to have the Midas touch."

Simpson noted that Segal initially sold a limited number of shares in Western Hanover at $50,000 per share and by the time 2001 dawned, those shares were selling for $240,000.

Dragon Again raced under the ownership of auto dealer Ed Mullinax, and Simpson took on the responsibility of selecting breeders to be offered shares.

That meant phone calls to breeders across North America with the goal of acquiring about 20 investors with good mares that fit to Dragon Again.

Stallion syndication in the Standardbred industry began in earnest in 1957. John R. Gaines, a young man full of enthusiasm for horse breeding, took note of the success of Demon Hanover, the trotter that had eluded Lawrence Sheppard a decade earlier. Demon now stood at Gay Acres Farm in Wooster, Ohio.

The pipe-smoking lawyer Bob Critchfield, a devotee of trotters with a small but select band of broodmares, owned Gay Acres. Gaines reasoned that if

Demon Hanover were exposed to a larger book of quality mares, he might well dominate the future of trotting.

Gaines approached Critichfield and offered him $505,000 for Demon Hanover, adding that he intended to sell shares in the horse to leading breeders.

Critchfield puffed on his pipe. He'd had other offers for Demon Hanover, but this was a bit different and he asked with bemused curiosity, "What's that extra $5,000 for?"

"Delvin Miller sold Adios for $500,000 and I want to top that price," explained Gaines.

Critchfield shook his head and said, "No, Delvin Miller is a friend of mine, and I won't do that. Let's make the price $500,000 even."

Gaines then enlisted the support of the some of the prominent breeders in harness racing and moved Demon Hanover to Walnut Hall Farm in Kentucky. After one season in the stud, Demon Hanover died suddenly, casting a pall on the practice of syndicating stallions.

When stallion syndication regained popularity in the 1960s, Hanover wasn't an avid player. Sheppard and later Simpson preferred to control the Hanover stallions. Typical was the deal in which Hanover had acquired one-third of Adios. The other partners were Max Hempt and Delvin Miller.

Hanover gained control of its stallions and shared ownership with a partner or two at most. In all cases, Lawrence Sheppard or John Simpson called the shots.

The owners of the best stallion prospects usually were delighted with this arrangement, knowing that a stallion could have no better opportunity than a stall at Hanover. Unlike other farms which acquired stallions almost indiscriminately and left them to fend for themselves in attracting mares, Hanover chose its stallions carefully and then supported them wholeheartedly.

The rising value of stallion prospects forced Hanover to alter its policies. When syndications regularly began to exceed $1 million, it became essential — and even desirable — to bring in a broader base of breeders to support a young stallion.

"You need the support of other good breeders with a young stallion," says Jim Simpson. "When you go into second and third-year doldrums before a stallion's offspring are on the track, you need support. Every stallion without exception has lower numbers or lower quality in his books in the second and third seasons."

Enlisting the support of other breeders also helps spread the cost and the risk associated in syndicating a stallion, but it's the broodmares that they can send to a stallion that makes them indispensable, Simpson points out.

"We don't want people who simply want to invest in a stallion share without sending mares," says Simpson. "Breeders with good mares — that's our mantra."

Just as Jim Simpson makes phone calls to potential syndicate members with Dragon Again, he's often on the receiving end of phone calls from syndicators anxious to have Hanover on board to support a young stallion.

The Hanover team listens with an open mind, weighing the ability of the individual, his fertility, and the sires stakes program to which his foals will be eligible. In the end, however, there is one overriding consideration.

"Commercial viability," says Simpson. "It's as simple as that. We have to determine if his offspring will have appeal in the sales ring."

Simpson points out that even if a stallion's offspring will have commercial appeal, if the shares are priced too high, it's not sound business to buy a share. In such cases Hanover may want to breed to the stallion by simply paying the stud fee. That involves a one-year commitment rather than the more substantial investment of a syndication share.

In 2001, Hanover Shoe Farms serves as the syndicate manager for 11 stallions and has agreements to stand No Nukes and The Panderosa. Things have changed a lot since Dillon Axworthy was the first Hanover stallion.

The person responsible for managing the syndicates and much of the business end of the farm operation is Jim Harvey, the farm's corresponding officer and manager of Information Systems. He is an important cog in the Hanover operations and his roots go back many decades.

Harvey's father Gene came to work as a private pilot for Lawrence Sheppard in 1965 when Jim was 14 years old. While the father was high in the clouds, young Jim was learning harness racing from the ground up, cleaning stalls in his free time from school.

The busiest time of the year for Gene Harvey was each autumn when the Hanover plane would be pressed into service to ferry horsemen to Hanover so that they could appraise the yearlings in action at the Hanover fairgrounds. He also flew Sheppard and Simpson wherever they needed to go, and assisted with record keeping in the office.

His studies at Temple University didn't hold much fascination for young Jim Harvey, so he spent a year rubbing horses for John Simpson's stable. He soon found himself coming back to the farm where he helped superintendent Hal Jones when teasing broodmares. He moved to JD's Twin Springs Farm and later managed Lana Lobell Farm's operation in Hanover.

In 1985 the position of corresponding officer at Hanover Shoe Farms opened and Jim Harvey learned about the position from his father. He wasn't sure that John Simpson would be willing to take him back on the payroll, but the headman welcomed him back.

"Mr. Simpson was a tough man," says Harvey. "If you didn't know an answer, you'd better tell him you didn't know because you couldn't fool him. Or tell him that you'd get him an answer quick. He was demanding, but his position required that."

Harvey was immediately thrust into an avalanche of record-keeping responsibilities at Hanover and he could see that computers were badly needed in the office. His father had introduced some basic computerization to Hanover in the past, but it was time to move the office into the modern era.

"Everything was being done by hand, and nothing was very efficient," he says. "When we first starting looking around for programs on farm management, there wasn't anything on the market that would suit our needs. We had over 1,200 head of horses on the farm at one time and none of the existing programs would accommodate that many horses."

So Harvey, along with Jim Simpson, started to learn about computer programming and developing databases. They designed the applications that the farm currently uses to track all the activity on the farm.

For example, Harvey can tell you that 28,020 medical services were performed on horses in 2000. He can tell you that 1,554 mares were bred that year and that over 1,700 were bred the following year.

From 1989 through mid-2001, Hanover had collected $26,851,000 in service fees. During that same period, 4,235 foals were born at Hanover.

Much of Jim Harvey's time is spent tending to the matters of the syndicated stallions at Hanover. There are, for example, 50 shareholders in Lindy Lane, 39 in Donerail, 36 in Arturo, 33 in Cam's Card Shark, and others in other Hanover stallions.

Harvey has seen the size of syndicate agreements grow as the lawyers who draw up such documents seek to cover a greater number of contingencies.

"At first we thought that the more general you could make an agreement, the better off you were because you could interpret it better," says Harvey. "We have a template here in our records that we use as a base and then add things depending on the owner of the horse."

At one time, most stallions were syndicated into 40 or perhaps 50 shares, but Harvey says that 120 shares are now a more common number.

"It seems that Tyler B was the first horse to be syndicated into more shares," says Harvey. "It was explained to me that Delvin Miller wanted more people to get into the stallion and that way the shares wouldn't be so costly. At the time, I wondered how I was ever going to keep track of 100 shares, but we just wrote another application."

When Hanover stands a stallion, its reputation for supporting it is such that some breeders almost automatically jump on board. The imprimatur of Hanover Shoe Farms is sufficient for others to invest their money, too, so many of the same names crop up among the shareholders in Hanover stallions.

Managing the syndicates involves collecting stud fees and Harvey spends much of his time working on behalf of the syndicates. The farm has always maintained a businesslike approach to paying its bills and getting its customers to pay their bills.

"It's not a business if you're not collecting the money," says Harvey simply.

When a mare's due date arrives, Hanover sends an invoice for the stud fee, realizing that the mare may not have foaled yet. The stud fee is payable when the mare has a live foal, and penalties for late payment don't begin until 30 days after the actual foaling date.

"Very few customers have any problem with our system," says Harvey. "We expect to be paid. Hanover has a reputation for collecting. There aren't too many people who get away without paying a service fee."

If a foal dies, the stud fee is waived if the owner of the broodmare provides Hanover with a statement from a veterinarian.

"We do that because we have a fiduciary responsibility to the syndicate," says Harvey. "We usually don't have any problems in this area. I remember billing one guy for six months and then he told me his foal died. We asked for a vet statement, and we found out that the foal was four months old when it died. So he eventually paid the stud fee."

John Simpson often summed up Hanover's approach to business by saying, "Fast pay makes fast friends." It's a philosophy that has endured at Hanover. The folks at Hanover like fast pay almost as much as they like fast horses.

Chapter 19

A New Look At The Ladies

In the late summer of 1997, Jim Simpson was elected president of Hanover Shoe Farms. Russell Williams was elected as president of the Standardbred Horse Sale Co., and remained as a vice-president of Hanover. Paul Spears was elevated to the position of Hanover's chairman of the board.

If Jim Simpson learned one thing from his father, it was the importance of maintaining Hanover's extraordinary broodmare band.

"From the beginning of this farm, broodmares have been the emphasis," Simpson stresses. "We have tried to acquire as many high-quality mares as possible. If the farm wants to stay successful, our philosophy will have to stay that way."

Simpson knows that most stallions are failures or disappointments at best, but if a farm has enough depth and strength in its broodmare band it can overcome such failures.

Earlier in the 1990s, Paul Spears had begun an ambitious program of upgrading the broodmare band, giving emphasis to mares with earnings in excess of $100,000.

"We had all these old mares from old families," says Spears. "We had a lot of mares with time trial records. Nobody wanted to buy yearlings from those mares."

Ironically, the farm's traditional emphasis on broodmares had caused both Sheppard and Simpson to fall victim to sentimentality.

Looking back on how his father differed from Lawrence Sheppard, Jim Simpson says, "I think Mr. Sheppard was a little more sentimental toward certain female families. I can remember some strong discussions — I wouldn't call them arguments — about culling mares from the family. It's not that Mr. Sheppard was opposed to culling mares, but he and Dad would get into a fuss about a certain individual. And Mr. Sheppard would always win."

That's as it should be, of course. Horses were far more than just a business to him. Sheppard tossed objectivity out the window when it came to horses like

Jim Simpson, the current president of Hanover Shoe Farms

Dean Hanover and the descendents of Miss Bertha Dillon.

Decades later in an interview in *Hoof Beats*, when John Simpson was asked what his greatest mistake in running Hanover, he paused for a long time. Then he said, "Well, I've gotten carried away with some fillies and mares out of certain female lines. I shouldn't have kept them around as long as I did. So I'd say my biggest mistake has been not culling more vigorously."

While the emphasis on broodmares remains, the type of broodmares found on the pages of the Hanover yearling catalog today are quite different than in the era of John Simpson or Lawrence Sheppard.

In the formative years, Sheppard built a broodmare band by keeping fillies from his best broodmares. He knew that a well-bred mare was like an annuity that paid off year after year when her offspring went to auction.

True, Sheppard was sentimental, but he could afford to be biased about the daughters and granddaughters of Miss Bertha Dillon. Such mares made up a disproportionate part of the Hanover broodmare band in the early decades.

Each year Sheppard and his closest advisors looked over the farm's yearling fillies to see which ones would be more valuable as future broodmares than as sale yearlings.

These fillies were then placed in training in hopes that they would further the accomplishments of their family, but no one ever lost sight of the fact that their real purpose was to join the Hanover broodmare band and follow the Biblical admonition to "be fruitful and multiply."

Thus during the 1950s and 1960s John Simpson trained countless fillies by stallions like Hoot Mon and Tar Heel, for example, that were retained by Hanover. Some of them became stakes winners; Romola Hanover and Brenna Hanover are two examples of Tar Heel fillies that Simpson trained and raced.

Romola Hanover is a mare that Dale Welk remembers fondly not only for the accomplishments of her offspring, but because she was so delightful to be around.

"She's one real nice one that sticks out in my mind," says Welk, who worked with the horses before moving into a maintenance role.

Hanover Shoe Farms rose to fame, it will be remembered, on the contributions of Miss Bertha Dillon, who came from a family of hot-tempered females, and Dale Welk says Hanover continues to have a few mares like that.

"I can name lots of mares who weren't so nice," says Welk. "Mitzy Hanover [by Tar Heel] was out to get you. She put a few people in the hospital. In recent years we've had Eager Min who is so tough she's kept by herself. Hilary Hanover was tough, and so was Angela D."

The great writer and pedigree expert Jim Harrison notes that Sheppard believed in the basics of breeding, knowing that Tar Heel on Adios mares was a money-making cross and the same was true with the Hoot Mon mares sent to Star's Pride.

"Just keep saving those Hoot Mon mares and we'll be all right," Sheppard once advised his assistant Harrison.

Unless a filly showed extraordinary talent, she was given only a perfunctory campaign. Many were lightly raced and then given a record in a time trial to demonstrate that she did have some speed. Simpson trained many sour-tempered Tar Heel fillies who were given time trial records below 2:00, then a badge of honor, and sent to the broodmare ranks with earnings of a few thousand dollars.

The practice of retaining fillies was once commonplace among major breeders. In this way they could keep select fillies without the cost of acquiring them at auction.

It was, however, a tradition that yearling buyers frowned on.

Murray Brown never warmed up to that policy because he could see what a negative impact it had on the fillies that Hanover sold. They were clearly perceived as the farm's second string.

"Customers don't like it when farms keep fillies," admits Jim Simpson, echoing a long-held complaint in the breeding business. "When we came up with a good filly in the racing stable, some people didn't like it much. There's a feeling that breeding farms that keep and race fillies are in competition with their customers. And there's some truth to that."

Another detrimental effect of such a policy is that it doesn't introduce new blood and new maternal families into the broodmare band. All the buyers of

Hanover yearlings were seeing were successive generations from the farm's foundation mares.

"Our consignments got stale," admits Murray Brown.

The farm's short-lived practice of "pairing" fillies is also history.

"Pairing the fillies removed the stigma attached to retaining fillies," says Brown.

"Any buyer could have any Hanover yearling filly under the pairs concept, and it still allowed the farm to keep seven or eight each year. That worked out great for a while and then the filly market went kaput."

The preferences of yearling buyers had changed by the 1990s and the management team realized that Hanover had to change to meet its customers' demands. Buyers preferred yearlings from mares that had more than just a fancy pedigree; they would pay the biggest bucks for yearlings from mares that were outstanding on the track, too.

Today all the fillies bred each year by Hanover are sold at auction. Simpson feels that it makes the job of selling yearlings far easier if Hanover can tell its customers, "There they are . . . the whole crop. They're all for sale. You pick the best ones.

"That allows us to come back and pick off fillies and mares when they are through racing," he continues. "They then have the records that we want. Sometimes we buy them without records."

John Simpson used his extensive array of contacts to buy exceptional race mares privately, but the new team opted to make more purchases at public auction.

So each year after the yearling sessions of the Standardbred Horse Sale in Harrisburg are completed, the parade of broodmares begins and that is when you'll find Jim Simpson, Russell Williams, Paul Spears, and their team reversing roles and buying instead of selling.

"Hanover Shoe Farms made the broodmare market from 1991 on," says Paul Spears. "We spent a lot of money at Harrisburg. We were looking for mares with proven racing performance."

"We've been pretty high-profile at the Harrisburg sale," agrees Simpson. "One major reason is that the yearling sale is over, and we know what our income from that is. We know where we stand financially. The broodmare offerings at Harrisburg have increased in quality and quantity, so it's not a bad place to shop."

Long before the sale is held, Murray Brown has scanned the broodmares entered and selects those that he thinks merit review by others. Many are called, but few are chosen. Dr. Jablonsky, Jim Simpson, Russell Williams, and Paul Spears inspect the mares and determine a target price for those that pass muster.

It didn't take Bridgette Jablonsky long to pick up the Hanover credo on broodmares.

"Mares make your farm; stallions don't," she says. "It was a tremendous asset to have Super Bowl and Albatross come along in the same year, but year after year, it is the mares that make a breeding farm."

Knowing the importance of broodmares, the final days of the Harrisburg sale are among the most enjoyable for the lady often called "Dr. J."

John Simpson Sr. on the track with Romola Hanover

"Those days are perhaps the two most important days of the year," says Jablonsky. "You have to pick the mares right. They'll be producing our future yearlings."

Hanover purchased over 50 mares for $100,000 or more in the 1990s, many of them at Harrisburg.

In 1995, the farm paid $250,000 for Beat The Wheel, then the fastest trotter ever in a race. You wonder what Lawrence Sheppard would have thought of spending twice as much on one broodmare as he'd spent for Tar Heel, but Beat The Wheel quickly rewarded Hanover. She was bred to Valley Victory the following year and had a colt named Berndt Hanover who was the sport's highest-priced yearling in 1998 at $400,000.

In 1998, Hanover bought Almost An Angel for $270,000, Divine Victory for $220,000, and Clover Hanover for $200,000. The following year at Harrisburg the big-ticket broodmares for Hanover were Triplet Hanover at $250,000 and Panned Out at $210,000.

In 2000, the farm's most expensive purchases were Cathedra at $270,000 and Water Star at $220,000.

The most expensive mares aren't always the best producers. Two queens of the Hanover broodmare band, Rich N Elegant at $12,000 and Daisy Harbor at $25,000, were obviously bargains.

"What we buy at Harrisburg in broodmares is about half of the total mares we acquire annually," says Simpson. "The other half of the mares are purchased privately." Brown agrees that the farm's current policy of acquiring mares when their racing days are done is the best method he's seen in his three decades there.

"There are some mares where you may overlook a weaker pedigree because of what a mare did on the track," says Murray Brown, citing Cami Whitestocking p, 4, 1:50.3 ($573,388) as an example. "She had great name recognition among the buyers."

When acquiring a mare privately, Hanover and other breeding farms have traditionally given credit to sellers on Hanover yearlings. That is, if a mare is valued at $100,000, the buyer might be happy to accept $50,000 in cash and $50,000 in credit on a Hanover yearling.

"Credit is not used as much as people probably think," says Simpson. "Everyone sees credit as a big advantage to the breeding farm. It's certainly not a disadvantage, but it's probably not what it is cracked up to be. When we give credit for a sale, it's money that we don't receive. It's nice to know that the $50,000 credit has to be spent on our yearlings, but I don't think that we can buy customers that way."

Murray Brown adds that the credit factor at yearling sales is much exaggerated.

"I think the total outstanding credit on Hanover yearlings isn't nearly as much as what people think," he says. "I would guess we go into each sale season with about $250,000 credit outstanding."

Hanover Shoe Farms maintains a broodmare band of approximately 400 mares. That number ebbs and flows with sales and purchases, retirements and deaths. It's a number that Jim Simpson is quite comfortable with.

Whether mares are acquired at public auction or privately, the Hanover team wants to know the physical traits of the individual they're buying because the yearlings will so often reflect the flaws of the mother.

In his era, John Simpson hated fillies that hit their knees as broodmare candidates, but the gait of harness horses has improved dramatically and Jim Simpson now finds conformation flaws as his greatest hang-ups.

"I don't like a calf-kneed mare," says Simpson, referring to a defect in which the front legs are bowed backwards, thus putting undue strain on the tendons. "That breeds on. It's like those horses are always going uphill.

"I remember that my father liked length in a mare, trotter or pacer," continues Simpson. "He also wanted a good-sized mare. Dad also wanted to see a filly display some natural speed in some part of the mile. It might only be an eighth of a mile, but he wanted to see a filly demonstrate some speed. That's true today, too."

Another change from bygone days is that the Hanover broodmares are mated to a variety of stallions in their reproductive careers. Years ago the farm's Adios mares seldom saw a stallion other than Tar Heel. The Hoot Mon mares invariably went to Star's Pride. Tar Heel and Bret Hanover mares usually went to Albatross year after year. Some mares were practically betrothed for life to one stallion.

For example, Kaola Hanover, a 1949 filly by Nibble Hanover, had 14 foals and all but one were sired by Tar Heel. That one exception was the Adios filly Kitten Hanover, which was retained by the farm for breeding purposes. Kitten Hanover had 16 foals, and all but one was by Tar Heel.

In the Shepherd-Simpson era, Hanover bred almost exclusively to its own stallions. When you saw the Hanover yearling consignment, you were seeing a reflection of the horses standing in the stallion barn at Hanover.

Booking the Hanover mares was much simpler in that era because there was no concern about gaining access to stallions, and many of the matings were just rubber stamped from the previous year.

What the consignment had in quality, it lacked in variety. Buyers eventually got bored seeing the same crosses year after year.

"It was a long time after I came to Hanover in 1967 before we ever bred a single mare to an outside stallion," recalls Brown. "There was a question of why should we send our mares to other stallions and help our competition. The first horse I recall Hanover breeding to that we didn't stand or have an interest in was Meadow Skipper."

"Those days are gone," explains Jim Simpson. "We switch sires as much as possible. We shuffle the deck. It appears that buyers like that. They want the unknown. If a mare hasn't produced a good performer by Sierra Kosmos, she might produce one by Lindy Lane.

"My father really started that by buying shares in outside stallions," continues Simpson. "In 2001, our mares were booked to over 40 different stallions.

It gives the consignment more variety. It gives people different sires stakes programs in our consignment."

Each year in December, the Hanover team sets aside virtually all other tasks and concentrates on some of the most important decisions of the year. They determine which mares will be booked to which stallions.

It is a process that should involve a crystal ball and ouija board because they are attempting to project how a mating planned in late 2001 will pay off when

Beat The Wheel at Meadowlands; she is the dam of Berndt Hanover, the highest-priced yearling in harness racing in 1998

the resultant foal walks into the sale ring in 2004. An even greater test will be when the foal races in 2005 and 2006.

"It's precision guesswork," says Simpson with a knowing laugh. The Hanover team comes to the meeting not with a crystal ball, but with notebooks and data on each mare and her offspring. Much of the preliminary work is done by Murray Brown and Bridgette Jablonsky.

The ultimate decisions are batted about by Simpson, Williams, Spears, Jim Harvey, and Ralph Lemmon.

"Murray makes his selections on marketability and how the foal might sell while Dr. Jablonsky concentrates on the physical characteristics of the mare and stallion," says Simpson.

Many other factors must be weighed. For example, a mare that has proven in the past to be a problem breeder is more likely to kept on the farm under Jablonsky's watchful eye instead of being shipped to New York where she may have to remain away from Hanover for a few months.

Disagreements in stallion selection invariably arise as the list of more than 400 mares is reviewed. These differences are always settled amicably, says Simpson, by yielding to someone with strong feelings. That person may have to yield on a later decision.

"Shuffling the deck" yielded a nice profit to the farm when tried with one stalwart member of its broodmare band.

"I remember the mare Ginger Belle," says Murray Brown, referring to the classy Speedy Crown stakes filly from the early 1980s. "She was booked every year to Super Bowl and the foals raced reasonably well. The foals were a bit small, but they would often sell in the $30,000 to $40,000 range."

One year Brown decided that since variety is the spice of life and ginger is a spice, she needed a new consort.

"Why don't we breed her to Sierra Kosmos?" he asked at the mating meeting. "What have we got to lose?"

Around the room, there were some murmurs of "Why would we do that?" but ultimately the others concurred. Ginger Belle dutifully got in foal and delivered a bay filly on April 27, 1997. After raising a dozen Super Bowls, Ginger Belle had a foal by a different sire, and what a beauty she was. When she sashayed into the sale ring as a yearling, the bidding reached $110,000.

In Ginger Belle's case, shuffling the deck left Hanover holding a queen.

Murray Brown says, "People want something new. I can't understand why buyers would give a significant bonus to breeding a mare to a stallion other than the one she's achieved success with. But they will. Just as buyers will overpay on first-crop stallions relative to the proven sires. You just scratch your head about it."

In the early 1990s, the directors of the U.S. Trotting Association, assembled at their annual meeting in Columbus, Ohio, approved rules allowing for the transport of fresh semen. It was a step that would revolutionize the procedures for breeding mares, allowing owners to save money and to avoid risks inherent in shipping mares and foals.

Traditionally, a mare went to the stallion. If Hanover booked mares to stallions in Kentucky, the mares — and often their foals — were loaded on vans and taken to the Bluegrass for the breeding season. Transporting horses is not only expensive, but also fraught with the potential for injury. Introducing a new mare and foal into an established horse herd also increases the potential for spreading disease.

It was done much the same way in the Thoroughbred business, but there was a noteworthy difference: Standardbreds were permitted to use artificial insemination in addition to live cover.

Once methods of preserving semen were perfected, it simply made sense to transport the semen from the stallion to the mare. It was certainly far less expensive and risky. Many small breeders felt, however, that the major breeding farms would do everything in their power to block approval of semen transport. The farms with stallions, small breeders felt, wanted the revenue that went along with boarding mares during the breeding season.

That proved not to be true. Farms have long contended that they didn't make money boarding horses, only by selling yearlings and stallion services. Boarding was labor intensive and the cost of farm labor is steadily increasing.

When semen transport went into effect, it proved to be a godsend for both large and small breeders. Neither would ever want to go back to the days when mares had to be shipped to distant farms.

"We love it," says Jim Simpson, referring to transported semen. "Conception rates are pretty close to having mares right here on the farm. If you get the semen in the mare within 24 hours, it's almost like being on the farm."

Hanover developed a Semen Ordering System (SOS) to better serve its customers. Stallions at Hanover are bred starting at 1 p.m. on Monday, Wednesday, Friday, and Saturday. A remote customer in Kentucky or Illinois can call before 11 a.m. that same day and receive semen for his broodmare the next day through an express delivery service.

Hanover's stallion station in New Jersey is a special situation because a foal conceived by semen shipped outside the state is not eligible to the New Jersey Sires Stakes. Therefore, semen must be picked up within the borders of the Garden State.

While New Jersey was certainly the sport's Mecca in the last two decades of the 20th century, its dominance was challenged when slot machines at tracks in Ontario began fueling purse increases as the calendar page turned to 2000.

Hanover was quick to seize the day. The farm began purchasing shares in Ontario-based stallions and began patronizing other stallions in that province to stay ahead of the game. Semen transport has made it much easier for American breeders to supply the stock to race in Ontario-sired events.

"We're breeding 60 to 70 mares in Canada in 2001 and they are never going to leave this farm," says Simpson. "That eliminates the expense of shipping those mares to Canada and boarding them somewhere and leaving our acreage fallow."

With the expansion of transported semen, the number of mares shipping to Hanover to be bred has dropped dramatically, as has the number of outside-owned mares boarded there. In any year, perhaps only 50 to 75 non-farm mares are boarded at Hanover.

Board rates in 2001 were $15 daily for broodmares, weanlings, and yearlings. If a mare had a suckling foal at her side, an extra two dollars was assessed. Those rates increased only modestly during the previous decade; boarding fees are not a significant source of income for the farm.

Ginger Belle and Sonny Dancer

"For those year-round boarders, our personnel treat them the same as our own mares, and, in fact, the farm crew barely knows the difference between the farm mares and those owned outside," says Simpson.

If a mare still has years of reproductive capacity ahead of her, but has not produced up to expectations at Hanover, she will likely find herself in a sale. Every farm has mares with the potential to produce top racehorses, but some simply fail to fulfill that potential. They are culled and sent to auction. Maybe they will prove successful for another owner.

When a successful broodmare's days of raising babies at Hanover are over, she isn't shuttled off to the nearest sale and sold for a pittance. Simpson, Williams, and Spears feel that they have earned the right to a comfortable and dignified retirement, so three spacious fields at the farm are set aside for these pensioners.

"The people who own this farm are truly horsemen," says Dr. Jablonsky. "They're not businessmen who simply decide that they like the limelight of being in the winner's circle. They realize that the mares have kept Hanover at the top, and they do everything possible to make their lives comfortable."

In the summer of 2001, there were 58 mares living as honored pensioners at Hanover. In one field you could find Adorna Hanover, Boutique Hanover, Bret's

Fancy, Farm Norah, Farmstead Belle, Friendly Gift, Heleta Hanover, Hilana Hanover, Jolita Hanover, Lyna Hanover, Maxine Marie, Meadow Beaut, Mighty Impressive, Moneta Hanover, Norah Dancer, Pammy Blue Chip, Rhoda Lobell, Skipper's Dream, Starqueen Hanover, Superlou, Time To Skip, Victoria Regina, and Victorious Lil.

In another field were Armis Blue Chip, Augusta, Barette Hanover, Betty N Hanover, Bretina Hanover, Chickasaw, Decent Interval, Finger Bowl, Gigi Barmin, Kathy Newton, Ledy Hanover, Marissa Hanover, Mis Roz, Nichole Hanover, Noble Claire, Rishbish, Roanoke, Romie Hanover, Southern Crown, Speedy Elma, Sunray Mimi, Super Queen, and Talia Hanover.

The smallest field of pensioned mares contains only a dozen mares, and they are Berlinda Hanover, Cedarwood Flight, Ebony Crown, Harriet Hanover, Highland Maiden, Historic Hanover, Lustra Hanover, Maxine Marie, Starglo Knight, Tarport Dottie, Tarport Mary, and Trinka Hanover.

The farm has provided a final resting spot for some of its greatest stallions and mares. It's directly across Route 194 from the main entrance to the farm. Dillon Axworthy, one of the founding stallions, was buried here after his death in 1939. Among the stallions that rest nearby are four giants of the modern Standardbred. Star's Pride and Tar Heel fittingly rest side by side, as do Albatross and Super Bowl. To walk past these graves and to realize the significance of these horses sends chills down the spine of any Standardbred devotee.

You will also find the graves of Mr. McElwyn, Billy Direct, Spencer Scott, Hoot Mon, Dean Hanover, Titan Hanover, Nibble Hanover, Sampson Hanover, Knight Dream, Armbro Nesbit, Hickory Smoke, and Tyler B.

The mares that sleep under this hallowed ground are familiar names to those who appreciate Standardbred pedigrees. Here is a partial list of these honored dead: Hanover's Bertha, Miss Bertha Hanover, Volga E, Justissima, Rose Scott, Miss Pierette, Helen Hanover, The Old Maid, Brenna Hanover, Barbara Direct, Spry Hanover, Delicious, Laurita Hanover, Arpege, Romola Hanover, Wendy Hanover, Descent, Noble Gal, and Brief Romance.

The legendary champion Rosalind, subject of the classic book *Born To Trot*, is buried here. Goddess Hanover, her daughter Cassin Hanover, and her granddaughter Elma also rest with these champions.

Ironically, the lady who started it all, Miss Bertha Dillon, is not buried at Hanover, but in another suitable location. She rests in the centerfield of The Red Mile, a track where countless descendents of Miss Bertha Dillon have found fame. She was in Kentucky to be bred when she died and a granite marker lists her accomplishments.

In 2001, Hanover bred 412 mares to 43 separate stallions standing not only in Pennsylvania, but also in New Jersey, Ontario, Kentucky, New York, and Delaware.

Some 74 trotting mares went to Hanover's own stallions Donerail, Lindy Lane, and Sierra Kosmos. But other trotting stallions getting access to Hanover's broodmare band were Angus Hall, Balanced Image, Berndt Hanover, Conway Hall, Credit Winner, Enjoy Lavec, Malabar Man, Mr. Lavec, Mr. Vic, Muscles Yankee, Self Possessed, Sir Taurus, SJ's Photo, Tagliabue, Valley Victory, Yankee Glide, and Yankee Paco.

The farm sent 185 pacing mares to its own stallions: Arturo, Ball And Chain, Big Towner, Cam's Card Shark, Dragon Again, No Nukes, The Panderosa, Western Hanover, and Western Ideal.

Hanover mares also went to such outside pacing stallions as Artiscape, Artsplace, Badlands Hanover, Cambest, Camluck, Grinfromeartoear, Island Fantasy, Jenna's Beach Boy, Life Sign, Magical Mike, Real Artist, Run The Table, Rustler Hanover, and Shady Character.

"Our philosophy is to have something for everyone," says Murray Brown. "I see this happen over and over and over again. A guy who is looking for a Pennsylvania-eligible yearling sees a yearling sired in Ontario in our consignment and winds up buying that. You want to have yearlings to attract as many different people as possible."

Based on Hanover's rising yearling sale averages, it seems to be working.

Russell Williams with some of Hanover's pensioned mares.
Hanover Shoe Farms credits its broodmares with its success.

Chapter 20

What Am I Bid For 'Im?

For almost a year, they have the most carefree time of their life. They are free to run and jump and fight and kick as much as they wish. Of course, they must slug through the snows of winter and the heat of summer, but never again will they enjoy the freedom of these undisciplined days.

They are the Hanover Shoe Farms yearlings, and each year almost 300 of them grow to maturity in fields that have been home to many champions in the past.

After they are weaned in the autumn, the yearlings are separated by sex and size. The colts stay with other colts and the fillies with other fillies. And since there is often considerable difference in the size and maturity of a February foal and a May foal, they are grouped by age. About 25 yearlings share a 50-acre field.

They have fences around their fields, of course, and painstaking attention is paid to their nutrition and health care, but otherwise they are free to be horses. That means that they will roughhouse much like any adolescents. A pecking order will often emerge early, and the leaders are likely to enforce their dominance with bared teeth or a swift kick.

Invariably, this results in bumps, scrapes, and knots that may diminish the value of some yearlings, but these horses are being raised to be athletes, not hothouse flowers. If they are to endure the rigors of training, they must first endure the rigors of being raised in the rough, a process that strengthens them both physically and mentally for the challenges ahead.

"From the time they are a week old and healthy, our foals don't see a stall until we bring them in to prep them eight weeks before the yearling sale," says Jim Simpson.

Periodically they are herded into a catch pen to have their hooves trimmed and to be de-wormed and vaccinated. The scene can often resemble a Wild West show as the yearlings resent the intrusion and restraint and fight back in every way possible. But the Hanover yearling crew has been down this road before and they take it all in stride. The individual yearlings may be different each season, but their antics are much the same.

Their names are much the same, too, because they all bear the Hanover surname. Lawrence Sheppard was not the first breeder to affix a farm name to his horses, but he did it on such a large scale and over such a long period of time that some people thought that Hanover was a breed of horse, not just one of many Standardbred farms.

Traditionally, a Hanover yearling will carry a first name that starts with the first letter of his dam's name. Thus, the great mare Descent had Hanover foals with the first names of Dawn, Desdemona, Davidia, Duran, Ditka, Davallia, Demilo, Doodles, Destiny, Degree, Dallas, Dandy, and Duchess.

World champion mare Noble Gal had Nobie, Noblesse, Noble, Ned, Newfi, Neil, Novella, Ninette, Nobleboy, Nanuet, Noxie, Nobella, Nowak, Nix, and Noble Gal — all with the Hanover surname, of course.

The remarkable pacing mare Rich N Elegant's first half-dozen foals were named Rustler Hanover, Royalflush Hanover, Richess Hanover, Rye Hanover, Red River Hanover, and Righteous Hanover.

A field of Hanover yearlings

Russell Williams is the high commissar of names for Hanover Shoe Farms and coming up with names for several hundred yearlings each summer is an onerous task. That has caused him to bend the rules occasionally and not use the first letter of the dam's name in choosing a name for the foal.

Thus the mare French Dressing has a foal named Mayonnaise Hanover; Sarah's Fergi has had a foal named York Hanover; Happy Fiddler has a son named Tevye Hanover; Kiss And Make Up has a son named Bolero Hanover; and Beat The Wheel has had Berndt Hanover, Beaumont Hanover, and Lady Luck Hanover.

This practice isn't really new to the farm as it was several decades before Lawrence Sheppard started his policy of using the first letter of the dam's name as the starting basis for the names of her offspring. In fact, Sheppard even used Hanover as a prefix in some of his early names, such as Hanover's Bertha and Hanover Maid.

The famed trio of Hanover Sisters are examples of the how loose the naming pattern was in the farm's early years. Bertha C Hanover's foals were Patricia, Betsy, Delphia, Appie, Charm, Sugar, Brenda, Colby, Dolores, Madge, Colin, and Desira.

Hanover's Bertha's foals were named Brownie, Shirley, Ann, Edgar, Gem, Empress, Beverly, Sparkle, and McElwyn.

Despite the expense, Hanover continues the practice of leading yearlings, which gives them exercise and enhances their value in the sales ring

Charlotte Hanover's foals carried such names as Knight, Norma, Henry Boyd, Evening, Ross, Taylor, Milt, Flicka, Elizabeth Ann, Clipper, Starlette, and Charmaine.

There was some family favoritism at work in the names of the yearlings, as well you might expect. Charlotte Hanover was named after Mrs. Sheppard and her daughter of the same name. The other daughters, Alma and Patricia, had fillies named for them, and a Dillon Axworthy colt foaled in 1928 was named Sonny Hanover.

There was the previously-mentioned Lawrence Hanover, and one of his sons was named Sheppard Hanover. Harper Hanover was named after Lawrence Sheppard's father, and there is a famous two-mile race in Sweden called the Harper Hanover Race.

Many people, famous and not-so-famous, in harness racing have had the honor of being the namesake of a Hanover yearling. There was the famed and aforementioned Dancer Hanover, but Hall of Famers Billy Haughton and Joe O'Brien had faster Hanover-bred pacing colts named for them, too.

Dale Welk recalls how pleased and proud his father was when Hanover named a Best Of All colt born in 1973 Welk Hanover. After working at the farm for so many years, the name meant a lot to the senior Welk.

"I don't think it would have mattered at all to my father if that colt had raced or not," admits Welk. "Just the honor of having a horse named for him meant a lot."

The Hanover yearlings are raised at a complex near Bonneauville, about nine miles west of the main farm, almost to Gettysburg. That might confuse visitors at first, but nothing is done without reason.

"There are 12 fields there," says Bridgette Jablonsky. "Having the yearlings so far away helps us control the spread of disease. We have a whole different crew working at the yearling farm. None of them take care of mares and foals. There are some problems that mares can live with that you absolutely don't want yearlings getting."

Having the yearlings so far away is also a blessing at weaning times, explains Dr. Jablonsky. Separating a young foal from its mother is always a traumatic time, but the adjustment process goes much smoother if the newly weaned foals are relocated far away from mama. Out of sight, out of mind, so to speak.

Jablonsky laughs when she thinks about the weaning process, which might often be seen as the Adams County Rodeo. It can be wild and woolly at times, but the process is handled professionally by the staff, minimizing the chance of injury.

"We should charge admission," she says with a chuckle. "We have silver goose-necked trailers and all of the partitions are removed. We wean about four fields or about 80 foals each day. The mares are rechecked for pregnancy and vaccinated and the foals get their neckbands on with their mother's number.

"We lead the first mare and foal onto the trailer and then we lead the mare back off the trailer," she says. "A couple men will restrain the foal to keep it from following her. Then we lead the next mare up to the loading chute and some men will push the foal onto the trailer. We just keep doing that until we have five or six weanlings in the trailer."

The trailer door is then closed and the truck heads west, taking the newly weaned foals to the Bonneauville yearling farm. They ride loose in the trailer. There is certainly a bit of separation anxiety, but they get over it quickly.

"There is really nothing in the trailer that they can get hurt on," says Jablonsky. "They're with babies that they've been raised with. We don't separate them from their buddies."

The weaning process isn't without its untoward moments, however, and Bridgette Jablonsky will never forget one athletic youngster that caused her some grief just a few months after she started working at Hanover.

"We were using a tall loading ramp at the time and I was holding one of the sides of the ramp," she recalls. "Halfway up the ramp, this one colt decided he wasn't going onto the truck. He reared and whirled, knocking down the sideboard I was holding. I went flying and I landed on my tailbone on concrete."

The colt took off running. When he encountered a five-foot fence in his path, he simply cleared it like a Grand Prix jumper. Just to show it wasn't a fluke he jumped the same fence again. By now the Hanover staff was in full pursuit, and the colt then jumped the fence from a standstill.

As Bridgette Jablonsky lay on the ground, wincing in pain, she marveled at how nimble and graceful this colt was. "He'll either make a really good racehorse or a good jumping horse," she mused.

The colt came through his escapade without injury but Jablonsky broke her tailbone.

That yearling was named Destry Hanover when he sold as a yearling, but he was renamed Union Guy and under that name he took a 1:50.1 mark and earned almost a half-million dollars in his first three seasons at the races.

Starting early each summer, the first group of yearlings, slated to sell at The Meadows in early August, is brought in for their first lessons in deportment. After this initial wave comes in, the yearlings cataloged to sell at the Garden State Sale in September are readied. After those yearlings find new homes, the herd of approximately 160 yearlings undergo preparation for the huge Harrisburg sale.

The fairgrounds in Hanover is the headquarters for this basic training period. Hanover Shoe Farms purchased the land many years ago after the local fair was discontinued. The farm uses it to accommodate mares shipping in to be bred during the breeding season. Once the breeding season is over, it belongs to the yearling crew.

The process is the same with each group: they must first get accustomed to being handled, groomed, and walked by the farm's yearling personnel. They must adjust to life in a stall, learning to stand in the crossties as grooms introduce them to the currying and brushing routine. It's all new to these youngsters who have been handled sparingly since birth.

There are the inevitable rebellions. Some colts and some fillies find that they simply don't like this loss of freedom and lash out in any way possible. These incidents don't last long in the hands of the Hanover crew which has seen just about every kind of errant behavior in a yearling.

One man who has certainly seen it all is Eddie Miller, the yearling foreman at Hanover Shoe Farms. He was 19 when he began working there in 1967. Miller is one of those rare people who has an uncanny insight into a horse's temperament and behavior. It's not something he learned in college, but in the school of hard knocks year after year with the Hanover yearlings.

Miller knows when to be gentle, and when to be firm. He knows that patience is perhaps the greatest virtue that a horseman can have. He also knows when it's time to enforce a little discipline with a rank yearling. He gets his point across without anger.

"I've never seen Eddie mad at a horse," says Jim Simpson. "I've seen him mad at people, but never at a horse."

After the youngsters are comfortable with being groomed, walked, and having their feet picked up for inspection, they graduate to the next step. They get a chance to show their stuff on the surface on the Hanover fairgrounds racetrack.

It's a process as old as harness racing itself. Because gait and overall carriage are so critical to success in harness racing, most trainers want to see a yearling in action before bidding on it. No horse ever won a race standing still, so it's important that prospective buyers get an idea of how a yearling moves.

For most of the 20th century, it was traditional for major Standardbred farms to show their yearlings in action while being led by a rider on a cantering horse. Such horses are always called "lead ponies" but they are, in fact, full grown horses kept specifically for this purpose.

The yearling is kept in check by a lead shank held by the rider, but has enough freedom and play to demonstrate its natural way of moving.

Simultaneously riding a cantering horse and showing a yearling on gait is a skill that few horsemen have, and even then it is usually acquired after years of practice. In the early stages, virtually all the yearlings will fight the restraint and get tangled up before learning the routine.

In the hands of an experienced, adept rider, a naturally-gaited Standardbred yearling can be a beautiful sight as he ignores his cantering partner and shows the gait and speed bred into him for generations. Many yearlings have shown such spectacular speed, gait, and presence that they have enhanced their value many times over.

Getting a yearling to that stage is a time-consuming process, and extraordinarily labor intensive. That is why many Standardbred farms have discontinued leading their yearlings, opting instead to merely turn the yearlings out in a paddock for prospective buyers. That method works fine for many farms, but it doesn't work for Hanover.

"Leading can be a real bother," admits Simpson. "It's expensive because we maintain about 30 riding horses year-round to help lead our yearlings. The rest of the year they do nothing."

Beyond the expense, it is a rare horseman who can lead a yearling and show it off properly. Hanover lost one of its trusted masters of this art in early 2001 when Billy Jessie retired after working there more than 42 years. He had been the farm's yearling foreman for many decades.

"Leading yearlings enhances their value in the sales ring," says Simpson. "Plus, they have so much energy that they need to get out each day and exercise. In the past we were leading each yearling every other day. They were not getting enough exercise. Now we lead them one day and put them on an exercise machine the next day."

Showcasing yearlings on the fairgrounds may help Hanover when they sell, but the biggest beneficiaries of the practice are the trainers and owners who take the time to come to Hanover to watch the process. Until late in the 20th century, it was commonplace for trainers to spend several days in Hanover to familiarize themselves with the array of yearlings to be offered at Harrisburg.

To be truthful, however, the pilgrimages that many horsemen made to Hanover were almost as much social as they were business because the relaxed atmosphere gave them a chance to "talk horse" with colleagues from around the country. The Hanover staff made sure they were treated hospitably.

Prior to the 1980s, there were seldom many races of importance after the Grand Circuit meet at Lexington ended in early October. The racing calendar has changed radically with the advent of the Breeders Crown and other late-season stakes. That left many trainers simply too busy to visit Hanover, but Jim Simpson sees a revival of interest as the new century begins.

"The traffic is picking up a bit," says Simpson. "The people who do make the trek to Hanover are serious buyers. It's a good investment of their time. I'm always amazed that more buyers don't go to a breeding farm, not just to Hanover, even when it's inconvenient. Trainers should be doing that more often."

One prominent Standardbred buyer who finds the trip to the Hanover fairgrounds rewarding in a financial and personal sense is Canadian businessman Robert K. Waxman. He has been a patron of the Hanover yearling consignment for several decades.

"They obviously raise a great horse at Hanover," says Waxman. "That underlies everything. There is nothing that I enjoy more than going to Hanover and watching yearlings lead. At first it was either by myself or with some friends, but in recent years it's been with my son. I love having crabcakes for lunch and spending time with Jim Simpson, Russell Williams, Murray Brown, and Ralph Lemmon."

Waxman continues by saying, "These are terrific people and I'm always happy to be associated with them. Dr. Jablonsky has been involved lately and Dr. Boyce in the past. I'm more inclined to buy horses from the people I have an association with."

Waxman recalls the fall day in 1985 when he first saw Ditka Hanover on the track at the fairgrounds. The son of Super Bowl from Descent had a pedigree that would attract the attention of any astute buyer, but when Waxman saw the horse in motion he was hooked.

"I knew from the first time I saw Ditka that I would try to buy him," recalls Waxman. "You could tell from his gait that he seemed to be an absolute natural."

Waxman's instincts were right. Ditka Hanover proved to be a sensational two-year-old, winning the Peter Haughton Memorial over a challenger named Mack Lobell.

Waxman says that he finds it useful to compare the form the yearlings display during his visit with the videotaped presentations available at sale time. He knows, and all buyers know, that a consignor won't show unflattering views of a yearling on videotape. Those buyers who travel to the fairgrounds can get their own unedited impression of the yearling in action.

"If you compare the live action to the videotape, I think you get a leg up on other buyers who don't go to the fairgrounds," he says. "You get to see these yearlings as they really are."

Waxman prefers to see yearlings exercised in a controlled manner on the lead strip as opposed to seeing them turned out in paddocks, which is the practice at many farms.

"I don't like to impose on farms to turn yearlings out," he says. "I can remember one farm that turned out its yearlings for anyone who wanted to see them. They had yearlings whose ankles were already puffy from being turned out in muddy paddocks or from stopping abruptly to avoid hitting a fence. You can damage a lot of yearlings that way. Leading is a better method."

Waxman has seen enough yearlings over the years to understand that while the Hanover yearlings didn't always have the spit and polish of other yearlings, particularly in past decades, only a foolish buyer pays for cosmetic beauty.

"I view horses differently today than I did back in the 1980s," concedes Waxman. "Most trainers and the buyers who can see what a horse will look like three or six months down the road are better off buying from Hanover. Some people are drawn to horses that look flashy the week of the sale, but some of those yearlings deflate when they're put in training."

One person who has seen a lot of yearlings step down the track at the Hanover fairgrounds since 1967 is Murray Brown. He sees a definite connection between speed at the fairgrounds track and speed later demonstrated at tracks across North America.

"Almost without exception, every great trotting horse that I can remember was a great leader," says Brown. "Sugarcane Hanover was certainly one that showed a lot, but so were Davidia Hanover, Legend Hanover, Chiola Hanover, Spartan Hanover, Lindy's Pride, and Quick Pay. Then there was Brisco Hanover; he could trot faster than any lead pony could run."

Brown says that the filly Somolli (then named Larmon Hanover) was an impressive filly on the lead strip, too. She didn't accomplish anything on the track, but she contributed immeasurably to the breed through her son Speedy Somolli and her female descendents.

Brown admits that the internationally renowned Delmonica Hanover was not a memorable trotter on the fairgrounds track, but she was acceptable.

"The only horse I remember that had no ability on the lead strip that turned out to be a good horse was Desdemona Hanover," says Brown. "She was a sister to Davidia Hanover, but everything that Davidia was, Desdemona was not. Davidia was small; Desdemona was big. Davidia was cheerful; Desdemona was anything but cheerful. Davidia could fly on the trot; Desdemona wanted to pace."

*Delmonica Hanover
as a yearling*

Brown says that his experience shows him that how pacing yearlings show next to the pony isn't as accurate an indication of how they will perform on the track.

"Any potential buyer is doing himself a great disservice by not watching yearlings lead at the fairgrounds," he says. "More than anything, the biggest factor is attitude. You want to beware of a yearling that pins its ears or swishes its tail."

Brown tells about a superbly bred Western Hanover colt that displayed a distinct lack of interest when he was ponied.

"Almost from the first day he was sour on the track at the fairgrounds," says Brown. "He got worse and worse. To get him to go, there would have to be a couple guys on ponies behind him chasing him. Even then he wouldn't go."

The youngster looked the part, however, and he attracted admirers at the Harrisburg sale. When buyers asked Brown about the colt before the sale, he was candid and conceded that he had he had some reservations about the yearling's attitude.

"The person who bought him hadn't seen him lead," says Brown. "And he didn't ask me about him. I think if he had seen this colt lead, he would have been turned off."

Each fall as children set go to go trick-or-treating and politicians make their final promises prior to election day, the Standardbred world focuses its attention on the Pennsylvania Farm Show Complex in Harrisburg, the capital of the Keystone State.

236

It's been that way for over a half-century as horse people — buyers, sellers, and those just simply curious — flock to Harrisburg to take in the sport's largest auction. If you're looking to buy a Standardbred, the Harrisburg sale, as it's commonly called, is an ideal one-stop shopping mall. If you can't find a horse that suits you in a week at Harrisburg, you'd probably better get out of harness racing.

Murray Brown is a whirling dervish during the Harrisburg sale, trying to attend to the myriad concerns of buyers, sellers, and anyone and everyone attending the sale. He must wear both his Hanover Shoe Farms hat and his Standardbred Horse Sale hat and it is a juggling act which he has perfected after more than three decades of practice.

Sale company president Russell Williams marvels when he watches Brown in action from his control center in a trailer at the Harrisburg sale.

"He'll be schmoozing with customers who come in, dealing with people who need decisions to be made, looking at the sale tickets that are brought to him, and watching the action in the ring on his TV monitor," says Williams. "He keeps all this going in his head. It's kind of scary. Not much slips through the cracks."

The month leading up to the mammoth Harrisburg sale is both the best of times and the worst of times for Brown. He loves seeing the horsemen and owners come to the fairgrounds to inspect that Hanover consignment, and he loves the sense of anticipation as all the elements of the sale come together.

He is, however, never without a nagging sense of doubt, a sense that some calamity could befall the world that could turn the sale upside down. Just as politicians don't like "October surprises" when they're campaigning, Brown frets about them as the sale approaches. Some might dismiss such worry as an exaggerated sense of paranoia, but Murray Brown needs only to say "October 19, 1987" to make his case.

"That was probably one of the worst days of my life," he says. It was the day when the Dow Jones Industrial Average dropped 23 percent in one stormy session. It was the worst day in Wall Street history, and rumors were rampant that economic chaos was just around the corner.

No one knew what waited around the corner for Wall Street, but Murray Brown knew the annual Harrisburg sale was just around the corner, only two weeks away. He knew that a plunging stock market spelled doom for his sale.

"I think it affected our sale by 20 percent that year," says Brown, still smarting from the wound years later. "In the horse business, your entire year depends on a sale that lasts a few days."

While no one appreciates the value of Murray Brown to the Standardbred Horse Sale Co. more than Russell Williams, he also has had the chance to appreciate Brown's inestimable value to Hanover Shoe Farms, too.

"I refer to Murray as our resident wizard," says Williams. "His tenure is really quite amazing. He came in at the end of the L.B. Sheppard era, then all through the Simpson period, and is still with us.

"When he first came to Hanover, Murray used to read the Sires & Dams book in the winter," marvels Williams. "Now he's on the computer all the time, so he adapted well to the changing times."

Williams says that Brown's value to both the sale company and to Hanover extends far beyond just pedigrees. Management leans on Brown for opinions on the value and commercial appeal of stallions and broodmares.

"With established farms like Hanover, there's a tendency to slip into a siege mentality where we think that just because we're Hanover we make the rules," says Williams. "There is a danger of losing touch and keeping the wrong kinds of stallions and mares. Murray has helped Hanover avoid siege mentality because he's very conscious of what's happening in the market."

Brown's knowledge of the marketplace is tested at each sale. Before each yearling enters the sale ring, he has an estimated sale price by its name. It's often remarkably close to the sale price, but it can also be far too conservative if a couple ambitious bidders decide they can't live without the same yearling. Inevitably, too, there are those yearlings expected to fetch a fancy price and the bidding falls far short.

"That disappoints me, but in a few days I'll get over it," says Brown. "In more cases than not, I'll find the reason it didn't bring what we thought it should. Sometimes there just isn't a reason."

While the Harrisburg sale is still the epicenter of Hanover's marketing mechanism, it also sells yearlings at the Adios sale held each August at The Meadows south of Pittsburgh and at the Garden State Horse Sale in New Jersey. Ordinarily, the yearlings consigned to these venues are those that won't bring top dollar.

"The yearlings sold at The Meadows are all Pennsylvania-sired yearlings, so we are hitting the target market for them," Jim Simpson says "These might be individuals with a problem. Their pedigrees aren't necessarily weak. In fact, a mare might have a yearling selling at The Meadows one year and at Harrisburg the next."

Simpson also knows that the constraints of space and manpower and market realities prevent the farm from selling these yearlings at Harrisburg.

"We have found that the saturation point for Hanover to sell yearlings at Harrisburg is around 160 head," says Simpson. "The yearlings sold at The Meadows would probably sell on Wednesday, the final day of the yearling sales at Harrisburg. That wouldn't help the sale, or help those yearlings."

Of course, the wonderful enigma of breeding horses is that the yearlings sold at The Meadows or sometimes in New Jersey don't know that they are sometimes labeled below average. They often outshine the headliners from Harrisburg. In 2000, for example, the runaway winner of the Breeders Crown for two-year-old trotting fillies was Syrinx Hanover, a daughter of Lindy Lane plucked off for a mere $8,500 at the Garden State Sale. She earned $680,797 as a two-year-old alone.

Through the good sales and those that weren't so good, Murray Brown has survived and come back the next year for more. But when the hammer falls on the final horse, a certain depression sweeps over him.

"The very worst day of the year for me is the Saturday after the Harrisburg sale," he says. "It doesn't matter if it's a good sale or a bad sale. It's just a terrible letdown for me. I have a feeling of great emptiness. After being with the yearlings every day for months, you get to know them and love them, and then suddenly they're gone, cold turkey."

While Brown wrestles with all the concerns of the Harrisburg sale, the farm's treasurer, Ralph E. Lemmon, Jr., is the president of the Garden State Sale in New Jersey. He downplays his role with characteristic modesty, however, preferring that manager Dale Welk get the visibility and credit.

"It's more important for the sale manager to be visible," he says. "He's the one looking at horses and dealing with customers."

Lemmon is one of those quintessential behind-the-scenes stalwarts that no business can do without. He's uncomfortable in the spotlight, but those closest to Hanover and the Garden State Sale Co. appreciate his value the most.

He's a local Hanover boy who went to work at the shoe company in 1970 after college and service to Uncle Sam. His boss was Paul Spears, and when Spears moved into a more active role at the farm in 1982, Lemmon moved with him.

He came to the farm just in time to see a colt named for him win the Triple Crown.

"Burnell Hesson was the corresponding officer before I came out to the farm and he sent me a copy of the registration certificate for Ralph Hanover," says Lemmon. "There was a note saying, 'Here's something you may be interested in.'"

Watching a colt bearing his name win the Triple Crown gave Lemmon great joy, but then he had to endure the good-natured ribbing from his colleagues when Ralph failed as a sire.

"They all told me that it figured that Ralph wouldn't be a good stallion," laughs Lemmon.

"We run the farm just like any other business," he says. "We buy stuff, we sell stallion services and yearlings, and we have to collect our bills. Sometimes people are perplexed when we charge late payment penalties. We take the responsibility to collect money very seriously."

There are some customers, however, who are always applying pressure to get a break, asking the farm to waive interest charges or grant a favor. It is often Lemmon and associate Jim Harvey who are thrust into the "bad cop" role of making that deadbeats pay up.

"A lot of people try to tell us that they'll pay when they get ready to pay," laments Lemmon, "and that doesn't sit very well with a business."

Lemmon worked very closely with Paul Spears, who was a numbers man himself and was very detail-oriented. He also worked for John Simpson, who was "more of a big-picture" person. Simpson would laughingly refer to Lemmon as a number cruncher, bean counter, pencil pusher, or other terms commonly used for accountants, but the wily old horseman was smart enough to appreciate the importance of accountants in a business.

Although Lemmon spends most of his time in the Hanover office, he enjoys the opportunity that yearling time presents to meet and greet Hanover customers.

"I try to get to the fairgrounds as often as I can," he says. "I see a lot of names on the books during the year, and it's nice to meet these people face-to-face. Plus, I learn things when I'm around our customers."

In addition to Ralph Hanover, Lemmon was a big fan of Dragon's Lair during his racing days. As an accountant, he couldn't help but love Albatross and Super Bowl for their contributions to the bottom line.

The most memorable race he's seen was the March of Dimes Trot in 1988, which he drove to see with Murray Brown. They were thrilled beyond words when Sugarcane Hanover upset the favorites.

"It was a tremendous race, and it was won by a horse that we had an affiliation with," he says. "It was great just to be there at Garden State that night. We won't see a race that good for a long time."

Bridgette Jablonsky doesn't have as many yearling sales as Murray Brown or Ralph Lemmon under her belt, but she still feels the same sense of excitement at sale time.

"Whenever we sell a yearling well, and I know it was well-prepped, that gives me a lot of satisfaction," she says. "The week before the Harrisburg sale is the worst week of my year and the week of the Harrisburg sale is the best week of my year. I love watching our yearlings sell well."

She enjoys following the Hanover yearlings once they leave the farm and go on to the racing wars, too.

"When one with the name Hanover races well, I think that we must have done something right," she says.

A casual comment by a trainer stayed with Jablonsky long after others may have forgotten it. It was made at a seminar for new owners sponsored by the U.S. Trotting Association in 1999. A trainer was speaking to a group of prospective Standardbred owners at a sale, explaining the vagaries associated with yearling selection.

As he appraised a Hanover yearling, the trainer paused and told the group, "When you buy a horse from Hanover, you know it's been raised right. That's one of the big advantages of buying from Hanover. You know that everything has been done to increase its chance of becoming a successful athlete."

Overhearing that remark, the 5'1" veterinarian suddenly felt 10 feet tall.

"That really made me feel good," she says.

Chapter 21

Some Things Stay The Same

Although harness racing has changed and the personnel at Hanover Shoe Farms have changed over the years, the basic integrity so fundamental to the farm's owners has not changed. Two incidents reflect how the integrity of Hanover has remain unaltered.

Long ago, a Hoot Mon mare named Lovely Hanover presented a not-so-lovely surprise to Hanover: Her 1963 foal by Hickory Smoke actually arrived in 1962. It was a late December foal, the kind of rare surprise that Mother Nature will play on breeders periodically.

Most farms begin their breeding season in mid-February, but only a few mares are cycling normally in the dead of winter and the pregnancies resulting from February breedings are limited. Since a mare's gestation period is usually 11 months and a handful of days, those foals usually arrive in late January.

Occasionally, however, foals will arrive far ahead of schedule. If the mare was due to foal early, that can place the foaling date perilously close to the January 1 birthday shared by all racehorses. And those unfortunate foals that arrive in late December are write-offs from a commercial breeder's perspective.

So when the farm superintendent at Hanover called Lawrence Sheppard late in December 1962, to tell him that Lovely Hanover's foal had arrived early, you can be sure that Sheppard was mightily upset.

Hoping to placate Sheppard, the caller made an egregious mistake. "Mr. Sheppard, you and I are the only two people that know about this filly being born early. I can keep her hidden for a few days until after the first of the year."

This hapless soul had said the wrong thing to the wrong man. Lawrence Sheppard exploded with indignation, and retorted, "If you and I are the only ones who know about it, that's one too many."

With a puckish sense of humor, the premature filly was named December Hanover and she was given to John Simpson, Jr., then a young trainer assisting his father. It would be nice to say that December Hanover later redeemed herself on the track or as a broodmare, but such wasn't the case.

On New Year's Day in 2001, Jim Simpson walked into the office at Hanover and thought he'd mistakenly stumbled into a funeral parlor. Everywhere he looked there were glum faces. "Who died?" he asked.

"No one," was the answer. "We had a foal last night."

"Oh, God," said Simpson, knowing that the farm had just incurred a financial loss. "What mare was it?"

It was the Speedy Crown mare Excella's Crown, a $105,000 acquisition just a few years earlier. She had been so anxious to greet her Sierra Kosmos son that she couldn't wait for January 1. She delivered 27 days ahead of her due date.

"Most of the time when mares foal that early, it's the result of a dystocia [difficult foaling] or something was wrong," says Simpson. "This guy came out ready for action, kicking, and bouncing off the walls."

When he was but a few hours old, however, the colt officially became a yearling. If he were to begin training in the fall of 2002, in his first season at the races he would be required to start in three-year-old events, a monumental handicap.

Jim Simpson understood that Hanover had no choice but to swallow hard, accept what nature had dealt, and take the financial losses that such an unexpected birth mean. The colt was offered for sale privately.

The people at Hanover know that such calamities are inevitable. Just a year earlier, the Breeders Crown-winning mare Hardie Hanover ruptured an artery and died a month after Hanover had paid $150,000 for her at Harrisburg.

Jim Simpson, Russell Williams, and Paul Spears don't spend much time fretting about such losses. In fact, while they are justifiably proud of Hanover Shoe Farms' many accomplishments in its first 75 years, they prefer to spend their time looking to the future instead of the past. They will talk about their hopes for their young stallions and mares, about new farmland they've acquired, or about the team of professionals they have running the farm.

They dream the same dreams as Lawrence Sheppard and John Simpson dreamed. Each mating, each foal, and each yearling represents a potential new superstar from Hanover; such are the dreams that sustain those who breed horses.

The long shadow cast by Lawrence Sheppard is very real at Hanover, even today. Current management feels an allegiance to the traditions of Hanover and an obligation to carry forth the quest for excellence.

That quest often means change, and under the leadership of Jim Simpson the farm has embraced change while adhering to an unchanging operating philosophy.

"In Jim you see an interesting blend of old and new," says Russell Williams. "He knows the eternal verities and practicalities of the horse business on one hand, and innovation on the other hand."

One example of Simpson's innovation, Williams says, was his decision to convert the sale pedigrees from an old Veritype machine to a personal computer.

"Jim wrote a software program that goes into the USTA database and sucks out all the current performance data for the offspring of our broodmares," says Williams. "Then it puts the information into the catalog pages so that it updates itself automatically."

Williams laughs when he says that a sure way to manipulate Simpson is to defend an idea by saying, "We've always done it this way." He knows that Simpson will immediately dismiss the old methods and seek a better solution.

While the innovative side of Simpson gives him an open mind to new ideas, his background as a horseman enables him to understand what is best for horse health.

"We had a little squabble about keeping the barns closed up all the time," recalls Williams. "Some of the workers probably felt it was easier to keep them clean that way, but Jim realized that horses need fresh air. So the doors stayed open."

Another change that Simpson made was to order the installation of wash stalls in the stallion barns. That came after a harrowing escape by one of the farms' stallions.

"We'd always bathed the stallions by leading them outside," says Williams. "Ideally we would have one person holding the stallion and the other one bathing the horse. Human nature being what it is, occasionally only one person is handling that task."

One day a Hanover stallion was being bathed by a handler and he suddenly broke loose. There was a large group of mares in a field across Route 194 and the stallion trotted across the highway to visit the mares.

"Fortunately he crossed the road when there were no cars coming," says Williams. "They caught him. That prompted Jim to order wash stalls. Little things like that might seem prosaic, but they're part of making a farm work."

Williams also credits Simpson with being the one "who turned Dr. J [Dr. Bridgette Jablonsky] loose on an unsuspecting world." Everyone at Hanover knew the risk of placing such trust in a young woman, and that surely wouldn't have happened in years past.

In the early 1990s, Paul Spears asked Simpson to investigate the use of exercise machines for yearlings and to purchase a few if he thought they could help

Hanover. Simpson did his homework and liked what he saw. Soon Hanover installed three exercisers.

"They are very helpful in yearling preparation," says Simpson, "and they actually put a yearling 'in training' prior to the sale. We've been very pleased with the exercisers. The buyer is actually getting a yearling that is much fitter than in the past."

Other changes under Simpson's tenure have been the use of electric fences in some broodmare fields.

Russell Williams might well be speaking about himself when he praises Jim Simpson.

"He's not egotistical," Williams says. "Jim realizes that being president isn't about him; it's about the farm."

Each year in December, the employees of Hanover Shoe Farms come together for a Christmas party at a local fire hall. It's a time to celebrate the season, to relax with their co-workers and spouses, and to review the accomplishments of the past season.

This is a night for fun. Long speeches are verboten. As president of the farm, however, Jim Simpson spends a few minutes thanking the employees for their loyalty, hard work, and commitment.

In 2000, Dale Welk used the holiday party to say something that had long been preying on his mind. Dale had lived on the farm ever since his birth in 1958 except for one month when he first got married and housing wasn't immediately available. No one knows Hanover Shoe Farms or its people better than Dale Welk.

He'd also had the chance to observe how other farms operated in his role as Director of Operations at the Harrisburg and Garden State sales.

At the holiday party Welk took the microphone and said, "With my traveling to different sales, I spend a lot of time with people from different breeding farms. These other farms all do a good job, each one in its own way."

Welk looked out over the crowd of almost a hundred people, many of whom he'd known for decades, and added, "After seeing how they operate, there's something that I have to say. Not only is Hanover the greatest name in harness racing, but I also think that we have the greatest group of people in harness racing."

Somewhere, Lawrence Sheppard and John Simpson were smiling.

About The Author

Dean A. Hoffman has been the Executive Editor of *Hoof Beats* magazine since 1981. Prior to that time he wrote on a free-lance basis for publications in the United States and Canada. He has followed harness racing closely since the early 1960s. His first trip to Hanover Shoe Farms came in 1967 while he was still in high school. He recalls the 31-year-old Nibble Hanover as well as Star's Pride and Tar Heel, who were then in their prime.

Hoffman is a native of Cincinnati and graduated cum laude from Ohio University. While in college he spent his summers as a groom for a Grand Circuit stable. In addition to his work at *Hoof Beats*, he was also an assistant manager at Stoner Creek Stud in the 1970s.

He has traveled extensively and visited harness tracks not only in North America, but also in Australia, Russia, Sweden, Germany, France, Norway, Finland, Denmark, and The Netherlands.

Photo credits

Many of the photos used in this book are from the collection of Hanover Shoe Farms or the personal collection of the author. Ed Keys, the veteran chief photographer for the United States Trotting Association, also deserves credit for his assistance in providing important photos.